Thatcher's Children?
Politics, Childhood and Society in the 1980s and 1990s

D0224284

13.95

k

HQ 792 .G7 T47 1996
Thatcher's children

231035

DATE DUE

DEC 0 3 1997	

BRODART   Cat. No. 23-221

JP: For Eddie and our son, Jack
SW: For my friend Kathleen Mannering, with love

OKANAGAN UNIVERSITY COLLEGE
LIBRARY
BRITISH COLUMBIA

Thatcher's Children?
Politics, Childhood and Society in the 1980s and 1990s

Edited by

Jane Pilcher and Stephen Wagg

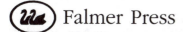 Falmer Press

(A member of the Taylor & Francis Group)
London • Washington, D.C.

UK	Falmer Press, 1 Gunpowder Square, London WC4A 3DE
USA	Falmer Press, Taylor & Francis Inc., 1900 Frost Road, Suite 101, Bristol, PA 19007

© J. Pilcher and S. Wagg 1996
© Front cover photograph: Nigel Tanburn, London

All rights reserved. No part of this publication may be reproduced, stored in a retrieval system, or transmitted in any form or by any means, electronic, mechanical, photocopying, recording or otherwise, without permission in writing from the Publisher.

First published in 1996

A catalogue record for this book is available from the British Library

Library of Congress Cataloging-in-Publication Data are available on request

ISBN 0 7507 0461 6 cased
ISBN 0 7507 0462 4 paper

Jacket design by Caroline Archer

Typeset in 10/12pt Garamond by
Graphicraft Typesetters Ltd., Hong Kong.

Printed in Great Britain by Biddles Ltd, Guildford and King's Lynn on paper which has a specified pH value on final paper manufacture of not less than 7.5 and is therefore 'acid free'.

Every effort has been made to contact copyright holders for their permission to reprint material in this book. The publishers would be grateful to hear from any copyright holder who is not here acknowledged and will undertake to rectify any errors or omissions in future editions of this book.

Contents

Contents

List of Tables and Figures

1   Introduction: Thatcher's Children?

Jane Pilcher and Stephen Wagg

Regarding Children

The French historian Philippe Aries first published his famous and important work *Centuries of Childhood* in 1959. Since then, sociologists around the world have, from time to time and with varying degrees of conviction, endorsed the book's central tenet, namely that childhood is socially constructed and is, thus, specific to certain times and places in human history. On the whole, however, they have been reluctant to take the matter much further and, as recently as 1990, it was argued that the sociological study of children and childhood was in its 'own infancy' (Chisholm *et al.*, 1990, p. 5). The criticism has been, not that there was a lack of research on children, but that the research which had been done was disproportionately concerned with the processes through which children became adults. It attended primarily to the development and social-ization of children in families and schools. The notion that children were *people* — acting, reacting and helping to create their own social worlds — has taken longer to establish (see Alanen, 1992).

In recent years, however, new approaches to the social study of children and childhood have been emerging. In a seminal account, Prout and James (1990) have, in effect, set out a new paradigm for the sociology of childhood. This paradigm is more interpretative. It challenges notions of the natural or universal character of childhood and it assumes instead that childhood is pro-cessual and perpetually in flux, subject to the understandings and experiences of children in their specific social contexts (Prout and James, 1990, p. 15). Two features of this new approach are particularly important. Firstly, childhood is now seen as an institution which represents the ways, varying across time and cultural place, in which the biological immaturity of children is understood. Secondly, there is a concern to 'give a voice', albeit by adult mediation, to chil-dren as social actors who are themselves engaged in constructing and recon-structing this institution (Prout and James, 1990, p. 8).

Also central to the new view of childhood is the importance, following Foucault (Foucault, 1972), that is now attached to 'discourse' — the concepts of children and childhood, the language through which these concepts are thought and expressed, and the social practices and institutions from which, ultimately, they are inseparable (Prout and James, 1990, p. 25). This concern with discourse defines the purpose of our book. Each writer has explored some dimension of the contemporary political discourses of childhood. While we accept fully the new view of children as active, reactive and creative beings, it would clearly be foolish to assume that they were active, reactive and creative in circumstances of their own choosing. Although, adapting Sartre, children will always make something of what is made of them, it is important, we feel, to look at the ways in which children have been framed, and their range of possibilities defined, in the dominant political language and practices of the late twentieth century.

During the 1980s and 1990s debates in Britain about social, political and economic affairs have been heavily circumscribed by the discourses of the New Right, which has made for a heightened public discussion of children and childhood. This discussion has taken place against a backdrop of important social and economic changes, which have been in train since the Second World War. For Alanen (1992, p. 6), these changes have brought a decreased significance of the traditional agencies of childhood (the nuclear family and the school) in relation to other agencies: child and youth services, the mass media and peer groups. It is the anxiety wrought by these changes that has found its most forcible and public expression in the discourses of the New Right. Indeed, children have often seemed to be at the heart of contemporary ideological wrangles. After all, in the most memorable political enunciation of the 1980s, Margaret Thatcher declared: 'There is no such thing as "society". There are men. And there are women. And there are families.' The assumed children of these 'families' have often appeared in the rhetoric of the New Right to hover between Heaven and Hell. In Heaven, the male head of their nuclear family, doubtless an entrepreneur now liberated from state control and trade union interference, provides them with love, discipline and selective education. In Hell, children are menaced by a gallery of social demons: single mothers, absent fathers, muddle-headed social workers failing to detect abuse, drug pushers, paedophiles, 'do-gooders' reluctant to punish young offenders, 'trendy' teachers, doctors prescribing contraceptives for young girls, media executives purveying violent and sexually explicit material, and so on. Most of the chapters in this book are intended to go beyond these often lurid and melodramatic representations.

For, while commentators on the right have dominated political debates about childhood during the 1980s and 1990s, the left has nevertheless made its presence felt. Thus, while many among the New Right have foretold of a disintegration of childhood, many on the left have been exploring the possibility of extending the boundaries of childhood. Here long-established anarchist-humanist traditions seem to have combined with newer notions of empowerment to produce an active and influential children's rights movement in several countries. In Britain, this manifested itself in successful campaigns on corporal punishment and bullying in schools, on child labour and on the rights of children both in local authority care and in hospital.

Thatcher's Children?

Although the book addresses other political discourses, *Thatcher's Children?* acknowledges the key role played by the New Right in the mounting debate about children and childhood in the 1980s and 1990s. The political New Right was, as it remains, a broad and diverse grouping which cannot be reduced to a single party or government (Levitas, 1986); nevertheless, the Thatcherism of the 1980s can be seen as both heavily informed by, and an important variant of, New Right ideology (Smith, 1994; Hayes, 1994). Despite the departure of Margaret Thatcher in 1990, few would dispute the continued reverberation of Thatcherism as an identifiable cluster of arguments and assumptions in British political culture in the 1990s. Described by Kingdom (1992) as an 'unstable amalgam' of neo-liberalism — in relation to the economy — and authoritarian conservatism on moral questions, the discourse of the New Right has continued to characterize the Conservative administrations of John Major.

Both inside and outside parliament, debates about the family are one area where the morally conservative discourse of the New Right has been especially influential. For the New Right, the traditional, self-reliant, patriarchal nuclear family is *the* central social institution and the condition of the family serves, therefore, as an index of the moral well-being of the wider society (Moore, 1992). In New Right discourse, the liberal political consensus, which was forged in 1945 and which supported the interventionist state, is seen to have undermined the family, and with it the moral and economic health of the nation. Hence the stated determination of recent governments to re-establish the private sphere of the family — with patriarchal authority in regard to gender and generation — over the public sphere of the state. The apparent contradiction in New Right thinking between economic freedom, on the one hand, and social and moral authoritarianism on the other, can be resolved by seeing these two strands as aspects of a broader logic: 'Individual freedom and choice were to be confined to the sphere of market relations, since in the social realm they had to rest upon a common cultural and moral foundation' (Hayes, 1994, p. 89).

The central importance of 'the family' in New Right ideology, then, has been well established (Fitzgerald, 1983; David, 1986; Abbott and Wallace, 1989, 1992; Durham, 1991; Smith, 1994). However, the comparably important place in this ideology occupied by notions of children and childhood has come under considerably less scrutiny. So we hope in this book to add not only to the body of work done within the new paradigm of the sociology of childhood but also to the literature on the politics of the New Right. Each chapter of this book examines political discourse, practice and invocations of 'the child' in relation to an important social issue.

Stephen Wagg's chapter looks at the post-war politics of British schooling, with particular reference to the period between the late 1970s and the mid-1990s. During this period, of which the Education Reform Act of 1988 is the major legislative landmark, children have been increasingly constructed in political

discourse as passive. In this passivity, they have been seen principally as vulnerable (to 'trendy' or, latterly, merely 'bad' teachers) or as beneficiaries of their
parents' search for 'good schools' and 'standards'. 'Parent power', the popular
rallying cry of right-wing educational politics in Britain since the 1980s and
the rhetorical seal set on the 1988 Act, is argued to have brought little genuine
enfranchisement in the 'new education market'. In the culture of this market,
the term 'child-centred education' has become a straightforwardly pejorative
one; nevertheless, as Wagg shows, efforts continue to be made to empower
the British schoolchild.

As a number of contributors show in their respective chapters, children
are mainly present in New Right discourse as instruments of wider political
concerns about the condition of society — concerns which have included the
relationship of the state to the private sphere, parental responsibility, support
for 'the family', law and order and sexual morality. The chapter by Karen
Winter and Paul Connolly addresses the apparent contradiction of the Children
Act of 1989, in which a Thatcher administration, rhetorically steeped in patriarchal 'family values', legislated apparently to extend children's rights. They
show that, within the Act, these rights relate to their dealings with social
service agencies, rather than with parents. Thus, the Act sits well with Thatcherite
concern over the decline of 'the family' and the evils of state intervention.

Nigel Parton's chapter also examines the 1989 Children Act, arguing
that it represents a shift in the relations and hierarchies of authority between
the different agencies involved in child protection. Child abuse, he suggests, is
constituted not as a medico-social problem, as previously, but as a socio-legal
problem. Parton's central point is that, because of the extent to which child
abuse is now perceived as a legal matter, too many cases are filtered out of
the system, for lack of sufficient forensic evidence. Moreover, following media
and public outcry at several killings of children by abusers (beginning with the
death of Maria Colwell in 1973), child abuse has become an issue of *publicity*
for the authorities. This, argues Parton, has strengthened official preoccupation
with serious cases and left many other children in need of protection vulnerable. In short, the Children Act of 1989 has failed to solve the problem of balancing state intervention with the protection of privacy in these matters.

In the area of crime and young people, Tim Newburn notes that policy
and practice during the ascendancy of the New Right has not been uniform.
Here, despite militant declarations on 'law and order', early Thatcher administrations generally approved constructive, non-custodial work with young
offenders. However, during the 1990s, in the face of proliferating moral panics
about lawless youth and children out of control, there was a return to punitive
custodial regimes for young offenders. This entails a new, or the return of an
old, construction of the young offender — as someone who 'knows what he's
doing' and can only be deterred by tough discipline.

But, if young people know what they're doing when they engage in
crime, we cannot, according to New Right ideology, assume the same awareness on their part if they choose to have sex. On this count, Jane Pilcher

considers the moral eruptions over children and sex that have been a persistent feature of the 1980s and 1990s and studies in detail the implications of the so-called 'Gillick Judgement'. She emphasizes the twofold paradoxical nature of the Gillick case: firstly, in that the Thatcher administration prevailed over the 'moral lobby'; secondly, because the conceptions of childhood implicit in the final House of Lords judgment are at odds with New Right notions, both of the family and of the child. A review of the legacies of the Gillick case, however, reveals, as Pilcher concedes, that these paradoxes, especially in relation to children's access to sexual knowledge and advice, are more apparent than real.

The fact that New Right campaigners such as Gillick have received less than full endorsement for their arguments from the courts must in part be due to the parallel strivings of the movement for children's rights. A brief history of this movement, outlining its central ideas, debates, proposals and policies is provided by Annie Franklin and Bob Franklin. They, like Wagg in Chapter 2, note the largely unsympathetic response of leading politicians to initiatives on children's rights. Successive Conservative governments in the 1980s and 1990s have disputed the need for a Commissioner for Children's Rights, arguing that the Children Act of 1989 was sufficient to guarantee such rights. This means, as Franklin and Franklin point out, that, politically, the prevailing view is that children have rights of *protection* but not of *participation*.

Carey Oppenheim and Ruth Lister attend to a vital contradiction in New Right thinking on the family and childhood. They focus on policies to alleviate child poverty introduced by Conservative administrations in the 1980s and 1990s, with particular reference to the Child Support Act. Their analysis shows that during this period the self-styled 'party of the family' presided over policies that in many ways deepened the disadvantage of children and their families. Moreover, the Child Support Act, while purporting to reaffirm patriarchal family values and bind errant fathers to their parental responsibilities, in fact led to a channelling of money toward the Treasury and away from needy children.

Turning now to media discourses on childhood, Bob Franklin and Julian Petley assess newspaper reportage of the case of James Bulger. Press characterization of this killing of a small child by other children signals, they argue, a broader concern about children and contemporary childhood. Indeed, they find that, in a sense, British journalists used this occasion to reiterate the crude notions of 'evil' and individual culpability and to place in the dock the whole idea of extenuating social circumstance — a change of political mood discussed earlier by Tim Newburn. Franklin and Petley throw the distinctive nature of these dominant British attitudes toward child criminality into sharp relief by comparing them, firstly, to the treatment of similar cases in nineteenth-century Britain and, secondly, to the handling of a virtually identical incident in contemporary Norway.

In the following chapter, Pat Holland looks at the ways in which television now speaks to, and provides for, children and she discerns in these new modes of address a symbolic realignment in the relations between childhood and adulthood. This, she suggests, helps to make the relations between actual adults and actual children even more problematic. She also notes the incursion of the values of 'childishness' into adult media, arguing that this does not necessarily translate into a greater understanding of the needs of children. Indeed, we are still subject to intermittent moral panics about children's relationship to the media, as new, often computer-related, forms develop children's knowledge and skills in areas where many adults feel they cannot follow. Furthermore, this knowledge and these skills are being associated with dangerous pleasures, rather than learning or self-improvement, and are being honed in an increasingly deregulated commercial and media environment. Here, once again, we see vividly the clash between the values of the protective, patriarchal family and the free market ethos of economic liberalism.

A similarly stark reminder of this contradiction is provided by Michael Lavalette in his study of contemporary child labour. Lavalette contends that no meaningful distinction can be made between 'children's work', a comparatively comforting phrase, and 'child labour', a term that suggests exploitation. At home and abroad there is clear evidence that the conditions dictated by neo-liberal economic policies have militated in favour of the oppression of child workers and against the preservation of childhood, as it is conventionally understood in the industrialized world. Lavalette examines these further contradictions in New Right politics and in the policies to prevent child labour, which many poor countries adopt but cannot afford to implement.

Finally, Julia O'Connell Davidson and Jacqueline Sanchez Taylor deal with a social and political issue wherein these contradictions can be seen at their most powerful and disconcerting: the role of children in sex tourism. In the British political life of the late twentieth century, three assumptions have been axiomatic: firstly, children have been styled as essentially asexual, to the point where it might be thought necessary to withhold knowledge of sexual matters — even via sex education — from them; secondly, those who seek to have sex with children have tended to be pathologized, especially in the popular press, as 'monsters' and 'paedophiles'; and, thirdly, part of the economic way forward popularly advocated for impoverished Third World nations has been for them to develop tourist attractions for holidaymakers from the Northern nations. Drawing on their research in Thailand and Cuba, however, O'Connell Davidson and Sanchez Taylor show how the planeloads of male tourists from the 'developed' world who come to such countries for sex with local children call the stereotype of the 'paedophile' into question. Instead, such tourists, whom the British Conservative government has so far been reluctant to prosecute, serve as a metaphor for layers of exploitative power relations: adult with child; males with female; white with black; and First World with Third.

We'd like, in conclusion, to thank Bob Franklin, Peter Golding, Keith Faulks, Martin Barker and Brian Milne for help in the putting together of this book and the staff of *Socialist Worker* and *The Teacher*, along with John Harris and Nigel Tanburn for assistance in finding a suitable photograph for the cover.

References

ABBOTT, P. and WALLACE, C. (1989) 'The family', in BROWN, P. and SPARKS, R. (eds) *Beyond Thatcherism*, Milton Keynes, Open University Press.

ABBOTT, P. and WALLACE, C. (1992) *The Family and the New Right*, London, Pluto Press.

ALANEN, L. (1992) *Modern Childhood? Exploring the 'Child Question' in Sociology*, Jyvaskla, Institute of Educational Research, University of Jyvaskla.

CHISHOLM, L., BROWN, P., BUCHNER, P. and KRÜGER, H. (1990) 'Childhood and youth studies in the United Kingdom and West Germany: An introduction', in CHISHOLM, L., BROWN, P., KRÜGER, H. and BUCHNER, P. (eds) *Childhood, Youth and Social Change*, London, Falmer Press.

DAVID, M. (1986) 'Moral and maternal: The family in the right', in LEVITAS, R. (ed.) *The Ideology of the New Right*, Cambridge, Polity Press.

DURHAM, M. (1991) *Sex and Politics: The Family and Morality in the Thatcher Years*, London, Macmillan.

FITZGERALD, T. (1983) 'The New Right and the family', in LONEY, M., BOSWELL, D. and CLARKE, J. (eds) *Social Policy and Social Welfare*, Milton Keynes, Open University Press.

FOUCAULT, M. (1972) *The Archaeology of Knowledge*, New York, Pantheon Books.

HAYES, M. (1994) *The New Right in Britain*, London, Pluto Press.

KINGDOM, J. (1992) *No Such Thing as Society?* Milton Keynes, Open University Press.

LEVITAS, R. (1986) 'Ideology and the New Right', in LEVITAS, R. (ed.) *The Ideology of the New Right*, Cambridge, Polity Press.

MOORE, R. (1992) 'Foreword', in ABBOTT, P. and WALLACE, C. *The Family and the New Right*, London, Pluto Press.

PROUT, A. and JAMES, A. (1990) 'A new paradigm for the sociology of childhood? Provenance, promise and problems', in JAMES, A. and PROUT, A. (eds) *Constructing and Reconstructing Childhood*, London, Falmer Press.

SMITH, A. (1994) *New Right Discourses on Race and Sexuality*, Cambridge, Cambridge University Press.

2 'Don't Try to Understand Them': Politics, Childhood and the New Education Market

Stephen Wagg

Keep movin', movin', movin', though they're disapprovin'
Keep them dogies movin', Rawhide
Don't try to understand 'em
Just rope 'em through and brand 'em
Soon we'll be livin' high and wide.

Theme from *Rawhide* (Lyrics by Ned Washington; music by Dimitri Tomkin; sung by Frankie Laine)

Compulsory education is one of the defining characteristics of modern childhood; to a degree, therefore, any politics of schooling is also a politics of childhood, with inevitable implications for the lives that children lead and for the way that childhood itself is understood. This chapter traces the politics of British schooling, with its changing pattern of legislative intervention and implied notions of the child, since 1945. Its main focus is on the period since 1979, one of unbroken Conservative government in Britain, but it argues that some important changes in the school lives of British children were in gestation some years before the word 'Thatcherism' had entered the lexicon of social commentary.

The chapter begins with an account of British schooling between the 1940s and the 1970s, touching on the main measures taken by government, and on the political and academic debates about British schoolchildren that took place over the period; I look then at the Education Reform Act of 1988 (the so-called 'Baker Act'), which, for good or ill, was, as Baker himself proudly claimed on several occasions, the most significant reform of the British education system since the Second World War. Then I consider the political aftermath of the Act, during which, with the Department of Education and Science under the tenure, first of Kenneth Clarke, then of John Patten, some of its consequences for schoolchildren and those charged with their education became clearer. Next I outline the response of the left in Britain to these changes, firstly in the academic world, secondly among those left intellectuals in Britain now discerning 'New Times' and, thirdly, within the broad movement for children's rights (discussed in greater detail elsewhere in this book by Annie and Bob

Franklin). Finally, I comment on the current politics of childhood-in-education in Britain in the mid-1990s, noting in particular key interventions by the Prime Minister John Major, the Leader of the Opposition Tony Blair, and their principal respective lieutenants, Gillian Shephard and David Blunkett.

I should add that much or most of what I have to say is necessarily not about children directly, but about what is said and done in their name. Political rhetoric in this area, however heady or vacuous, necessarily reveals assumptions about 'the child' and it's these assumptions, and the changing discourses and political mythologies of which they have been a part, that are my main concern throughout. None of the more powerful discourses or mythologies has attended to children *as subjects*; indeed, although one of the central axioms of the contemporary politics of British schooling is that providers of education are now beholden to 'consumers', these consumers are taken to be, not the children concerned, but their parents.

After Butler, Before Baker: Unpicking the Post-war Settlement

The contemporary British school system was forged in the political consensus of late war time: the Education Act of 1944, presented by R.A. Butler, President of the Board of Education in the coalition government, established secondary education for all children to the age of fifteen. The act was one of the first to enshrine in legislation the now widely endorsed concept of 'equality of opportunity', between the social classes in this instance. 'We must make sure', stressed the Prime Minister Sir Winston Churchill in a broadcast to the nation the previous year, 'that the path to the highest functions throughout our society and empire is really open to the children of every family.' These families, constituting the nation, were explicitly racialized, Churchill informing his audience that the future of the world, with its 'scientific apparatus' lay in the hands of the 'educated races' (Cootes, 1984, p. 87). The act, however, was not prescriptive as to the nature of secondary education to be provided in each district and this was a matter of clear political contention.

In most areas it was decreed that children should move from the newly designated primary schools to different types of secondary school, according to their performance in the 'Eleven Plus' examination. The Eleven Plus was a test format which had been available to British teachers since the introduction of the Free Place scheme in secondary grammar schools in 1907 and it was rooted in the then prevailing notion of the child as inheritor of its 'intelligence quotient'. This notion had, before the Second World War, generally been seen by its exponents as a progressive measure, favouring the 'naturally gifted' child over the rich child of modest intellect (Bernbaum, 1967, pp. 80–1), although now on the left it is regarded as a reactionary, unscientific and class-based device (Rose, Kamin and Lewontin, 1984, Ch. 5). According to their performance in the Eleven Plus, children in the state sector were allocated either to grammar schools, or to modern schools, or, in a minority of cases, to technical schools. Local authorities were sustained in the framing of this provision by the influential Norwood Report of 1943, which had declared, quite arbitrarily and without evidence, that there were three types of child: one that liked learning 'for its own sake', one that relished only 'applied' learning and one who 'deals more easily with concrete things than with ideas' (Maclure, 1973, pp. 201–2).

A handful of local authorities used their new powers under the 1944 Act to introduce comprehensive secondary schools: that is, schools academically unselective in their admissions policy. This was principally in rural areas, where scattered populations were thought to be insufficient to support a sixth form based on selection, and, for the most part, in the immediate post-war period, comprehensive schooling was a demand of the left alone. The Labour Party Conference of 1944 had voted for comprehensive schooling, but the Labour government elected the following year had demurred: the orthodoxy, both in the party leadership and the Department of Education, was that the grammar schools remained the best chance for the able, working-class child.

There had, however, been strong agitation within the Labour Party since the 1930s (Bernbaum, 1967, p. 58) for some form of unitary secondary schooling and rank-and-file anger at the obduracy of the Attlee government culminated in the unanimous passing of a resolution at the party conference of 1947, warning the minister, George Tomlinson, not to 'perpetuate under the new Education Act the undemocratic traditions of English secondary education' (Simon, 1991, pp. 104–8).

The movement for comprehensive secondary education gained steadily in strength through the 1950s, drawing in large numbers of the more liberally-minded educationists, politicians, teachers and parents. The growing support for comprehensive secondary schooling marks the further consecration of 'equality of opportunity' as a political ideal, assumed in, and held out to, the electorate. The child, as bearer of this ideal, was now conceived increasingly as a *social being*, whose educational progress was dependent, not on natural endowment, but on *culture*: teachers, peers, parents and the rest. The sociological literature that reviewed schooling in the 1950s and early 60s varied in its perspective, certainly. Some, notably J.W.B. Douglas' influential *The Home and the School* which was first published in 1964, were heavily positivistic. Douglas' book was based on survey research and laden with tables and statistical appendices; its children are the passive receptacles of social class difference and their school experience mediated almost wholly through test results (Douglas, 1964). Others, like Jackson and Marsden's widely cited *Education and the Working Class*, featured the schoolchild as *subject* — albeit, in Jackson and Marsden's case, through the device of adults recalling their schooldays. Contrary to the expressed wish of many of their respondents, who had progressed successfully, via the Eleven Plus, into middle-class occupations and saw no need for reform, Jackson and Marsden call for the introduction of comprehensive schooling: '. . . we hope our voice is the voice of the last grammar school generations: for something better can be done' (Jackson and Marsden, 1966, p. 247).

The new academic consensus in these matters, therefore, was that the educational performance of schoolchildren was *socially constructed*, and not the product of biologically given intelligence rising to the surface. This married well with the emergent ethos of an increasingly technocratic Labour Party, out of office since 1951 and convulsed by successive 'Must Labour Lose' debates. Labour leaders now saw comprehensive education as the principal motif of a fresh Britain, based on talent, openness and merit. Anthony Crosland, Secretary of State for Education in the Labour government which came narrowly to power in 1964 and whose book *The Future of Socialism* (Crosland, 1956) was seen as a blueprint for the new party philosophy, informed his wife soon after the election: 'If it's the last thing I do, I'm going to destroy every fucking grammar school in England . . . And Wales. And Northern Ireland' (Crosland, 1983, p. 148).

In 1965, the first Wilson government, aware of the narrowness of its majority and of strong residual support for grammar schools in each major political party, opted for a departmental circular, rather than legislation, to guide Crosland's three national targets toward comprehensive schooling. Circular 10/65 asked local authorities to draw up plans to introduce comprehensive schools in their area. The essentially supplicant nature of this measure meant, importantly, that local authorities and individual schools could interpret the word 'comprehensive' as they pleased. Although enough to persuade the now-retired Butler that Labour's approach was 'obsessive' and 'doctrinal', rather than 'empirical' (Butler, 1973, p. 125), Circular 10/65 in practice allowed local education planners real latitude. Some, indeed, evaded comprehensive reorganization altogether but, crucially, many of those that complied with the circular did so on the basis of *internal selection* — that is, streaming. So, although the point was reached around 1973 when over 50 per cent of state schoolchildren of the appropriate age were in a school labelled 'comprehensive', in practice very few of these schools engaged solely in 'mixed ability teaching': most of them selected within their pupil population at some stage (Bellaby, 1977, p. 12). Moreover, a good many schools after 'going comprehensive' nevertheless maintained many elements of their previous cultural identity, grammar or modern (Bellaby, 1977, pp. 80–3).

This matter of internal selection lies at the heart of the political debate about children and secondary schooling between the mid-1960s and the late 1970s. For many on the radical left and for a large cadre of academic commentators, the child in school was seen as enmeshed in a complex and ongoing labelling process: consignment to a low stream was, like the poor IQ score and the Eleven Plus 'failure' before it, conceived as the first step on the road to a self-fulfilling prophecy. Books like David Hargreaves' *Social Relations in a Secondary School* were very influential here (Hargreaves, 1967). They were important, not only in discussing the low expectations that may result from streaming children, but in the simple validation of the schoolchild's experience and of the dissident subcultures in which such children often sought consolation. Indeed, this became something of an academic theme: in *Learning to Labour*, one of the most cited education books of the 1970s, a bunch of low-stream secondary modern school boys in the West Midlands — sensitively understood, if extravagantly theorized, by the researcher Paul Willis — storm onto the unskilled job market in a hail of expletives and defiant male bravado (Willis, 1977). While such lads were pushed to the margins of school life, the implication was, equality of opportunity did not exist.

For the right, the essential fear was of social *contagion*: 'able' children would be obstructed in their progress by contact, in the same classroom, by pupils of the wrong sort, who 'didn't want to work', 'would slow the others up', and so on. Moreover, a taken-for-granted school culture, as part of an equally taken-for-granted national culture, was felt to be under threat, menaced, in particular, by increasingly relativist accounts of school knowledge (e.g., Young, 1971). In the burgeoning number of Marxist analyses, this knowledge was depicted as merely incidental to the reproduction of class relations (Althusser, 1971; Bowles and Gintis, 1976). Linguists asserted that no correct use of language could be defined (Labov, 1973; Rosen, 1974; Stubbs, 1976) and the anarchist Catholic priest Ivan Illich called for school to be abolished altogether (Illich, 1971).

A series of Black Papers now appeared, the first in 1969. These collections of articles were compiled, variously, by Brian Cox, Professor of English at Manchester University, Tony Dyson, another teacher of literature, and Rhodes Boyson, an historian, head of Highbury Grove School in London and aspiring politician of the populist right. The papers themselves were written in a paradigm of Leavisite anxiety that learned, 'good' culture was being dismembered. Boyson (1995) wrote later:

> My concern was the preservation of culture and good academic education wherever they existed, irrespective of whether this was in a tripartite, a bipartite or a comprehensive system. I was first and foremost an educationalist concerned for high standards, as I still am. (p. 88)

Children, perceived in the Black Papers as unstable creatures in need of firm guidance, should be brought back to the traditional verities: there should be spelling, punctuation and a clear sense of right and wrong. 'Discipline' and 'standards', now assumed to be declining in schools, must be restored. These two words have remained staples of political and media discourse on schooling ever since. Moreover, the notion that the good order of school life was being subverted by one malign cultural influence or another is one to which Conservative politicians, and their allies in an increasingly self-parodic popular press, have had frequent recourse since the late 1960s. The cultural politics of which the makers of the Education Reform Act of 1988 subsequently availed themselves emerged at this time, and they became part of a central element in 'Thatcherism' — rhetorical invocations of 'Sixties permissiveness'.

Don't Try to Understand Them: The 'Baker Act' and the Politics of Decline

It's now no more than a truism to observe that Britain in the 1970s was a society in decline. The decline had deep historical roots (Gamble, 1981; Overbeek, 1990) but it did not become a manifest fact of British political life until this decade. The rise in international oil prices during the early part of the decade and the growing uncompetitiveness of British industry precipitated a crisis of the corporate state that was first explicitly recognized by the third Wilson government of 1974: Anthony Crosland, now Secretary of State for the Environment with responsibility for public spending on local government services, declared memorably in 1975: 'The party's over' (Crosland, 1983, p. 295). The period of decline is also the period of the breaking of the post-war political consensus and the rise of the 'New Right' (Levitas, 1986). The ideas and prescriptions of the New Right have had clear reverberations, both material and ideological, in the lives of British schoolchildren.

The late 1960s and early 1970s saw a number of moral panics about children and cultural subversion. The activities of the 'hippy' movement and the open advocacy by leading popular cultural figures of sexual freedom and the decriminalization of consciousness-changing drugs caused disquiet in ruling circles, where there was particular concern about the likely effects on the young. This concern is thought to have provoked the prosecution for drug offences of three members of the Rolling Stones in 1967 and of three editors of the 'underground' magazine *Oz* in 1971: Issue 28 of this sexually explicit magazine (designated *The School Kids Issue*, June 1970) had been edited by young volunteers aged between 14 and 18 and *Oz*'s editors were charged with attempting to corrupt the morals of young children, a serious offence normally associated with child molesters. They were convicted and sentenced to prison terms, although the sentences were suspended on appeal (Palmer, 1971).

The editors of *Oz* had tapped into a small but perceptible movement, among older children and sympathetic adults, which sought greater personal freedom for those of school age. The popular press at the time of the *Oz* episode were also angrily denouncing *the little red schoolbook*, which political activists were said to be selling to impressionable schoolchildren. Published in Copenhagen, primarily associated in the tabloid social landscape with pornography, the *lrs* aimed to explain school life to the young, offering advice on learning, teachers, punishment, pupils, the exams system and so on. There is much advice on drugs and sex, intelligence, gender discrimination and how to form a school council. Children are encouraged to demand their rights 'but be polite' and they are informed that 'All grown-ups are paper tigers' (Hansen and Jensen, 1971). Many of the issues raised in the book were taken up by the National Union of School Students (see Franklin and Franklin, Chapter 7 in this book) which flourished briefly in the mid-1970s and whose magazine *Blot* dealt in matters such as 'bunking' [off school], exams, 'wanking' and the scrapping of school uniform. NUSS issued a twenty-seven point policy statement after a national conference in October 1972, which must rank as one the most uncompromising and idealistic statements of liberation philosophy ever seen in British educational politics (see Figure 2.1). It is also a mirror image of Conservative education policy since 1979: almost all the things which NUSS called for have been specifically removed or prevented.

Figure 2.1: NUSS Policy Statement as Amended by National Conference 28/29 October 1972

NUSS exists to protect and advance the interests of school students and in so doing to seek student-teacher co-operation on common issues pertaining to the following:

1. To work for a co-educational comprehensive system of education with the phasing out of all grammar schools, public schools, direct grant and secondary modern schools and the abolition of streaming inside existing comprehensives and end all divisions on the grounds of class, sex, race or religion, and physical handicap as far as possible.

2. To promote greater democracy inside schools eventually leading to school committees of teachers, students, parents and non-academic staff subject to instant recall, and representatives of the local community controlling the schools and organising the curriculums; representation of students, teachers, parents and non-academic staff on local education committees.

3. To work towards the abolition of the role of boards of school governors, but *in the short term*, making them more representative of the local community including staff, students and parents.

4. To work towards the abolition of compulsory religious education and religious assembly, to be replaced by optional discussion periods or unbiased cultural/religious education. Also to work towards the abolition of compulsory physical education and all forms of military training in schools.

5. To work towards:
(a) The speedy abolition of corporal punishment and the prefect system, and to encourage an increase of student responsibility and self discipline in schools.
(b) All forms of discipline to be under the control of a school committee and all school rules to be published.

6. To campaign for a greater rate of expansion of expenditure on schools — especially on school buildings and facilities — to meet the increased demand caused by the raising of the school leaving age.

7. To campaign for increases in teachers' salaries, and better conditions, with an immediate reduction in class size, to a maximum of 25 in the short term, and with more and better trained teachers, all attending regular refresher courses.

8. Increased availability of school facilities to the local community developing schools as centres for sport, arts, meetings and youth clubs.

9. To work towards a fair measurement of ability, incorporating a mixture of continuous assessment, oral and course work (open book), project work and an examination, to replace the present examinations-based system, and to consider new methods of selection for higher education.

---

10. To fight for the immediate re-introduction of free school milk for pupils under 16, and to eventually obtain a free school meals service and free public transport to and from school.

11. A minimum living wage for all students over the age of 16, i.e., to enable life independent of parental support.

12. To fight unemployment amongst school leavers and to fight for better training conditions for those at work and for an improved Youth Employment Service geared towards *All* school leavers, staffed and employed by the broad Labour Movement.

13. To fight for free state nursery schools as a right, and the phasing out of private nursery schools.

14. To fight for freedom of speech, assembly and the end of censorship of school magazines, clubs and societies and the banning of non-academic and confidential fields (sic) in schools, and that students be allowed to see any references about themselves, sent to further education establishments or prospective employers.

15. To defend the rights of any school student (whether or not a member of the union) and teacher against victimization.

16. To achieve beneficial relations with teaching unions and all trade union organisations.

17. To secure recognition that the basic human rights apply equally to all school students.

18. To campaign for better sex education and free contraceptives to be available for everyone over the age of consent.

19. To work towards the abolition of compulsory uniform, but to have suitable alternatives to uniform grants, students having the right to determine their own appearence at school.

20. To campaign for better conditions for school students in part time employment, including guarantee of tenure and a minimum legal wage.

21. Higher education should be open to all those who desire it and are prepared to study.

22. (a) To press for more immediate teaching of English to immigrant children, while retaining their national identity.
(b) To press for more bi-lingual teachers.

23. To fight for the same freedom to be given in boarding schools as to those living at home.

24. To fight for the free movement in and out of the school grounds and buildings during break, lunchtime, and free periods.

25. The Union believes that school students should be encouraged to prepare voluntarily for lessons at home, rather than be forced to do extra work at home to supplement school lessons.

26. To encourage each branch to take active part in local youth councils and similar organisations.

27. To campaign for the right of school students of all ages to have a 'Common Room' and to have facilities of relaxation similar to those enjoyed by teachers and sixth-formers.

In 1976, the national politics of childhood-in-education in Britain acquired the toxic mixture of fact, reactionary fantasy and lurid, tabloid-assisted speculation that has characterized it ever since (Holland, 1992, pp. 76–81). This was occasioned by the William Tyndale affair, in which the staff of a primary school in the north London borough of Islington had in the early 1970s fallen foul of many parents in trying to implement a progressive educational regime. Although the dissatisfaction of parents, inspectors and some staff was real enough, it could not explain the extraordinary national prominence to which the affair was raised. A Queen's Counsel was appointed to conduct an inquiry into the matter (Auld, 1976); several of the teachers indicted in the matter wrote a book in their own defence (Ellis, McWhirter, McColgan and Haddow, 1976); and two journalists from the *Times Educational Supplement* judged in a third account of the affair that the claim of teachers to professional status was shown, through this incident, to be 'ambiguous'. In such situations 'market forces' would intervene in the form of parents willing to 'vote with their feet' (Gretton and Jackson, 1976, pp. 124–5). The William Tyndale episode had ramification way beyond Islington and long after 1976. As Brian Simon (Simon, 1991, p. 446) observed, it brought teaching into disrepute and called the autonomy of teachers, schools and local authorities into question. Tyndale was followed by a steady flow of stories in the British popular press telling of 'bad teachers' who must be dismissed (SACK SCHOOL DUNCES ran a typical headline in the *Daily Express*, 16 July 1977) and the need to return to 'the three R's' (School Without Walls/Corner House Bookshop, 1978).

In 1976, the recently elected Prime Minister James Callaghan made a speech at Ruskin College, Oxford in which he spoke of children being overly prepared for their social role and not well enough schooled for their work role: 'Many schools', he recalled later,

> had developed experimental methods of learning, more centred on the child and less on the subject. When I visited I saw many happy, alert children far less repressed than I had been and occupying themselves with a wider range of activities. But were they also acquiring skill in handling the basic tools of knowledge they would need in later life? (Callaghan, 1987, p. 409)

Thus Callaghan, while appearing to welcome the greater vitality and self-possession engendered by child-centred learning, nevertheless accommodates the newly constructed national mood on schooling, with its key signifier, 'the three Rs'. The editors of the Black Papers were now, apparently, the authors of a new political consensus on the educational politics of childhood. The first sentence of Black Paper 1977 reads:

> In April 1969, Mr Short, then Secretary of State for Education and Science, said that the publication of the Black Paper was one of the blackest days for education for 100 years. He described our criticism of

informal education as 'archaic rubbish'. In October 1976, Mr Callaghan, the Prime Minister, attempted to steal our clothes, which have always been freely available. (Cox and Boyson, 1977, p. 5)

These clothes formed a paradigm for thinking about children in school roughly as follows: children were not, and should not be, self-determining creatures — they needed firm instruction, 'discipline' and 'standards'; these commodities were part of a national culture, independent of party politics and now under threat; this threat came, variously, from Labour politicians peddling the comprehensive ideal, from educational bureaucrats and from teachers who were 'progressive', 'trendy' or merely 'bad'; the nature of this threat was, chiefly, that it undermined the simple distinction between correct and incorrect, especially in humanities subjects such as English and history, where the spectre of cultural relativism was now raised; such 'progressive' pedagogy had brought school leavers onto the job market inadequately prepared for work; parents were assumed to share this analysis and to want a greater say in the conduct of schooling as a consequence; the school lives of children were judged now primarily in terms of their parents' *aspiration*, and education seen as a means specifically to social mobility and self-advancement, rather than to personal enlightenment or the tools of citizenship. Not to accept this paradigm was seen, increasingly, as failing the nation's children.

Once the paradigm was established and the Labour Party defeated in the General Election of 1979 a steady stream of proposals from emboldened right-wing commentators and 'think tanks' began to be made available to government. If the radical educational left, never a serious force in British schools, was now no more than a figment of the fevered imaginations of *Daily Express* readers, the far educational right received direct access to Downing Street. By the mid-1980s, not only were such groups calling for the complete dismantlement of the post-Butler system, but they had discovered new malign influences in the lives of the apparently long-suffering British schoolchild: left-wing local education authorities bent on the politicization of the curriculum. Children, it was alleged, were now being subjected to a range of leftist propaganda, such as anti-racism, anti-sexism and 'peace studies', while traditional values like heterosexuality and the Christian religion were being undermined (see particularly The Hillgate Group, 1986, 1987; Flew, 1987). While the popular press eagerly espoused the cause of teachers apparently in conflict with what they styled 'loony left councils' (Curran and Petley, forthcoming), the third Thatcher administration was putting an Education Reform Bill before parliament.

Both the substance of the Education Reform Act of 1988 and the pretext for its introduction, are anticipated in a tract called *Whose Schools? A Radical Manifesto*, issued by the right-wing Hillgate Group in 1986. Margaret Thatcher borrowed directly from its rhetoric when informing the Conservative Party Conference the following year that some British schoolchildren were now being taught 'anti-racist mathematics, political slogans, that they had an inalienable right to be gay and that our society offered them no future' (quoted in Simon,

1988, p. 18). The 'Baker' Act could thus be presented as putting an end to this state of affairs and as banishing all the dangerous progressivism of the previous two decades. The main provisions of the act are well known: a national curriculum of ten compulsory subjects, arranged around a core of three — English, maths and science; the provision for state schools to 'opt out' of local authority control and instead become maintained by direct government grant; 'open enrolment', giving schools the right to admit, and by implication to reject, as many pupils as they pleased; and the submission of children to regular tests, the results of which must be made public.

Baker had invited comment on his proposals from an array of interested parties; most of it was ignored and, indeed, withheld from public scrutiny until it was published in book form by a former television journalist (Haviland, 1988). When he presented the bill to the House of Commons in December 1987 he cited low skill levels in the workforce as a principal motive; referring to Callaghan's Ruskin speech of 1976, he claimed that 25 per cent of the long-term unemployed were now 'functionally illiterate'. But the central thrust of the government's case was that the bill would empower parents. Indeed, Baker later rendered his project at the DES as one of breaking the hold on education of its 'producers' — local authorities, teachers, teacher unions and leftish civil servants within his own department, who favoured comprehensive schooling — and transferring power to its 'consumers' defined in this instance as parents and business people (Baker, 1993, Chapters 8 and 10). Children, throughout the lengthy rationalizing of the new measures, remained the property of protective parents — Baker himself wrote of 'TV and radio networks . . . only too happy to include speeches from the most militant and rampant teachers whom parents would not want to see anywhere near their children' (Baker, 1993, p. 175) — and they provided, for the most part, a suitably emotive pretext for action: 'Our children deserve better'. The active participation of children in the ordering of school life was specifically curtailed in Baker's bill: pupil governorship for under-18s was abolished and proceedings of the committee stage of the bill reveal no obvious opposition to this from Labour MPs.

Children's representation in school government does take place in other European countries, such as Spain, France and Norway (Children's Rights Development Unit, 1994a). In Britain a further Education Act in 1993 confirmed parents as the 'consumers' of education. That these consumers might enjoy any genuine sovereignty in the matter of their children's schooling was, however, always in doubt.

Baker Days: Politics, Children and the New Educational Market

The term 'parent power', so often the ideological sound and fury surrounding the 1988 Act, seldom carried much conviction outside the government and its more ardent supporters and advisors. Although Labour were unlikely, once in office, to disturb the reforms, the Shadow Education Minister Jack Straw argued in the Commons that the proposals should be called the 'Education (State Control) Bill', for the many powers it vested, not in parents but in the Secretary of State. Former Premier Edward Heath argued in the same debate that: 'Parent power is just a political slogan. It has no real meaning for today's education system' (House of Commons, 1 December 1987) and Sir Ian Gilmour, a member of the first Thatcher cabinet, some years later perceived that:

> Parental choice is really a misnomer. Parents can express their prefer-
> ence for a particular school, but that is what they could, and did, do
> before. Unlike chocolate manufacturers, schools cannot hugely expand
> their production — they are constrained by the size of their buildings . . .
> (Gilmour, 1993, p. 206)

Opting out, argued Gilmour, would *decrease* parental choice because local authorities, also working now to a High Court ruling that forbad them to place applicants from their own area ahead of those from neighbouring LEAs, simply wouldn't be able to offer much choice. LEA schools would in time form the bottom of a revived three-tier system, below independent schools and 'opted-out', grant-maintained ones (Gilmour, 1993, pp. 209–10).

The political task of educating the parents claimed to have been enfranchised by the Act fell initially to Kenneth Clarke, appointed Education Secretary in 1990 in the first Major cabinet. In September 1991, he issued a 'Parents' Charter', one of a flurry of such charters to emanate from the Major administrations: this one asserted parents' right to information on the 'perform-ance' of each school — including truancy, examination results and the destina-tion of leavers (Meikle, 1991). Clarke's stay at Education was brief; he moved to the Home Office in 1992 and was replaced by John Patten. Schools policy under Patten did not differ greatly from that of his immediate predecessors, Clarke and John MacGregor (1989–90) and, since it was circumscribed by the voluminous reform act of 1988, it was not likely to. But his term of office provided a remarkable piece of political theatre and it was during this period that the main implications of the Act became clear.

John Patten sprang straight from the pages of Patrick Wright's *On Liv-ing in an Old Country*, a book about how ideas of Englishness and a mythic national past reverberate in the present times of confusion and decline (Wright, 1985). Patten, the child of a gardener and a domestic servant and educated in a state school (Bates, 1993) had, like a number of upwardly mobile males of post-war generations, developed a persona apparently based on the imaginary English gentleman; his clipped, early nineteenth-century aristocratic diction could have gained him a small part in a television costume drama. But such a pre-democratic presentation of self created havoc in his dealings in the edu-cation world, not least with parents, who, according to his party's own rhetoric, had just been brought to power in the government of schools.

Patten's initial strategy was the same as Clarke's had been: to defend the position of the new education market by invoking, regardless of their purchase on the current situation, the various monsters of Black Paper mythology. Both Clarke and Patten had frequent recourse to the word 'trendy', claiming, time and again, to have detected 'fashionable theories' at work in schools which obstructed children's access to sensible 'chalk and talk' teaching methods; this became a pretext for appointing a succession of educational activists of the far right to government advisory bodies on schooling (Judd and Crequer, 1992). There followed in 1993 a series of threats-to-our-schoolchildren which had to be addressed. In February he suggested that the National Union of Teachers and the National Association of Schoolmasters Union of Women Teachers represented old-fashioned trade unionism and that their members were more interested in causing trouble than in educating children (*Guardian*, 8 February). The following month he announced that tests conducted the previous summer under the Baker Act had revealed unacceptable reading levels in a third of 14 year olds (*Guardian*, 12 March). In June, possibly concerned about the excess of 'theory', the minister proposed conscripting a 'Mum's Army' of non-graduates into the teaching of children under seven (*Guardian*, 10 June). In October, Patten published proposals to extend the 'spiritual, moral and cultural aspects of pupils' development' by giving collective worship and, specifically, Christianity a more central place in the curriculum (*Guardian*, 12 October). Later the same month, as part of the government's grotesque 'Back to Basics' campaign, he turned his attention to single mothers, suggesting that schoolchildren with such parentage had a diminished sense of right and wrong (*Guardian*, 26 October). In November, Patten, in separate statements, claimed that one adult in ten was still 'functionally illiterate' (*Guardian*, 16 November) and that one schoolchild in eight was absent from school without leave for at least half a day in the school year — he castigated one quarter of schools for not supplying figures for the new 'truancy league tables' (*Guardian*, 18 November). Three weeks later, he warned teachers of sex education to make clear to their young charges that marriage took precedence over single parenthood, and heterosexuality over homosexuality (*Guardian*, 7 December). Then, in January 1994 he issued a draft document on school discipline, which was, as his department admitted, simply a re-issue of existing guidelines (*Guardian*, 5 January).

But this attempted moral crusade could conceal neither the very serious fractures in British educational life after Baker, nor the material consequences for children and their families. Opposition to the Act's principal requirements — testing, opting out and the publication of league tables — seemed furious and widespread. Teachers' unions successfully boycotted the government's test programme for the summer of 1993, chiefly on the ground that they were unworkable. On 2 June, Patten addressed the annual conference of the National Association of Head Teachers and was not only loudly barracked from the floor but informed by the association's president that many of the things he was doing were 'wrong'. Two months later, government advisor Sir Ron Dearing announced simplification both of the tests and of the national curriculum (*Guardian*, 3 August).

Moreover, parents, the acknowledged focal point of government strategy and the purported beneficiaries of Patten's various initiatives, seemed even less satisfied than teachers with the new arrangements. In particular, a majority were opposed to the tests, which, Patten had acknowledged in March of 1993, could be used for selection (*Guardian*, 3 March). Polls showed opinion evenly divided in the spring of that year but as early as the beginning of May the National Confederation of Parent Teacher Associations was warning that huge numbers of parents would allow their children to call in sick on the day of the tests (*Guardian*, 1 May). Furthermore, research by Exeter University appeared to show parental support for the teachers' boycott growing during the summer. Importantly, the Exeter survey revealed an unwillingness among parents to adopt Patten's critical perspective on contemporary schooling; indeed, 70 per cent were happy with the tuition provided. On the whole, they had no complaint about the atmosphere in their child's school, nor about its teachers, nor about the educational standards achieved; any dissatisfaction generally touched more material aspects of school life, such as the state of buildings and grounds (Judd, 1993). (Patten actually relaxed school building standards about ten days later — *Guardian*, 16 June).

So, if it had ever been the intention of the Major government to use powerful themes such as standards, values and discipline to drive a wedge between teachers and parents, the wedge did not materialize. Indeed, the depth of parents' opposition to the new system was noted on the far left, where *Socialist Worker*, organ of the Trotskyite Socialist Workers' Party, ran a series of optimistic headlines (e.g., SCHOOLS REVOLT SHAKES TORIES, 10 April 1993) and interviews: 'John Patten is just ignoring what the parents are saying,' said a Suffolk teacher, 'The parents have been brilliant' reported a teacher from Hertfordshire (20 March).

However, taken in the round, the response of the broader left to the Baker Act and its implications for children has been considerably more accommodating. I conclude this section with a brief account of this response.

After the crushing defeat of the Labour Party in the General Election of 1983, there were increasing calls for a 'rethink' on the left. In the field of education such voices were raised most notably in a collection of short essays entitled *Is Anyone Here From Education?* (Wolpe and Donald, 1983). Actually written in the run-up to the election it contained arguments by leading cultural spokespeople of the left, such as Stuart Hall (Hall, 1983) and Richard Johnson (Johnson, 1983) for a new political language in which to discuss schooling. It also included a number of attempts to argue that the established left had not had all the best ideological tunes: Anne Showstack Sassoon, for instance, endorsed some version of 'parent power', hitherto an exclusively Conservative slogan (Showstack Sassoon, 1983), while Valerie Walkerdine raised polite doubts about child-centred education, a central theme for radicals of the 1960s (Walkerdine, 1983).

When the Education Reform Bill was published by the third Thatcher administration, its most decisive critic was Brian Simon, veteran of the Communist

Party and Britain's most respected educational historian. Simon condemned the Bill as a vindictive measure, designed simply to break the power of local authorities and to re-establish an hierarchical system of schooling; comprehensives had been working well, with strong local support (Simon, 1986, 1987, 1988). But other contributions to the debate in the pages of *Marxism Today*, the Communist Party journal, were more ambivalent. Angela McRobbie offered a feminist defence of 'parent power' (McRobbie, 1987) and Andy Green emphasized the need to defend and enhance state education itself — a concept considerably more entrenched in other industrialized countries (Germany, Sweden, France, Holland, Japan . . .) than in Britain, but disparaged in Thatcherite rhetoric. The British system, according to Green, was fragmented and backward. Socialists, therefore, should not oppose a national curriculum; nor should they hold with too much cultural relativism (Green, 1988, 1991).

By the early 1990s, with the declaration of 'New Times' by intellectuals clustered around *Marxism Today* and the embracing of 'postmodernism' by many academics in the British social sciences, previously sympathetic writers felt they must now reject the certainties of Simon and the Seventies left. Eminent among these was James Donald. Donald was one of the few openly to challenge the venerable Simon. Reviewing the final volume of Simon's *Studies in the History of Education* he charges the author with building his narrative 'around unexamined categories of "the people" and "progress" ' (Donald, 1992a, p. 136) and, in his own book *Sentimental Education*, he offers his own way forward for those who rejected free market schooling. *Sentimental Education* draws centrally on the French philosopher Michel Foucault, whose adherents hold that social actors are constituted and categorized through the vocabularies commonly used to describe them, Donald (1992b) seeks to 'deconstruct' the familiar characterizations of the educational argument:

> My aim is . . . to question the existing boundaries of education, and to ask how certain narratives and categories are instituted as authoritative. In asking who has authority over education, for example, I would not take the conventional actors of liberal politics — parents, children, employers, parties, classes, governments — at face value. Rather, I would question how the staging of political dialogue produces these categories as collective actors with common interests: that is, how the terrain of educational debate is constantly made and remade. (p. 15)

Donald examines some of the concepts that have dominated the debate about schooling — the hope of progressive educationists for the self-possession of schoolchildren, the possibility, raised by Raymond Williams in *The Long Revolution* (Williams, 1961) that public education might promote a common culture . . . — and concludes that they are both difficult to define and impossible to realize. Donald, his deconstruction done, calls, more modestly, for the Conservative governments' disciplinary vocationalism in the field of education to be challenged by a 'critical vocationalism [which] would begin by asking what concepts, knowledges and intellectual skills would be necessary for understanding how economies work, in order to develop the potential for autonomy in the shaping of a career':

> Under any foreseeable democratic socialism, labour markets will continue to operate, and they will be characterised by degrees of inequality and antagonism. The question is how might education and training help to maximise the possibilities for autonomy and contest the inequitable and discriminatory practices of employment that exist at present? This implies neither the old socialist dream of liberating the full capacities of man through labour, nor its neo-liberal equivalent of entrepreneurial self-fulfilment. (Donald, 1992b, pp. 162, 164)

Elsewhere, however, child-centred work in relation to schooling continues to be done, chiefly under the rubric of children's rights. Here, many of the objectives of the old left in the matter of schooling have been salvaged, using the political vocabulary of the time, in the form of legal entitlements.

The *UK Agenda for Children* (Children's Rights Development Unit, 1994b), which was written to assess the extent of Britain's compliance with the principles of the UN Convention on the Rights of the Child after the British government ratified the convention in 1990, was co-edited by Peter Newell, once a teacher at the White Lion Free School in Islington. The *UK Agenda* . . . contains a long section on education which argues, among other things, that children have a right not to suffer discrimination in admissions, racism, unwarranted exclusion, bullying or, in the case of private schools, corporal punishment (such punishment became illegal in state schools under the Education Act of 1986, a measure emanating from a ruling in the European Court, not from government policy).

As the new education market takes hold on children's lives, several of these issues will have a sharper relevance: disguised discrimination in admissions is expected to be rife as schools strive to raise their standing in the eyes of 'consumers'; similarly teachers, conscious of the various league tables to which they are now subject, have recently called for greater powers of exclusion (*Guardian*, 22 September 1995).

Although the government is a signatory to the UN Convention, it has persistently argued that all the conditions of the convention are already being met in Britain and that, in the specific case of schooling, the various education acts preclude 'children's rights' as such. The Children's Rights Office reports no conspicuous support for children's rights, at school or elsewhere, in the House of Commons but a number of bodies are sympathetic, including the National Union of Teachers, the Campaign for State Education, the Advisory Centre for Education and Schools Councils UK, a body offering training assistance to schools thinking of setting up a school council and, thus, involving children in some way in the running of the school (Haigh, 1994). It is believed that around one seventh of primary, and one third of secondary, schools have such councils.

This work, of course, has the central and longstanding aim of establishing that schoolchildren are, after all, just people and a vivid illustration of this simple fact occurred in September 1995. A pupil thought to be a 17-year-old sixth former in a Scottish school turned out to be a man of 32; despite the customary lip-licking tabloid speculation, his friends asserted that he had been in every way an ordinary member of the school (*Guardian*, 23 September).

Major, Blair and the Games We Play: Schooling and Politics in the Mid-1990s

Several things are clear, and important to note, about the relationship between politics and schooling in Britain at the end of the century. Firstly, in British political culture the language of government is increasingly the language of public relations: policies which manifestly lack public support — indeed, which arouse clear antagonism — are deemed merely to have had an inadequate presentation. Thus, despite widespread parental anger at their main provisions and about the maintenance of schools in general, the education reforms were preserved in all their fundamentals. Instead, in 1994, the unpopular Patten was replaced with the more emollient Gillian Shephard and the following year, in the ultimate vocationalist gesture, Major merged the departments of education and employment.

A policy document thought to have been written by Shephard and leaked to the press in September 1995, is couched almost wholly in the vocabulary of political advertising: there is talk of 'a perception that schools are underfunded', which can be countered by words that people find attractive 'such as standards, discipline and chaos'. Shephard warns that some existing policies will cost the votes of maturing children 'and those of their parents' (*Guardian*, 15 September). Here education appears simply as a means to electoral success and 'good PR', with no external social purpose.

Secondly, and in this connection, schooling has moved nearer the centre of the national political stage and now contends with 'law and order' in the ceaseless quest for good poll ratings and 'feel good factors'. In 1994, Prime Minister John Major drew cheers from the Conservative Party Conference when he promised to 'put competitive games back at the heart of school life', thereby creating the subtext of an army of feminists and feckless progressives tampering with the national grit (Hargreaves, 1995). The following summer, Major gave an extended interview to Bruce Anderson in the *Times* in which he revealed that education was top of the government's agenda and spoke of 'a feeling in this country that we listen too much to the experts and too little to ordinary people' (Anderson, 1995). He urged schools to opt out of local authority control, something that 'ordinary people' seemed determined not to do: only 1,073 out of 24,000 schools had done so.

Thirdly, curricular politics continued to be dominated by right-wing notions and personnel. In 1992, Brian Cox, co-editor of all the Black Papers, had talked of a new trend to derogate teachers and impose curriculum 'which the best teachers know to be narrow and bigoted'; he had, he said, heard a rumour that right-wing Conservatives had been promised 'control of education' in return for their cooperation over the treaty of Maastricht (Cox, 1992).

In the summer of 1995, Nicholas Tate, Head of the School Curriculum and Assessment Authority appealed for a greater emphasis on narrative, Britishness and national heroes in the teaching of history. Around the same time, Shephard moved to appease accusations that a rise in examination passes actually meant a fall in standards, through 'grade inflation'; she set up an enquiry (*Guardian*, 10 August). Two days later Ofsted, the privatized school inspectorate, criticized teachers' reports for being too positive and failing to mention weaknesses. And in October, at the party conference, Shephard unveiled a working party to promote 'better' spoken English; in a symbolic rebuttal of cultural relativism its head turned out to be Trevor McDonald, a television newsreader, who, although born in Trinidad, had as a boy taught himself to speak like the voices on BBC radio's World Service (*Guardian*, 12 October). A former advisor, by contrast, warned of the educational dangers of increasing class sizes (*Guardian*, 16 October).

Fourthly, the Leader of the Opposition, Tony Blair gave an unmistakable personal endorsement to the notions of 'opting out' and 'parental choice'. He and his wife elected in 1994 to send their son Euan to an opted-out school eight miles from the family home. Blair's response to the inevitable furore which greeted the decision was instructive: 'Any parent wants the best for their children. I am not going to make a choice for my child on the basis of what is the politically correct thing to do' (*Guardian*, 2 December 1994). Blair's reaction was important not merely because it was the understanding of his colleagues that Labour policy was to oppose opting out and, once in power, to return the schools concerned to local authority control; but he implies, by invoking the notion of 'any parent', that his response, being rooted in some kind of common sense, is the only 'real' one, and that other responses are mere posturing.

The Conservatives made much of this decision during 1995. At their conference of that year an expansion was announced of the Assisted Places Scheme (introduced in 1980) whereby gifted children from state schools have places bought for them in private schools by the government. Labour were opposed to this scheme and Deputy Prime Minister Michael Heseltine castigated Blair for his hypocrisy in wanting opportunities for his own son but 'denying them to others'.

Blair's Education Spokesman, David Blunkett responded to this confusion with an ugly and inchoate populism. On Channel Four News (4 October 1995) he made the clearly contradictory undertaking, on the one hand, to equalize funding between opted-out and local authority schools, if Labour come to power; but, on the other, to root out the many teachers guilty of holding low expectations of the working-class pupil, the problem being 'not poverty, but the poverty of our education'. 'I'm sick and tired', he added, 'of people wearing their hearts on their sleeves when, literally, tens of thousands of youngsters are not getting the education they deserve'.

For twenty years, it seems, the leading politicians of education in Britain have ridden some prairie of the imagination, their hands resting in twitchy anticipation on their Colt 45s. The medicine shows, hawking non-standard English or empathetic history from the back of a covered wagon will be ridden out of town; the misguided cowpokes of child-centred education will learn the unsentimental lore of the trail — children are like steers: you don't try to understand them. And the many real men, women and children who still call for fairness, dignity and the prompt repair of leaking roofs in their schools will get short shrift. One's tempted to think that Sir Keith Joseph, Thatcher's second Education Secretary, maybe had a point when he once remarked of state schooling: 'I don't think we know how to do it' (Green, 1991).

Acknowledgment

I'd like to thank Bob Carter, Pat Holland, Jenny Hargreaves, Gerison Lansdown, Jane Pilcher and Schools Councils UK for help in the preparation of this chapter.

References

ALTHUSSER, L. (1971) 'Ideology and ideological state apparatuses: Notes towards an investigation', in COSIN, B.R. (ed.) *Education: Structure and Society*, Harmondsworth, Penguin Books/Open University Press, pp. 242–80.

ANDERSON, B. (1995) 'Major tells nation to seize opportunity', *The Times*, 24th August.

AULD, R. QC (1976) *William Tyndale Junior and Infants Schools: A Report to the Inner London Education Authority*, London, ILEA.

BAKER, K. (1993) *The Turbulent Years: My Life in Politics*, London, Faber and Faber.

BATES, S. (1993) 'When the blue chips are down' [Profile of John Patten] *The Guardian*, 5th April.

BELLABY, P. (1977) *The Sociology of Comprehensive Schooling*, London, Methuen.

BERNBAUM, G. (1967) *Social Change and the Schools 1918–1944*, London, Routledge and Kegan Paul.

BOWLES, S. and GINTIS, H. (1976) *Schooling in Capitalist America*, London, Routledge and Kegan Paul.

BOYSON, R. (1995) *Speaking My Mind*, London, Peter Owen.

BUTLER, Lord, R.A. (1973) *The Art of the Possible*, Harmondsworth, Penguin.

CALLAGHAN, J. (1987) *Time and Chance*, London, Collins.

COOTES, R.J. (1984) *The Making of the Welfare State*, Harlow, Longman.

CROSLAND, A. (1956) *The Future of Socialism*, London, Jonathan Cape.

CROSLAND, S. (1983) *Tony Crosland*, London, Coronet.

COX, B. (1992) 'Curriculum for chaos', *Guardian*, 15th September.

COX, B. and BOYSON, R. (eds) (1977) *Black Paper 1977*, London, Maurice Temple Smith.

CHILDREN'S RIGHTS DEVELOPMENT UNIT (1994a) 'Children's rights and education: How we can achieve change'. Unpublished paper.

CHILDREN'S RIGHTS DEVELOPMENT UNIT (1994b) *The UK Agenda For Children*, London, CRDU.

CURRAN, J. and PETLEY, J. (forthcoming) *Loony Tunes: The Media and Local Democracy*, London, Routledge.

DONALD, J. (1992a) 'Dewey-eyed optimism: The possibility of democratic education', *New Left Review*, No. 192, March/April, pp. 133–42.

DONALD, J. (1992b) *Sentimental Education: Schooling, Popular Culture and the Regulation of Liberty*, London, Verso.

DOUGLAS, J.W.B. (1964) *The Home and the School*, London, McGibbon and Kee.

ELLIS, T., MCWHIRTER, J., MCCOLGAN, D. and HADDOW, B. (1976) *William Tyndale: The Teachers' Story*, London, Writers and Readers Publishing Cooperative.

FLEW, A. (1987) *Power to the Parents: Reversing Educational Decline*, London, The Sherwood Press.

GAMBLE, A. (1981) *Britain in Decline*, London, Macmillan.

GILMOUR, I. (1993) *Dancing with Dogma: Britain under Thatcherism*, London, Pocket Books.

GREEN, A. (1988) 'Lessons in standards', *Marxism Today*, January, pp. 24–30.

GREEN, A. (1991) 'No marks for education', *Marxism Today*, June, pp. 32–5.

GRETTON, J. and JACKSON, M. (1976) *William Tyndale: Collapse of A School — Or A System?* London, George Allen and Unwin.

HAIGH, G. (1994) 'Voices of reason' [on Schools Councils] *Times Educational Supplement*, 27th May.

HALL, S. (1983) 'Education in crisis', in WOLPE, A. and DONALD, J. (eds) *Is Anyone Here From Education?* London, Pluto Press.

HANSEN, S. and JENSEN, J. (1971) *The Little Red School Book*, London, stage 1.

HARGREAVES, D.H. (1967) *Social Relations in a Secondary School*, London, Routledge and Kegan Paul.

HARGREAVES, J. (1995) 'Gender, morality and the national physical education curriculum'. Paper given to Leisure Studies Association conference on *Leisure, Sport and Education*, University of Brighton, Eastbourne, 14th September.

HAVILAND, J. (1988) *Take Care, Mr Baker! The Advice on Education Reform which the Government Collected but Withheld*, London, Fourth Estate.

HILLGATE GROUP (1986) *Whose Schools? A Radical Manifesto*, London, The Hillgate Group.

HILLGATE GROUP (1987) *The Reform of British Education: From Principles to Practice*, London, The Claridge Press.

HOLLAND, P. (1992) *What is a Child? Popular Images of Childhood*, London, Virago.

ILLICH, I. (1971) *Deschooling Society*, London, Calder and Boyars.

JACKSON, B. and MARSDEN, D. (1966) *Education and the Working Class*, Harmondsworth, Pelican.

JOHNSON, R. (1983) 'Educational politics: The old and the new', in WOLPE, A. and DONALD, J. (eds) *Is Anyone Here From Education?* London, Pluto Press.

JUDD, J. and CREQUER, N. (1992) 'The right tightens grip on education', *Independent on Sunday*, 2nd August.

JUDD, J. (1993) 'Parents shun school testing', *Independent on Sunday*, 6th June.

LABOV, W. (1973) 'The logic of nonstandard English', in KEDDIE, N. (ed.) *Tinker, Tailor . . . The Myth of Cultural Deprivation*, Harmondsworth, Penguin.

LEVITAS, R. (ed.) (1986) *The Ideology of the New Right*, Cambridge, Polity Press.

MACLURE, S. (1973) *Educational Documents: England and Wales, 1816 to the Present Day*, London, Methuen.

McROBBIE, A. (1987) 'Parent power at the chalkface', *Marxism Today*, May, pp. 24–7.

MEIKLE, J. (1991) 'Clarke's schools charter "will educate parents"', *Guardian*, 28th September.

OVERBEEK, H. (1990) *Global Capitalism and National Decline: The Thatcher Decade in Perspective*, London, Unwin Hyman.

PALMER, T. (1971) *The Trials of Oz*, London, Blond and Briggs.

ROSE, S., KAMIN, L.J. and LEWONTIN, R.C. (1984) *Not in Our Genes: Biology, Ideology and Human Nature*, Harmondsworth, Pelican.

ROSEN, H. (1974) 'Language and class', in HOLLY, D. (ed.) *Education or Domination?* London, Arrow Books.

SCHOOL WITHOUT WALLS/CORNER HOUSE BOOKSHOP (1978) *Lunatic Ideas: How Newspapers Treated Education in 1977*, London, Corner House Bookshop.

SHOWSTACK SASSOON, A. (1983) 'Dear Parent . . .', in WOLPE, A. and DONALD, J. (eds) *Is Anyone Here From Education?* London, Pluto Press.

SIMON, B. (1986) *Defend Comprehensive Schools*, London, Communist Party of Great Britain.

SIMON, B. (1987) 'Lessons in elitism', *Marxism Today*, September, pp. 12–17.

SIMON, B. (1988) *Bending the Rules: The Baker 'Reform' of Education*, London, Lawrence and Wishart.

SIMON, B. (1991) *Education and the Social Order 1940–1990*, London, Lawrence and Wishart.

STUBBS, M. (1976) *Language, Schools and Classrooms*, London, Methuen.

WALKERDINE, V. (1983) 'It's only natural: Rethinking child-centred pedagogy', in WOLPE, A. and DONALD, J. (eds) *Is Anyone Here From Education?* London, Pluto Press.

WILLIAMS, R. (1961) *The Long Revolution*, London, Chatto and Windus.

WILLIS, P. (1977) *Learning to Labour: How Working Class Kids Get Working Class Jobs*, Farnborough, Saxon House.

WOLPE, A. and DONALD, J. (eds) (1983) *Is Anyone Here From Education?* London, Pluto Press.

WRIGHT, P. (1985) *On Living in an Old Country: The National Past in Contemporary Britain*, London, Verso.

YOUNG, M.F.D. (ed.) (1971) *Knowledge and Control*, London, Collier-Macmillan.

3 'Keeping It in the Family': Thatcherism and the Children Act 1989

Karen Winter and Paul Connolly

Introduction: Thatcherism and the Family

At the heart of the Thatcherite project lay the ability successfully to capture the sense of insecurity and social upheaval that was being increasingly experienced in Britain from the late 1960s onwards and articulate this into a new hegemonic project. The advent of the global recession during this time was bound to hit Britain particularly hard. Many of its traditional industries were becoming obsolete and the constraints imposed by its existing technological base meant that the only option left for Britain, as it strove to be competitive and remain profitable, lay in the wholesale restructuring of its economy. As new technological systems were slowly introduced, large sections of existing employment, particularly in the manufacturing industries disappeared and were only partially replaced by an increase in the amount of part-time and temporary work offered in the service sector industries (Urry, 1989; Murray, 1989; Overbeek, 1990; Mitter, 1986). The growing sense of social upheaval that accompanied this was compounded not only by the still resonating effects of the slum-clearance programmes of the 1960s, where whole communities were broken up and people were isolated from their neighbours, but by a capitalist logic which required a fundamental reassessment of the welfare state and its provisions. Not only did the growing levels of unemployment place increasing demands on the welfare system but there were strong fiscal pressures on the government dramatically to cut and rationalize its welfare spending (Jones, 1989).

It was at this point that the internal contradictions of the social democratic consensus were laid bare as the state was forced to shed its welfare role and, in the depths of economic crisis, come increasingly to discipline and control labour (Hall, 1983). It was on the very site of these contradictions that Thatcherism gained ground. The growing sense of insecurity and social upheaval that accompanied Britain's decline were translated into a new discourse that appropriated the 'language of experience, moral imperative and common sense' (Hall, 1983). The widespread experiences associated with Britain's economic decline — unemployment, industrial disputes and an increasingly coercive and intruding state — were all re-worked through the language of 'Being British' and the need to reverse 'our' national decline. It was a decline, according to such a discourse, that was not simply economic but essentially political and moral as well (Parekh, 1986). As Hall (1983) argues:

> 'Being British' became once again identified with the restoration of competition and profitability; with tight money and sound finance . . . the national economy debated on the model of the household budget. The essence of the British people was identified with self-reliance and personal responsibility, as against the image of the over-taxed individual, enervated by welfare 'coddling', his or her moral fibre irrevocably sapped by 'state handouts'. (p. 29)

Thus Britain's economic decline therefore came to be understood through the weaving together of a whole host of factors (Parekh, 1986). In economic terms, it was the result of the burden of the public sector and lack of entrepreneurs and individual initiative and incentive while, politically, it was associated with 'our' loss of national fighting spirit brought on by the multicultural eroding of 'our' sense of national identity and patriotism. Underlying all of this, however, was moral decline associated, in the first instance, with 'our' over-reliance on the state and the loss of those virtues of self-help and thrift. It was this that undermined our entrepreneurial spirit and our sense of national pride and it was here that discourses on the family played a central role in the Thatcherite project. It was the family that provided the basic 'building block' of society where we learnt 'right from wrong'. Based upon a patriarchal structure and characterized by heterosexuality and within the context of marriage, it was here that children learnt about sexual morality, the importance of deferring to experience and the basic values that made up 'our' national identity (Morgan, 1985; Fitzgerald, 1983; Abbott and Wallace, 1989).

However, it was precisely this institution of the family that had suffered the most under the dangerous values promulgated during the 'permissive sixties'. The state had progressively taken away the rights and responsibilities that had traditionally been placed with parents (Abbott and Wallace, 1989) and had, in turn, created a new set of values within the family, based around those of selfishness and dependency (Fitzgerald, 1983). Not only were children being increasingly taught these new values but were also being given the wrong role models through the breakdown of marriage and the proliferation of 'inadequate family structures and poor family practices' (Morgan, 1985; p. 82). It was in this context that the underlying principles associated with the government's approach to the family came to be expressive of the broader tensions that existed within the Thatcherite project between neo-liberalism and neo-conservatism. On the one hand, then, there were calls for the state to retreat from interfering in the family and, as far as possible, to re-establish it in the private sphere and thus place it out of reach of the dependency culture (David, 1986a; Golding and Middleton, 1982). However, what was meant by 'the family', alluded to above, was defined in very restrictive terms. A second principle therefore emerged in Thatcherite rhetoric that laid stress on the government encouraging the natural values and caring instincts of motherhood and the associated naturalness of patriarchal life (Fitzgerald, 1983; David, 1986b). Indeed this 'interventionist' strand has come to predominate in recent years with the arrival of the Child Support Agency (see Oppenheim and Lister, this volume) and the scape-goating of single parent families.

It is within this context of the importance given to the traditional, patriarchal family unit in Thatcherite discourse that the emergence of the Children Act 1989 presents itself as an inherent paradox. The stress on 'children's rights' that have been associated with the Act stands in stark contrast with the patriarchal values of order, obedience and submissiveness that are traditionally expected of children. It is this apparent contradiction that will form the focus for this chapter. What we will argue is that there is no inherent paradox and, rather, through looking at the history of the Act, at its basic provisions and at how it works in practice, the chapter will conclude that it actually relates quite closely to the broader Thatcherite project.

Social Workers, Moral Panics and the Antecedents to the Act

In trying to understand the emergence of the Children Act 1989 we can point to three underlying factors that can help us explain its timing, nature and form. The first factor relates to a detailed review process that began in earnest in 1984 with the Parliamentary Select Committee (Social Services Committee, 1984) setting out on its task both to modernize and to rationalize child care and family law. This occurred in relation to a growing number of research studies (see Parker, 1980; DHSS, 1985) which highlighted the legislative minefield that had been created by the ad hoc implementation of a number of different legislative acts all relating to child care and families and all themselves originating at different times and over differing concerns (see also Lyon and Parton, 1995). In addition there were concerns regarding the poor quality of social work practice in the field of child care following the creation of generic social service departments under the Seebohm reforms (Seebohm Committee, 1968). It was noted that there was both a failure to work in partnership with parents and an over-reliance on compulsory measures (DHSS 1985; Social Services Committee, 1984). In many ways it was this general review process that made further legislation, in some form, inevitable. Secondly, we can also identify a growing politics, expressed both in Europe and by pressure groups within Britain such as *Justice for Children* and the *Children's Legal Centre* which increasingly came to organize itself around a discourse on rights. Here we find an emphasis on the imbalance of power in local authority decision-making processes between family members and professionals of statutory child care agencies. In this there was a feeling that professionals acted out of the need for self-preservation rather than closely assessing the competing needs and views of family members which, in turn, manifested itself in what was perceived to be an over-reliance, among social workers, on compulsory measures available in family and child care legislation (Lyon and Parton, 1995). This lack of accountability to family members and of an insensitivity to their needs was particularly noted in relation to children whose wishes were opposed to those of their parents or the social services agency (Lyon and Parton, 1995).

It was through the growing influence of this discourse on rights, especially in relation to children, that the legislation to emerge would come at least in part also to develop a language of children's rights. However, the particular nature and form that the legislation eventually took — in the form of the Children Act 1989 — can, as we have argued, only be understood within the broader Thatcherite project that was being constructed. Here, we are particularly thinking of the themes of state intervention and familial decline that came to be refracted through a number of moral panics concerning social work intervention in the period leading up to the formulation and implementation of the Act. It is to these that we now turn.

Between 1980 and 1987, inquiries into the circumstances surrounding the deaths of Jasmine Beckford, Tyra Henry and Kimberley Carlile took place after these children died as a result of injuries inflicted on them by their parents/step-parents and during the course of social work involvement with the families. During this period, social workers and their agencies were widely described in the British media as incompetent (Franklin and Parton, 1991b, 1991c) and lacking insight, initiative, common sense and intelligence (Finnis, 1986; Franklin and Parton, 1991c; Geach, 1982). Moreover, they were said to adopt a 'casualness' in their professional attitudes and practice (Franklin and Parton, 1991c, p. 17). A particular example of this was the 'rule of optimism' as highlighted in the report on the death of Jasmine Beckford (Blom-Cooper, 1985) whereby social workers were said to be guided in their attitude and practice by a belief that difficulties experienced by families leading to 'high risk' situations for children would simply ease and/or resolve themselves over time. This, it was argued, led to intervention of an inappropriate focus where dangers posed to children were at best minimized and at worst ignored. This, in turn, occurred because of social workers' failure fully to understand and use their authority (as prescribed in family and child care legislation) to appropriately deal with 'high risk' situations.

A shift in emphasis, away from the incompetence of social workers towards the unaccountability of their actions, was made in 1988 with the publication of the report of the inquiry into the events in Cleveland (Butler-Sloss, 1988). Here concern emerged over the large increase in the number of children apparently having experienced sexual abuse. This was the diagnosis reached following controversial medical examinations carried out on a number of children which, in many instances, were later revealed to be fundamentally flawed. A number of themes emerged out of this. Firstly there were accusations of 'empire building' levelled at social workers whose actions were seen as simply securing themselves more job-security, money and power (Nava,

1988; McIntosh, 1988; Franklin and Parton, 1991c). Secondly, it was argued that social workers were actively seeking to undermine the family as an institution. This was partly articulated by the local MP Stuart Bell whose portrayal of the parents as essentially victims of unwarranted state intervention gained widespread and largely uncritical media coverage and was also reproduced through the claim that the social work profession had been hijacked by 'ultra-feminist' and 'anti-family' elements (Franklin and Parton, 1991c). Alongside this there emerged a theme that reversed the original allegations and focused, instead, on the 'abuses' of the social workers themselves who, in a rather zealous and obsessive manner, were perceived to force children to undergo unnecessary and intimate medical examinations (Nava, 1988; Franklin and Parton, 1991a, 1991b, 1991c; Winter, 1992). Finally, underlying all of these themes was a concern as to the perceived unaccountability of social workers and their practice; being unaccountable to parents, children, other professionals and legal institutions.

These themes concerning the evils of state intervention were again resurrected, at the time the Children Act 1989 was being implemented, through the moral panics surrounding the events in Nottingham, Rochdale and, in particular, the Orkneys, all of which concerned allegations of ritualistic/satanic abuse (see Winter, 1992). In relation to the Orkneys, they were concerns that coalesced around two basic themes: the denial of abuse and the dangerous and detrimental effect of social work intervention on families and local communities. As regards the former, the whole notion of ritualistic/satanic abuse was undermined by associating its very idea with zealous American evangelical groups whose 'foreign theory', already discredited in the US, was now finding favour with gullible social workers in Britain. Here, social workers were described as both 'naive', 'awfully misguided' and 'muddled' in the British press while also full of 'zeal', 'malice', 'hysteria' and 'arrogance' (Winter, 1992, p. 21). It was therefore not the community that was to blame but social workers and their adherence to fashionable ideologies.

It was here that the press created a space for a more fundamental attack on the training and values underpinning social work more generally. The accusations found in the earlier moral panics over their 'anti-family' and 'ultra-feminist' ideological stance in relation to the Cleveland affair were rehearsed once more here and developed into a more broad and sweeping attack. The *Daily Mail* (6 April 1991, p. 5), for example, referred to 'pseudo-sociological knowledge . . . [and] zealous ideology' associated with the social work profession while their training was seen as 'absurdly impractical, extraordinarily woolly and dangerously ideological'. This was set in stark contrast to the 'common sense' that, according to the then Health Secretary, Virginia Bottomley, they appeared to have left behind (Winter, 1992, p. 25). It was this lack of common sense that the *Sun* (6 April 1991, p. 6) focused on in contrasting the young, inexperienced and ideologically driven social worker with Esther Ranzten, a television presenter who had set up the confidential telephone advice line, Child Line who was portrayed as being far more experienced because of her age and because she was a mother. It was within this context of the undermining of social workers' professional integrity that the *Daily Telegraph* (11 April 1991, p. 6) called for more 'mature' people to enter the profession and appealed to the common sense and experience of 'street-wise grannies'. For the *Daily Mail* (5 April 1991, p. 5), the lessons of the Orkneys were clear, as their headline stated: 'After the latest shameful indictment of our arrogant, incompetent social workers: sack the lot and start again.'

However, it was not the inexperienced and gullible nature of social workers that concerned the British press but their detrimental effects on families and local communities. It was, therefore, the undermining of the family that proved to be of most concern, leading to headlines such as: 'Satan Busters are Devils in Disguise' and references to the social workers' 'heavy-handed and ham-fisted' approach which operated as a 'Salem's Witch-Hunt' (see Winter, 1992, p. 20). The *Sun* (6 April 1991, p. 6) wrote of how 'we all dread the thought of a stranger breaking into our homes at night and kidnapping our children and that's exactly what happened.'

Central to this was a focus on the effects of these events on the families themselves and the local community. Reference was made to the quiet lives of families in the community (*Daily Mail*, 6 April 1991, p. 6) and parents who were 'trapped in the nightmare of Satanism allegations' (*Daily Mail*, 6 April 1991, p. 6). Once again, social workers were criticized for being unaccountable and not listening to the views of the parents or children. Their 'abuse' of the children was described in relation to the children being 'dragged from their families at dawn . . . and bundled off to secret locations' and then subject to 'relentless pressure little short of brainwashing to make them admit the abuse' (*Daily Mail*, 5 April 1991, p. 5). Interestingly, the discourse on children's rights was invoked in relation to the description of siblings being separated and held in isolation while in the care of social services; not being allowed visits or letters. The *Independent* (5 April 1991, p. 4), for instance, wrote of how the children were 'not even granted the rights of convicted murderers'.

It was these discourses expressed through a number of moral panics about specific incidents of social work intervention that set the terms of reference both for the writing of the Children Act 1989 and, equally importantly, its implementation. While the general review process and the increasing influence of the discourse on rights help us understand the timing of the Act and its advocacy of children's rights, the way that these rights have been codified and understood within the Act can only be understood through the dominance of these attacks on social worker intervention. Here, we are already given clues as to the nature of children's rights in the last set of quotes where they should have a right to question and resist social work intervention. Importantly, no mention was made of their rights within the family. It is this development of children's rights within the Act against the general concern with state intervention and the breakdown of the family that will now be outlined through a review of the main provisions of the Children Act 1989.

The Children Act 1989

Before looking at children's rights as defined within the Act it is useful to provide the context set by its other main provisions. Here we can begin to trace the moral panics over social work intervention as they have become embedded within the legislation. Two main points are worth drawing out in relation to this: the underlying commitment to the family as set out in the Act; and the need to limit and restrain social work intervention. As regards the former, the role of the family in the care of their children is reinforced in the Act in several ways. Most obviously, it is clearly stated within the Act that the best place for children to be cared for, if at all possible, is within their own family (HMSO, 1989, p. 1). This is reinforced in the way that the notion of parental responsibility and its associated duties and tasks is very broadly defined and there is provision for parental responsibility to be delegated to the unmarried fathers of children (HMSO, 1989, p. 1). This emphasis on the family as the most suitable and natural environment for children is also underlined by the clear preventative and supportive role given to social services agencies in relation to children and families; various duties are placed on these agencies to identify children in need (Children Act 1989, sched. 2, paras 1 and 3) and offer a range of supportive services to families of such children (Children Act 1989, s17(1)(a), sched. 2, para. 8),[1] so that these children can, wherever possible, remain in the care of their parents (Children Act 1989, sched. 2, paras 4, 6, 7(a) and 8).[1]

This refocusing of the role of social service agencies can be seen as part of a broader theme within the Act of redefining and restricting social work intervention. Although setting out social workers' duties to try and support and maintain children within the family unit as far as possible, it does acknowledge that there will be some parents who fail in their patenting tasks and whose children therefore have been or are likely to be at risk in some way (Children Act 1989, s47(1)(a) and (b)). In this situation, the Act makes clear the duty incumbent on social service agencies to intervene and lists a range of legal options available to social service agencies to be used when appropriate/necessary (HMSO, 1989, pp. 14–43 and 60–73). However, such intervention is more clearly prescribed than previously. On the one hand, the 'threshold criteria' for state intervention has been increased so that, under the Act, intervention is only justified when 'the child concerned is suffering, or is likely to suffer, significant harm' (Children Act 1989, s47(1)(b); HMSO, 1989, p. 6). Interestingly, the assessment of such relies on criteria which favour the medical model of abusive families (HMSO, 1989, pp. 24–26), a mechanism which pathologizes families, reinforces the belief that abuse is confined to a few inadequate families and also that these families can be easily identified and their children protected (Lyon and Parton, 1995).

On the other hand, the restrictions on social work intervention are also evident in the increasing emphasis on legalism within the Act. There is a clearer authority in law regarding issues of child care with the result that legitimate state intervention has to satisfy the legal requirements of the court and a much greater role has been given to the courts in deciding what is in the best interests of a child (Winter, 1992). It is here, in the increased legalism of the Children's Act, that we see the discourse on rights take shape. In relation to parents not only do social workers have a duty (Children Act 1989, s22(4)(b) and (c)) to ascertain and give due consideration to their wishes and feelings, but parents also have their own rights to challenge intervention by appealing, for example, against the granting of an Emergency Protection Order (Children Act, 1989, s45(8); HMSO, 1989, p. 70). In addition, a duty is imposed on social service agencies when placing a child: to place within the extended family wherever possible (Children Act 1989, s23(b)); to place near the parents' home (Children Act 1989, s23(7)(a)); and/or to facilitate contact between parents and the child where possible (Children Act 1989, sched. 2, para. 15(1)). Here we see most clearly the influence of the themes relating to the perceived 'abusive' and 'intrusive' nature of social worker intervention that emerged most prominently in relation to the Cleveland affair and resurfaced with the Orkneys where children were put in foster placements some distance away and had no contact with their parents.

What we see from this broad outline is that the Act not only gives prominence to the importance of the family as the natural and most appropriate environment for the child to be raised but also reinforces this through the emphasis on legalism and, within this, on setting out a range of parents' rights. Although it is recognized that abuse is likely to occur, the incidence of this is confined to a few deviant families and the Act clearly quashes any idea that it is more fundamentally related to the patriarchal structure of the family unit. The Act, then, while setting out provisions for the protection and care of children who are 'at risk' does so in a way that is meant to support and reinforce the family. As Lyon and Parton (1995) argue:

> . . . the identification of the actually or potentially dangerous individual or family provides the mechanisms both for ensuring that children are protected whilst also avoiding unwarrantable intervention . . . it offers the promise of identifying, isolating and removing children permanently who are in high risk but also ensures that the innocent and low risk are left alone. (p. 46)

Children's Rights

It is against this broader ethos of the Children Act 1989 that we can now more fully understand the particular way that children's rights have come to be codified and defined within the legislation. The actual emphasis on children's rights does, by default, begin to undermine the traditional familial relationship between parent and child. Rather than children simply being regarded as the mere possessions of their parents, the evocation of children's rights does come to define them more as individuals in their own right, to whom parents have a number of legal responsibilities (Bainham, 1990; Lyon and Parton, 1995). Whatever the precise nature of those rights and responsibilities as set out in the Act, this does represent a significant shift and will be discussed further in the concluding part of the chapter. For the moment, however, it is worth looking in more detail at how these 'rights' have been codified in the Act which, according to Bainham (1990), can be set out into three broad categories: provisions which seek to accommodate children's views; provisions which entitle children to act independently in a legal capacity; and those provisions relating specifically to 16- and 17-year-olds.

As regards the first of these, the Act places a duty on the court (Children Act 1989, s1(3)(a)), local authorities (Children Act 1989, s22(4) and (5)), voluntary organizations (Children Act 1989, s61(2) and (3)) and persons running registered children's homes (Children Act 1989, s64(2) and (3)) to have regard to the wishes and feelings of the child. Steps must be taken to ascertain these views before any decision can be made in respect of them (Children Act 1989, s22(4)) and due consideration must be given to the children's wishes before any decision is finalized (Children Act, 1989 s22(5)(a)). Furthermore, social service agencies have a duty, in relation to the children already in their care, to ascertain the views of that child before any review is held in respect of their situation and also that they have a duty to inform that child of the outcome of that review (Children Act 1989, s26). Moreover, local authorities have a duty to establish a complaints procedure for all children defined as being in need and/or cared for by that authority (Children Act 1989 s26(3) and (4)) and to publicize their procedures adequately (Children Act 1989 s26(8)). It is important to note, however, that within all of these circumstances a child's age and level of understanding have to be taken into account (Children Act 1989 s22(5)).

There are also provisions under the Act to facilitate the representation of children's views in court settings. One example of this is the provision that allows for children to give evidence, even if they do not understand the Oath, so long as they are shown to understand the need to be truthful and are of a level of understanding to warrant evidence being given (Children's Act 1989 s96(1) and (3)). Moreover, appointments of *Guardians ad Litem* (GAL) (Children Act 1989, s41(1)) have also become more extensive under the Act with the dual function of safeguarding the interests of the child and ensuring that the child's wishes are successfully articulated.

The second set of provisions, as listed above, allow for children to act independently in a legal capacity although, importantly, and as previously, they are provisions that are dependent on age and level of understanding (Children Act 1989, s22(5)). Within these provisions a child can apply: to be represented independently of a GAL (Children Act 1989, s41(4)); to have the appointment of a GAL terminated (Children Act 1989, s6(7)(b)); for discharge of a Care Order (Children Act 1989, s39(1)), and; for the discharge and/or variation of a Supervision Order (Children Act 1989, s39(2)). Furthermore, a child can also refuse to submit to a medical examination as directed by the court under a Child Assessment Order (Children Act 1989, s43(1)), Emergency Protection Order (Children Act 1989, s44(7)), Care Order (Children Act 1989, s38(6)) and Supervision Order (Children Act 1989, sched. 3, para. 4(4)) where they are of a significant understanding to make an informed decision.

Finally, in relation to 16- and 17-year-olds, Section 8 orders should no longer have an effect after a child is 16 years old (Children Act 1989, s91(10)) and no order should be made after this age. Furthermore, under the legislation there is no longer any mechanism for compulsory care orders for 17-year-olds because of restrictions on wardship proceedings (Lyon and Parton, 1995). In addition, 16-year-olds no longer have to rely on social workers but can refer themselves for accommodation and local authorities have a duty to provide such accommodation if that person is 'in need' and/or when their welfare would otherwise be likely to be 'seriously prejudiced' (Children Act 1989, s20(3)).

Thatcherism and Children's Rights

Having outlined the main tenets of the Children Act 1989, and of children's rights more specifically, we are now in a position to return to our basic concern of trying to reconcile what appeared to be a fundamental paradox between this focus on children's rights and the broader commitment to the traditional, patriarchal family within Thatcherite discourse. What we want to reiterate here is that, far from there being any fundamental contradiction, the particular way in which children's rights have been codified and expressed within the Act are closely related to Thatcherism's concern both with the decline of the family and with the 'evils' of state intervention. This is quite clear when we come to look at the particular rights that children have been granted.

With few exceptions, the principal provisions in the Act are concerned with the child's rights in relation to the state rather than to their parents. Although the Act includes a definition of parental responsibility and its associated tasks and duties, these are defined in such a broad and abstract way that there are no specific guidelines or legal requirements for parents detailing their parental role and responsibilities. Rather these are negatively defined inasmuch as the Act simply focuses on the consequences for parents and the state if they fail in their patenting tasks. It is interesting to compare this with other agencies who may happen to become involved in the care of a child whose roles and responsibilities are set out in great deal. It leads us to the question, as Bainham (1990) rightly points out:

> . . . if judges, local authorities, voluntary organisations and others are to have legal duties to ascertain and take into account the views of children it is surely reasonable to inquire why it was not thought possible or appropriate to expect the same of parents. (p. 312)

Of course, the answer to this is that if the state felt it necessary to set out in law what the parents' roles and responsibilities were in the care of their children then this would be tantamount to admitting that parenting is not something that 'comes naturally' but rather that parents and families require the guidance and support of outside agencies from time to time. It is not so much that Thatcherite discourse has been against state intervention *per se* — as we have seen in ongoing debates about the sanctity of marriage, single parent families and those surrounding parental responsibility and the Child Support Agency — rather they are against the type of intervention that brings into question the 'naturalness' of family life. It is this defence of the family that also lies behind the Act's advocacy of the medical model of abuse and its belief that abusive behaviour is confined to only a small percentage of inadequate and deviant families. As before, to admit otherwise would be to suggest that abuse is in some way related to the very nature and patriarchal structure of the family.

However, of those parents that are seen to 'fail' and whose actions necessitate state intervention, then the Act is quite detailed in setting out their rights, as parents, in relation to social services agencies. In this its primary aim is to set limits to and severely restrict state involvement in all but the few deserving cases. It is here that the underlying thrust of children's rights can also be located. Being rights that are predominantly concerned with their relationship with social services agencies, they can be seen as instruments in warding off the unwarranted attentions of social workers and allied professionals and so acting as a safeguard in maintaining the integrity of the family unit. They are, in other words, a third line of defence beyond the restrictions to social services intervention and parental rights found in the Act, to limit and keep at bay the 'abuses' meted out by social workers and the state. Rather than conflicting with Thatcherite discourses on the family, children rights so defined have actually become a central tool in maintaining and reproducing those traditional perceptions of the family.

One of the inherent contradictions in the Act in relation to children's rights is that it comes to conceive of children only partly as individuals in their own right and continuously counterbalances this with the need for those involved to assess the child's age and level of understanding. It is within this framework that we can understand the increased set of rights afforded to 16- and 17-year-olds which reflect the perception that individuals of this age are no longer children but adults responsible for their own actions. A contradiction appears, however, in relation to the rights of younger children. While children may exercise their 'rights' by protesting at being removed from the family home or being subject to a medical examination, these protests can be overruled by appealing to the child's age and lack of understanding. Here we see the influence of traditional socialization and developmental models of childhood which construct children as being cognitively unable to make decisions of that nature (Jenks, 1982; Wagg, 1988; James and Prout, 1990; Chisholm, Buchner, Krüger and Brown, 1990; Ambert, 1995).

Overall then, children's rights amount to little more than their right to remain within the confines of their family, wherever possible, and to express an opinion on their future. However, as we have seen, these opinions are largely confined to social services intervention and are not meant to facilitate children's criticisms of the ways in which their parents care for them. Furthermore, given the continued dominance of these traditional models of childhood, the views which children do express are open to very loose interpretation and can easily be dismissed as being socially naive. However, in drawing children into a discourse on rights, then, it does at least create the space within which these discourses and the child's position within the family can be progressively challenged. For the first time, the law has alluded to the notion of children as individuals in their own right, albeit in theory rather than practice, and it is this aspect of the Act that at least presents some hope for the future in building a more appropriate and comprehensive system of rights for children.

Note

1 Throughout this chapter, the letter 's' included in references to the Children Act 1989 denotes the particular section of the Act followed by its relevant subsections in brackets. Similarly, 'Sched.' denotes the particular schedule to be found at the end of the Act and 'para' the specific paragraph of that schedule.

References

Abbott, P. and Wallace, C. (1989) 'The family', in Brown, P. and Sparks, R. (eds) *Beyond Thatcherism: Social Policy, Politics and Society*, Milton Keynes, Open University Press.

Ambert, A. (ed.) (1995) *Sociological Studies of Childhood, 7*, London, JRAI Press.

Bainham, A. (1990) 'The Children Act 1989, adolescence and children's rights', *Family Law*, **20**, pp. 311–14, August.

Blom-Cooper, L. (1985) *A Child in Trust: Report of the Panel of Inquiry Investigating the Circumstances Surrounding the Death of Jasmine Beckford*, London, Borough of Brent.

Butler-Sloss, E. (1988) *Report of the Inquiry into Child Abuse in Cleveland*, Cmnd 412, London, HMSO.

Chisholm, L., Buchner, P., Krüger, H. and Brown, P. (eds) (1990) *Childhood, Youth and Social Change: A Comparative Approach*, London, Falmer Press.

David, M. (1986a) 'Moral and maternal: The family and the New Right', in Levitas, R. (ed.) *The Ideology of the New Right*, Cambridge, Polity Press.

David, M. (1986b) 'Morality and maternity: Towards a better vision than the moral right's family policy?' *Critical Social Policy*, **16**, 6, pp. 40–56.

DHSS (1985) *Social Work Decisions in Child Care: Recent Research Findings and their Implications*, London, HMSO.

Finnis, N. (1986) 'Twice across the divide', *Social Work Today*, 8 December, p. 6.

Fitzgerald, T. (1983) 'The New Right and the family', in Loney, M., Boswell, D. and Clarke, J. (eds) *Social Policy and Social Welfare*, Milton Keynes, Open University Press.

Franklin, B. and Parton, N. (1991a) 'Victims of abuse: Media and social work', *Childright*, **75**, pp. 13–16, April.

Franklin, B. and Parton, N. (eds) (1991b) *Social Work, the Media and Public Relations*, London, Routledge.

Franklin, B. and Parton, N. (1991c) 'Media reporting of social work: A framework for analysis', in Franklin, B. and Parton, N. (eds) *Social Work, the Media and Public Relations*, London, Routledge.

Fry, A. (1991) 'Reporting social work: A view from the newsroom', in Franklin, B. and Parton, N. (eds) *Social Work, the Media and Public Relations*, London, Routledge.

Geach, H. (1982) 'Social work and the press', *Community Care*, **27**, pp. 14–15.

Golding, P. and Middleton, S. (1982) *Images of Welfare*, London, Martin Robertson.

Golding, P. (1991) 'Do gooders on display: Social work, public attitudes and the mass media', in Franklin, B. and Parton, N. (eds) *Social Work, the Media and Public Relations*, London, Routledge.

Hall, S. (1983) 'The great moving right show', in Hall, S. and Jacques, M. (eds) *The Politics of Thatcherism*, London, Lawrence & Wishart.

HMSO (1989) *An Introduction to the Children Act 1989: A New Framework for the Care and Upbringing of Children*, London, HMSO.

James, A. and Prout, A. (eds) (1990) *Constructing and Reconstructing Childhood*, London, Falmer Press.

Jenks, C. (ed.) (1982) *The Sociology of Childhood*, London, Batsford Academic.

Jones, K. (1989) *Right Turn: The Conservative Revolution in Education*, London, Hutchinson Radius.

Lyon, C. and Parton, N. (1995) 'Children's rights and the Children Act 1989', in Franklin, B. (ed.) *The Handbook of Children's Rights: Comparative Policy and Practice*, London, Routledge.

McIntosh, M. (1988) 'Introduction to an issue: Family secrets as public drama', *Feminist Review*, **28**, pp. 6–15.

Mitter, S. (1986) *Common Fate, Common Bond: Women in the Global Economy*, London, Pluto Press.

Morgan, D. (1985) *The Family, Politics and Social Theory*, London, Routledge and Kegan Paul.

Murray, R. (1989) 'Fordism and post-fordism', in Hall, S. and Jacques, M. (eds) *New Times: The Changing Face of Politics in the 1990s*, London, Lawrence & Wishart.

Nava, M. (1988) 'Cleveland and the press: Outrage and anxiety in the reporting of child sex abuse', *Feminist Review*, **28**, pp. 103–22.

Overbeek, H. (1990) *Global Capitalism and National Decline: The Thatcher Decade in Perspective*, London, Unwin Hyman.

Parekh, B. (1986) 'The "New Right" and the politics of nationhood', in Cohen, G., Bosanquet, N., Ryan, A., Parekh, B., Keegan W. and Gress, G. (eds) *The New Right: Image and Reality*, London, Runnymede Trust.

Parker, R. (ed.) (1980) *Caring for Separated Children: Plans, Procedures and Priorities*, Report of a Working Party commissioned by the National Children's Bureau, London, Macmillan.

Karen Winter and Paul Connolly

Seebohm Committee (1968) *Report of the Committee on Local Authority and Allied Personal Social Services*, Cmnd 3703, London, HMSO.

Social Services Committee (1984) *Children in Care* (HC360), March, London, HMSO.

Urry, J. (1989) 'The end of organised capitalism', in Hall, S. and Jacques, M. (eds) *New Times: The Changing Face of Politics in the 1990s*, London, Lawrence & Wishart.

Wagg, S. (1988) 'Perishing kids? The sociology of childhood', *Social Studies Review*, **3**, pp. 126–31.

Winter, K. (1992) *The Day They Took Away Our Children: Ritualistic Abuse, Social Work and the Press*, Monograph 113, Norwich, Social Work Monographs.

4 The New Politics of Child Protection

Nigel Parton

During the last twenty-five years, child abuse has been seen as a significant and growing social problem and has been the subject of considerable media and political interest and argument. While it is generally agreed that it is a problem which we should do something about, there has been intense argument about what we should do and how we should do it. A central issue is the mandate, accountability and priorities of the various health, welfare and legal agencies and their interrelationships. In this respect an analysis of these developments and debates provides a key insight into the changing role of the state during this period and, in particular, into the changing relationship(s) between the family and various state agents, and the shifting political auspices under which they operate. While I will argue that it is quite inadequate to explain these changes simply in terms of the impact of Thatcherism or the New Right, the changing political contexts are crucial in understanding the contemporary nature and tensions of the child protection system, and its impact(s) on the adults and children who are on the receiving end and the professionals, particularly social workers, who operate it.

My central argument is that there has been an important shift in the relationships and hierarchies of authority between different agencies and professionals in key areas of decision making. While at the moment of its modern (re)emergence in the 1960s, child abuse was constituted as essentially a medico-social problem where the expertise of doctors was seen as focal, increasingly it has been constituted as a socio-legal problem, where legal expertise takes pre-eminence. Whereas previously the concern was with diagnosing, curing and preventing the 'disease' or syndrome, increasingly the emphasis has been placed upon investigating, assessing and weighing 'forensic evidence'. While social workers and social service departments in England have been seen as the lead and key agency throughout this period, the focus and priorities of their work has become constituted in quite new ways. More particularly the problem, of child abuse, or rather the way we respond to it has been 'legalized'.

The purpose of this chapter is to outline and analyse the main factors that have influenced and circumscribed the policies and practices we now call child protection and to explain how these differ from what went before. More particularly, I will identify the central contradictions and tensions which have been embedded in policies and practices and the various unintended consequences to which policy-makers are now struggling to respond. The child protection system is in crisis and it is very unclear what the future holds. The question which has to be addressed and which has been a central issue for the liberal state since the mid-nineteenth century is how can we devise a *legal* basis for the power to intervene into the private family to protect children, which does not convert a sizeable proportion of families into clients of the state? Such a problem is posed by the contradictory demands of, on the one hand, ensuring that the family is experienced by its members as autonomous and that it remains the primary sphere for rearing children, while on the other recognizing there is a need for intervention in some families where they are seen as failing in this primary task. Moreover, these demands must be met in a context where such laws are supposed to act as the general norms applicable to all (Parton, 1991). What will become evident is that current arrangements are getting this balance badly wrong even according to the essential principles and criteria set out in the Children Act 1989 and the various official guidances that go with it.

The Emergence of Child Abuse as a Socio-Medical Reality in the Context of Welfare Reformism

The establishment of the local authority child care service in the post-war period can be seen as a particular instance of the growth and rationalization of social interventions associated with the establishment of the welfare state at that time (Rose and Miller, 1992). The key innovations of welfarism lay in the attempts to link the fiscal calculative and bureaucratic capacities of the state. This was to encourage national growth and well-being via the promotion of *social* responsibility and the mutuality of *social* risk and was premised on notions of *social* solidarity (Donzelot, 1988).

A number of assumptions characterized welfarism: the institutional framework of universal social services was seen as the best way of maximizing welfare in modern society and the nation state, which was seen to work for the whole society, was the best way of procuring this. The social services were instituted for benevolent purposes, meeting social needs, compensating socially caused deprivations and promoting social justice. Their underlying functions were ameliorative, integrative and redistributive. Social progress would continue to be achieved through the agency of the state and professional intervention so that increased public expenditure, the cumulative extension of statutory welfare provision and the proliferation of government regulations backed by expert administration, represented the main guarantee of equity, fairness and efficiency. Social scientific knowledge was given a pre-eminence in ordering the rationality of the emerging professions who were seen as having a major contribution to developing individual and social welfare, and thereby operationalizing increasingly sophisticated mechanisms of social regulation.

The practice of state social work with children and families, from the immediate post-war period until the early 1970s, was itself imbued with a considerable optimism for it was believed that measured and significant improvements could be made in the lives of individuals and families via judicious professional interventions. Social work operated quietly and confidently and in a relatively uncontested way, which reflected a supportive social mandate. It was allowed wide professional discretion. It harmonized with a central plank of the post-war reconstruction which was the belief that a positive and supportive approach to the family was required so that the state and the family should work in part-nership to ensure that children were provided with the appropriate conditions in which to develop.

The high point of this optimistic growth and institutionalization of social work in the context of welfarism came with the establishment of local authority social services departments in 1971. This reflected the view of the Seebohm Report (1968), which was that social problems could be overcome via state intervention by professional experts. These experts were assumed to have the necessary social scientific knowledge and skills in the use of relationships and Seebohm envisaged a progressive, universal service available to all and with wide community support. Interventions in the family were not conceived as a potential source of antagonism between social workers and individual family members — whether parent(s) or child(ren). Social workers were not seen as having interests or rights distinct from the unitary family itself. When a family required modification this would be via casework, help and advice and if an individual did come into state care this was assumed to be in their interests. The law was not seen in any significant way as constituting the nature of social work, or significantly informing the skills required of social workers, or the types of relationships deemed appropriate for work with clients. When more coercive methods were drawn upon, these were primarily seen as a tool for fulfilling the more significant therapeutic goals.

The way child abuse was defined, explained and responded to from the early years of its modern (re)discovery was dominated by the 'disease' of the public health model (Parton, 1985, chapter 6). As the Beckford Report com-mented, quoting the work of Henry Kempe, 'Child abuse is a disease whose carrier is the parent and whose victim is the child' (London Borough of Brent, 1985, p. 88). With such a model it was assumed that child abuse was an illness and that clinical medico/scientific procedures were the best way of explaining, identifying and responding to it. Medical professionals, particularly paediatri-cians, radiologists and child psychiatrists, together with social workers, were seen as providing the crucial expertise in discovering child abuse and in diag-nosing, preventing and treating it. It is assumed that child abuse is a reality which has been hidden and requires medical science to uncover.

Such an approach was crucial in influencing the development of official policy and practice throughout the 1970s and early 1980s. The system of child abuse management was effectively inaugurated with the issue of a Department of Health and Social Security circular in April 1974, in the wake of the Maria Colwell inquiry (DHSS, 1974). The roles of paediatricians, GPs, health visitors and social workers were seen as vital and the social services department, as the statutory child care agency, central. The police at this stage, were not seen as crucial and it was a further circular in 1976 (DHSS, 1976) which recommended that a senior police officer should be included on all area review committees and case conferences.

The Collapse of the Welfare Consensus in Child Care

However, the optimism and confidence evident in social work and the welfarist child care system more generally was increasingly subject to critique from the mid-1970s onwards and these criticisms increased during the 1980s. Some of the anxieties emanated from within social work itself and concerned the apparently poor and even deteriorating quality of child care practice in the newly created social service departments (Parker, 1980). More widely however, a whole variety of different concerns were developing which became increasingly important in influencing the parameters of the debate as it developed. While the criticisms represented somewhat different, though overlapping, constituencies, their net effect was to undermine the optimistic welfare consensus in child care.

First, from the 1960s onwards, with the growth of the women's movement and the recognition of violence in the family, it was recognized that not only may the family not be the haven of tranquility it was assumed to be, but that women and children were suffering a range of abuses at the hands of men. Much of the early campaigning was directed to improving the position of women and it was only from the mid-1970s with the growing concerns about sexual abuse, that much of the energy was directed to the position of the children (Parton, 1990). Such critiques helped to disaggregate the interests of individual family members and supported the development during the period of the Children's Rights movement (Freeman, 1983; Franklin, 1986, 1995). During the 1980s this was to find a common ground with the more traditional child-rescue sentiments and received their most explicit expression with the establishment of ChildLine in late 1986.

Secondly, there was the growth from the late 1960s of a more obviously civil liberties critique which concentrated upon the apparent extent and nature of intervention in people's lives that went unchallenged in the name of welfare (see Taylor, Lacey and Bracken, 1980; Morris, Giller, Szwed and Geach, 1980; Geach and Szwed, 1983). Increasingly, lawyers drew attention to the way the administration of justice was unfairly and unjustly applied in various areas of child care and argued that there was a need for a greater emphasis on individual rights. These interventions were manifested in the establishment of a number of pressure groups including the National Association for One Parent Families, Justice for Children, the Children's Legal Centre and the Family Rights Group.

During the mid-1980s, the parents' lobby gained its most coherent voice with the establishment of Parents Against INjustice (PAIN). It was to prove influential in ensuring that the rights of parents and of children to be left at home, free of state intervention and removal, were placed on the political and professional agendas. As a result, state intervention, via the practices of health and welfare professionals, as well as parental violence was identified as being actively and potentially abusive.

It was child abuse enquiries that provided the major catalyst for venting major criticisms of policy and practice in child care and the competencies of social workers. While these were evident from 1973 onwards, following the death of Maria Colwell (Secretary of State for Social Services, 1974; Parton, 1985), they gained a new level of intensity during the mid-1980s via the inquiries into the deaths of Jasmine Beckford (London Borough of Brent, 1985), Tyra Henry (London Borough of Lambeth, 1987) and Kimberley Carlile (London Borough of Greenwich, 1987). It was public inquiries which provided the vehicles for political and professional debate over what to do about child abuse in a very public way and in the full glare of the media (Franklin and Parton, 1991; Aldridge, 1994). Not only did they provide detailed accounts of what had gone wrong in the particular cases but they commented critically on the current state of policy and practice more generally and made recommendations as to what should be done (DHSS, 1982; DoH [Department of Health], 1991).

Up until the mid-1980s the thirty plus enquiries had all been concerned with the deaths of children at the hands of their parents or caretakers. All the children had died as a result of physical abuse and neglect and had often suffered emotional neglect and failure to thrive. The child care professionals, particularly social workers, were seen to have failed to protect the children with horrendous consequences. Rather than see the deaths as resulting simply from individual professional incompetencies they were usually seen as particular instances of the current state of policy, practice knowledge and skills and of the way systems operated and interrelated (Hallett and Birchall, 1992). Crucially, however, social workers were seen as having been too naive and sentimental with parents and as having failed either to protect the interests of the children to use the statutory authority vested in them.

The emphasis in recommendations was to encourage social workers to use their legal mandate to intervene in families to protect children and to improve practitioners' knowledge of the signs and symptoms of child abuse so that it could be spotted in day to day practice. However, the Cleveland inquiry (Secretary of State for Social Services, 1988) set out a quite different set of concerns and circumstances, with new interpretations of what was wrong and how we should respond. This time it seemed the professionals — paediatricians as well as social workers — had failed to recognize the rights of parents and had intervened prematurely into families where there were concerns about sexual abuse. While again the reasons for the crisis were seen as residing primarily in inter-agency and inter-professional misunderstandings, in poor coordination and communication, and in the legal context and content of child abuse work, the emphasis was rather different. Now not only did the law itself need to be changed but there was now a perceived need to recognize that professionals should be much more careful and accountable in identifying the 'evidence', legally framed, for sexual abuse and child abuse more generally. It was not simply a question of getting the right balance between family autonomy and state intervention but also getting the right balance between the power, discretion and responsibilities of the various judicial, social and medical experts and agencies. In this respect the judical experts were seen to be central: for the law and legal thinking needed to be brought to bear in decision making which had such fundamental consequences for children and parents, and hence the family, which was seen as being fundamentally undermined by the events in Cleveland.

Thus while quite different in their social location and their focus of concern, we can see a growing set of constituencies developing from the late 1970s which criticized the post-war welfarist consensus in relation to child care and the medico/scientific dominance in relation to child abuse. These were most forcefully articulated in and via child abuse inquiries. What emerged were arguments for a greater reliance on individual rights firmly located in a reformed statutory framework where there was a greater emphasis on legalism. Within this emphasis, the rule of law as ultimately judged by the court, takes priority over those considerations which may be deemed, by the professional 'experts', as optimally therapeutic or 'in the best interests of the child'.

Such developments need to be located in the context of the more wide-ranging changes that were taking place in the political environment. During the 1970s an increasing disillusionment was evident about the ability of the social democratic state both effectively to manage the economy and to overcome a range of social problems via the use of wide-ranging state welfare programmes. The growth of what has been termed the Radical or New Right (Levitas, 1986), proved particularly significant in shifting the nature of political discourse in the 1980s. For the New Right, the problems in the economic and social spheres were closely interrelated. They were seen to emanate from the establishment and increasing pervasiveness of the social democratic welfare state. The prime focus for change was to be the nature, priorities and boundaries of the state itself. The strategy consisted of a coherent fusion of the economic and the social. It had its root in an individualized conception of social relations whereby the market is the key institution for the economic sphere, while the family is the key institution for the social sphere. The family is seen as an essentially private domain from which the state should be excluded but which should also be encouraged to take on its natural caring responsibilities for its members — including children. The role of the state should thus be reduced to: (a) ensuring that the family fulfils these responsibilities, and; (b) ensuring that no-one suffers at the hands of the violent or the strong.

Freedom, while central, is constructed in negative terms as freedom from unnecessary interferences. Clearly, however, a fine balance has to be struck between protecting the innocent and weak and protection from unwarrantable interference — particularly from the state. In such circumstances, the law becomes crucial in defining and operationalizing both 'natural' rights and 'natural' responsibilities. Not only must it provide the framework for the underwriting of contracts between individuals and between individuals and the state; it must also aim to make the rationale for intervention by state officials into the natural spheres of the market and the family more explicit and their actions more accountable.

Recent Legislative Changes and Practice Guidances

It is in this context that we need to understand the Children Act 1989. In many respects the Act was not consistent with other pieces of social legislation that were being introduced at the time. Many of its key principles seemed to be much more in keeping with the premises of social democratic welfarism than with the Thatcherite New Right. The Act took much of its inspiration from the Short Report (Social Services Committee, 1984), and the Review of Child Care Law (DHSS, 1985b). Consequently the central principles of the Act encouraged an approach to child care based on *negotiation* with families and *involving* parents and children in *agreed* plans. The accompanying guidance and regulations encouraged professionals to work in *partnership* with parents and young people. Similarly the Act strongly encourages the role of the state in *supporting* families with children in need, in preventative work and thus keeping the use of care proceedings and emergency interventions to a minimum.

However, the Act was centrally concerned with trying to construct a new set of balances, related to the respective roles, of various state agents and of the family, in the upbringing of children. While it would be inappropriate to see the legalisation as a direct consequence of Cleveland and other child abuse inquiries, it was child protection that was in effect its central concern (Parton, 1991). Notions of individual rights and legalism framed the legislation in ways which were not evident previously.

The other key elements to emerge were the *criteria* to be used for making decisions. The assessment of 'high risk' has become central (Parton, 1991, chapters 3 and 5). In the Children Act, 'high risk' is framed in terms of 'significant harm'. The criterion for state intervention under the Children Act is 'that the child concerned is suffering, or is likely to suffer significant harm' (Section 31 (2) (a)). For the first time the criteria for state intervention include a prediction of what may or is likely to occur in the *future*.

Since the mid-1970s the idea of dangerousness or the identification of 'high risk' has become a major topic in discussions of reforming systems of state social regulation more generally (Bottoms, 1977). Assessments of actual or potential 'high risk' become *the* central concern. However, in a context where the knowledge and research for assessing and identifying 'high risk' is itself contested and where the consequences of getting that decision wrong are considerable, it is not surprising that it is seen as inappropriate to leave that decision to the health and welfare experts alone. The decisions and the accountability for making these decisions needs ultimately to be lodged with the court and be based on forensic 'evidence'. So, while assessments of high risk are central, they are framed in terms of making judgments about what constitutes actual or likely 'significant harm'. The implication is that legal considerations and the weighing of forensic evidence cast a shadow over child abuse work and child care more generally, but that they are subjected to checks and balances via the need to work in partnership with children and families and with a range of agencies and professionals.

Law and order agencies have thus moved centre stage in a way that was not evident previously. For example, the key investigating statutory agencies are now explicitly the police and social services and it is seen as essential that there is an early 'strategy discussion' to plan the investigation, the role of each agency and the extent of joint investigation (Home Office, 1991, para. 28). It is stated that such cases, 'involve both child care and law enforcement issues' (Home Office, 1991, para. 5.14.4).

Social workers are still central but not as caseworkers or counsellors but as case managers or key workers, coordinating and taking central responsibility for assessing 'risk' and monitoring and evaluating progress. This takes place in a context where official procedures govern the carrying out of the work, thereby, potentially making policy and practice more explicit and accountable; this accountability is essentially to the parents and, to a lesser extent, to the children, on the one hand, and the court on the other. This is not to say that all cases go to court, but that the court and the legal gaze effectively dominates child protection work and thereby constitutes what child abuse is. This has been reinforced by the practices and procedures set in place following the Criminal Justice Act (1991), and the *Memorandum of Good Practice* (Home Office, 1992). The mechanisms for gathering forensic evidence for the purposes of the criminal prosecution of offenders and the civil protection of the child have effectively been combined (Wattam, 1992).

The *Memorandum of Good Practice* attempts to harmonize 'the interests of justice and the interests of the child' (Home Office, 1992, foreword), for it had long been recognized that the criminal courts were not able to provide an appropriate vehicle for receiving the evidence of children, who were usually the key witnesses in prosecution cases. Not only were the children not believed, but the processes of giving evidence, examination and cross-examination could themselves be seen as abusive of children. In 1988, the government decided to allow child witnesses to give evidence from outside the courtroom via a special television link to ease the anxiety of child witnesses. This was extended in the Criminal Justice Act 1991. For the first time, video recordings of earlier interviews with police and social workers could be played to the court as part of the trial. The *Memorandum of Good Practice* produces guidance about how this can be done. While attempting to be sensitive to the child this ensures, crucially, that the video constitutes forensic evidence that will stand up in a criminal court.

The introduction of the Criminal Justice Act provisions, together with the

Memorandum of Good Practice, has not only greatly centralized and under-lined the role of the police in child protection, it has legalized policy and practice ever further. We can thus understand the contemporary nature of child protection work as the need to identify 'high risk' in a context where notions of working together are set out in increasingly complex yet specific procedural guidelines and where the work is framed by a narrow emphasis on legalism and the need for forensic evidence.

The Current Crisis in Child Welfare

The various changes heralded, and in part introduced, by the Children Act 1989 have done little to avert the crises which continue to dominate child care policy and practice. The number and range of public inquiries has not subsided and child abuse tragedies of both under and over intervention continue to feature in the media. They have almost come to characterize and represent the cultural and communal malaise of Britain in the 1990s.

What is also now evident, and much more central to my analysis here, is that day-to-day policies and practices have not lived up to the aspirations and central principles of the Act itself. In a book published in 1991, *Governing the Family*, following the passage of the legislation through Parliament, but prior to its implementation in October of that year, I tentatively looked to the future and set out two possible scenarios (Parton, 1991, chapter 7). One scenario was framed essentially by child welfare and the other by child protection. In the former, policy and practice would be driven by an emphasis on partnership, participation, prevention, family support and a positive rethink of the purposes and uses of care. The emphasis would be on *helping* parents and children in the community in a supportive way and would keep notions of policing, surveillance and coercive interventions to a minimum. In effect, policy and practice would be driven by Part Three of the Act. The other scenario was that it would be priorities driven by child protection which would dominate — in effect Part Five and Section 47 in particular — and concerns about investigating and identifying 'significant harm and the likelihood of significant harm'. While I hedged my bets a little in *Governing the Family* I was clear that it would very likely be the latter scenario which would dominate future policy and practice.

While I am in great sympathy with the central principles of the Act and, as I have already suggested, it was not from the same political stable as other pieces of social legislation of the time, one had to be realistic about its history and the political context of its introduction. I was thus always pessimistic about its chances of success. My pessimism was informed essentially by two factors. First, while it is inappropriate to see the Act as resulting simply from the child abuse inquiries of the 1980s, there is no doubt that child abuse inquiries provided the essential *political momentum* for change and for the shaping of key elements of the subsequent legislation. But, secondly, the legislation was being introduced in a very hostile climate. This is a very small and insignificant piece of legislation when put alongside the dramatic changes that have taken place over the last seventeen years in the economy: increases in social inequality, changes in social security, the undermining of local government, the various legislation and destabilization in schools, health services and so on and which are analysed in detail elsewhere in this book. All of these changes have had a direct and indirect impact on the lives of children and thereby on the policies and practices of the child care services.

There is now a general recognition that it is concerns about child protection which have become dominant and that these are having very deleterious outcomes for the children and families involved (Audit Commission, 1994). In effect, the central philosophy and principles of the Children Act are being undermined in day-to-day policy and practice. Not only are the child welfare and family support aspirations and sections of the Act being implemented partially and not prioritized (DoH, 1994) but children are being left vulnerable and unprotected because the child protection system is overloaded and is not coping with the increased demands made of it. It is child protection which is the dominating concern and this is framing child welfare policy more generally so that, increasingly, it is felt that too many cases are being dragged into the child protection net. It is now clear that just four years after the implementation of the Act that there is a crisis and we are again having fundamentally to reconsider the issues which the legislation was meant to address.

Probably the major factor in identifying this crisis, and setting out its key elements and parameters, has been the completion of a number of research studies funded by the Department of Health (Dartington Social Research Unit, 1995), together with a number of other studies which have come up with similar findings. I will outline two of the studies to illustrate the impact and outcomes of child protection policies and practices. Gary Denman and David Thorpe (1993) studied the careers of 100 child protection cases in a Welsh local authority from the point of initial allegation for a period of nine months (the 100 cases constituted a 100 per cent sample for the period of study). They found that over half of all the allegations were not substantiated after investigation. While over a half of both physical and sexual abuse allegations were substantiated, only 20 per cent of allegations of neglect were ever substantiated — five out of twenty-six cases. Furthermore, five of the six cases where the allegation included neglect along with other allegations were not substantiated (see Table 4.1). Within the forty-four substantiated/at risk cases there were eight cases where there was no continued involvement. These eight cases, together with forty-five not substantiated, constituted nearly two thirds of allegations which did not result in any continuing involvement by the agency. In addition, of the remaining thirty-six substantiated cases, a further six were closed within two weeks of the allegation being made. Of the remaining thirty cases, only one half (fifteen cases) were placed on the Child Protection Register. Clearly a considerable amount of activity, time and resources were put into this sifting process.

Denman and Thorpe (1993) also analysed the cases in terms of the family

Table 4.1: Initial allegation of child abuse by final decision following investigation (From Denman and Thorpe, 1993, p. 14)

Allegation	Final Decision Substantiated	Decision Not Substantiated	Total	% Total
Physical Abuse	23	17	40	40
Sexual Abuse	13	10	23	23
Neglect	5	21	26	26
Grave Concern	2	2	4	4
Physical Abuse/Neglect	1	4	5	5
Sexual Abuse/Neglect	0	2	2	2
Totals	44	56	100	100%

Table 4.2: Family structure of reported cases of child abuse (From Denman and Thorpe, 1993, p. 15)

Family Structure	Allegations	%
Biological Parents	26	(26%)
Reconstituting Family	22	(22%)
Single Female Parent	40	(40%)
Single Female Parent (Extended Family)	4	(4%)
Single Male Parent	4	(4%)
Other	3	(3%)
Not Known	1	(1%)
Total	100	(100%)

composition of the households involved (see Table 4.2). What is evident from Table 4.2 is that 40 per cent of all referrals were made on single female parent families. When we add the four single male parent families and the four cases where a single female parent was living with her extended family we can see that 48 per cent of all referrals involved single parent families. Denman and Thorpe (1993, p. 15) add that 'furthermore, the records show that in most cases, not only were they caring for children alone, but they were doing so in a context of financial difficulty.' Thirty-five per cent of the allegations involving single female parents living along were for neglect and this increased to 45 per cent if allegations where neglect was a part of the initial allegation were included. As we have already seen, allegations of neglect are the least likely to be substantiated and the least likely to receive continued social work involvement.

A very similar pattern emerges from another but much larger study on the operation of child protection registers (Gibbons, Conroy and Bell, 1995). A central objective of the research was to describe the process that led to a child's name being placed on a register. Detailed study took place in eight different English authorities (two outer London boroughs, four inner London boroughs and two counties). Over a sixteen week period in 1992, children referred for investigations were identified and their progress through the child

Table 4.3: *Operation of filters in child protection system (From Gibbons, Conroy and Bell, 1995)*

ENTRY POINT	1,888		42 'Lost' cases
New Incident			
FIRST FILTER	1,846	(100%)	478 (26%)
Checks			
SECOND FILTER	1,368	(74%)	925 (50%)
Further Investigation			
THIRD FILTER	433	(24%)	128 (7%)
Child Protection Conference			
RETAINED IN SYSTEM AFTER CONFERENCE	315	(16%)	
OF WHOM ON REGISTER:	272	(15%)	

protection system was tracked for up to twenty-six weeks through social work records and minutes of conferences. Most of the 1,888 referrals (44 per cent) were for suspected physical abuse, followed by suspected sexual abuse (28 per cent) and neglect (21 per cent) or fears for the child's safety (4 per cent). Only 3 per cent of referrals involved allegations of emotional abuse without other forms of maltreatment.

Less than a third of the children lived with both natural parents and there were high levels of social deprivation. However, children investigated for sexual or emotional abuse were in generally better material circumstances. About two thirds of the families were already known to the social services department, and nearly half had experienced previous investigations. A substantial minority of parents had histories of criminal behaviour, substance abuse or mental illness. Domestic violence was recorded in over a quarter of the cases.

The process whereby cases are quickly filtered out and receive no service or no 'protection' is even more apparent in this study (see Table 4.3). Of the original 1,888 allegations forty-two were lost from the outset and could not be traced. However another 478 (26 per cent) were filtered out by social work staff at the duty stage without any direct contact with child or family. This might have involved discussions with the senior social worker and telephone calls to other agencies. Cases were more likely to be filtered out at this initial stage if: the allegations concerned neglect, rather than physical or sexual abuse; the abuse was thought to be physically less serious; the alleged perpetrator was not in the household; the source of the allegation was anonymous or from a lay person; and there had been no previous contact with social services.

The second filter was the investigation itself, where the senior social worker or manager was seen as the crucial decision-maker. About two thirds of the cases actually investigated (925 of 1,368) investigated) were filtered out and never reached an initial child protection conference. The nature of the abuse, and the source of the referral, were again influential as were any previous history of suspected maltreatment and any recorded or parental problems such as criminality or substance abuse.

The third filter was operated by the initial child protection conference. In

51 per cent of the conferenced cases the child was registered, 10 per cent were already on the register, 10 per cent were deferred and 29 per cent were not registered. Compared with those not registered, cases placed on the register had more previous investigations of abuse, and had more indications of poverty, parental deviance and domestic violence.

Gibbons, Conroy and Bell (1995) conclude that about six of every seven children who entered the child protection system at referral were filtered out without needing to be placed on a child protection register. In a high proportion (44 per cent of those actually investigated) the investigation led to no actions at all. *There was no intervention to protect the child nor were any other family support services provided either.* In only 4 per cent of all the referred cases were children removed from home under a court order during the investigation. This is a very different picture to the one painted by the Cleveland, Orkney and Rochdale inquiries. The further one moves away from forensic evidential concerns, the less are interventions likely to take place. Thus in 65 per cent of the neglect referrals (392 in total) the researchers could not identify any protective actions nor any mobilization of support. Yet the children had the highest number of poverty indicators and just as many indicators of vulnerability as those referred for physical abuse or, especially, sexual abuse. Thus the commonest picture was of children not reaching the threshold for child protection proceedings, but not getting any preventive help either (Gibbons, 1993).

These studies demonstrate that only about 15 per cent of child protection referrals ever find their way onto a child protection register, the rest being filtered out much earlier in the process and usually receiving neither protection nor any other service. Now it might be argued that this resource-intensive and time-consuming system of investigations and filtering is worthwhile if the most dangerous cases are being identified. Unfortunately the Department of Health research found little or no evidence for this. In effect, the child protection system, as I have argued throughout, is inherently defensive and conservative. It reflects the procedural, legalistic mentality which is concerned with accountability and with insuring against public inquiry and opprobrium if things are seen subsequently to go wrong. As I have argued throughout this chapter it is an almost inevitable outcome of its history and the political contexts in which it has developed. Unfortunately what we have is now a child welfare system almost completely dominated by concerns about child protection which does little to actually protect *children* and which does little or nothing to meet their needs either. As we have seen in the studies by Denman and Thorpe (1993) and Gibbons, Conroy and Bell (1995), a disproportionate number of those dragged into the child protection net are from the poorest sections of society and are often from single parent households. All that is offered is minimal surveillance and monitoring, for the primary concern is with investigating forensic evidence rather than with identifying unmet need.

Yet it is apparent, as is discussed at greater length elsewhere in this book, that there has been a considerable growth in poverty and deprivation amongst children and families in this country since the late 1970s. The poorest families in Britain have suffered a cut in their real income between 1979 and 1990 of 14 per cent, whereas the average family had an increase of 36 per cent. Similarly, between 1979 and 1990–91 the numbers of children living on less than half the average income trebled to 3.9 million, a third of under 16-year-olds (Households Below Average Income 1979–1990/91, 1993). Numerous reports and surveys have been published demonstrating: the increased social isolation and insecurity; growing inequalities in income and wealth; poor housing and homelessness and the impact of unemployment; and the reduced levels and access to social security in recent years (Barclay, 1995; Hills, 1995). All this when local government, the voluntary sector and other areas of health and welfare services are subject to reduced resources and almost perpetual reorganization.

Conclusions

Perhaps the clearest example that there is now official recognition that the child welfare system is in crisis and is increasingly riven with tensions and contradictions is the recent report by the Audit Commission (1994). In effect, the report argues that the aspirations and central aims of the Children Act are not being achieved and it makes recommendations to try to move policies and practices forward. It is argued that children are not receiving the help they need because local authority and community child health services are poorly planned and coordinated, resulting in much of the £2 billion being wasted on families who do not need support. Central to the Report's recommendations is that local authorities and the health service should produce strategic children's services plans to target resources more effectively. The recommendations for change are borrowed virtually wholesale from the field of community care. The focus should be on identifying and assessing need, then producing flexible and non-stigmatizing services, although these may not be provided by social workers. 'One stop shops' are another option for local communities, with a particular emphasis on care managers who coordinate provision. More emphasis could then be placed on prevention and less on reactive interventions, and reliance on expensive residential services could be reduced.

However, the report completely fails to locate the current problems in any wider political analysis of why the current problems have come about. These problems cannot be divorced from other much more significant social and economic policies and transformations. As a consequence its recommendations for change not only miss the point but are likely to make the situation worse. There is a real danger that social services and health authorities will be given responsibility for solving problems which are well beyond their remit and resources and other social and economic policies will be let off the hook. Developments in Britain have a direct parallel with similar changes in the USA where the trends and contradictions are even more evident (Lindsey, 1994).

We can now summarize what the essential factors have been which have contributed to this situation.

Firstly, the nature of the problem of child abuse has been officially broadened well beyond its original conception of the 'battered baby syndrome' (Dingwall, 1989) and now includes neglect, physical abuse, emotional abuse and most recently 'organized' abuse (Home Office, 1991). The definitions are essentially broad and all inclusive and while we do not have a mandatory reporting system, health and welfare professionals may be found morally and organizationally culpable if they do not report their concerns to an appropriate investigating agency, essentially social services departments.

Secondly, and directly related to this, public, professional and political awareness has grown considerably. This was reflected in the 1980s by the tremendous increases in the number of cases on child protection registers. Perhaps of greater significance, however, is the dramatic increase in referrals requiring investigation — now estimated at running at about 160,000 per year (Dartington Social Research Unit, 1995).

Thirdly, this broadening definition and growth in awareness and referrals has taken place in a context where social workers and others now have a clear responsibility not only to ensure that children do not suffer in the family but also that parental responsibility and family autonomy are not undermined. The notion of child protection subsumes within it not only the protection of child from significant harm but also the protection of the parents and family privacy from unwarrantable state interventions (see Winter and Connolly, this volume).

Fourthly, however, these developments have taken place in a changing economic and social environment which has had a direct impact on social services departments and social work practice with children and families. The amount of need and the number of potential clients has grown as increasing sections of the population have become marginalized from the mainstream of the economy, and the incidence of poverty, deprivation and insecurity has grown. However, not only have other state health and welfare services had insufficient resources for the demands made of them but social service departments have been subject to continual resource constraint and cut back.

This increased actual and potential demand in the context of reduced resources means that social services departments are finding it almost impossible to develop the more wide-ranging preventative family support strategies included in the Children Act 1989. Priorities and choices have to be made, not just between the more traditional child welfare responsibilities and responding to child abuse, but also choices and priorities in relation to child abuse itself. It is in this respect that the investigation of 'high risk' takes on its particular purchase and gets to the heart of what it is to do child protection work. The focus becomes differentiating the 'high risk' from the rest, so that children can be protected, parental rights and responsibilities can be respected, and scarce resources directed to where they will, in theory, be most effective. Resources and skills are focused on investigating, assessing and sifting out 'high risk', particularly when 'high risk' cannot be clearly demarcated. Where there is insufficient knowledge to demonstrate that the family or situation is safe, systems of monitoring, observation and surveillance take on a major significance.

The child protection system has been set up essentially to identify actual or significant harm and this is dominating the provision and priorities of child welfare services more generally. Increasingly the priorities are framed according to legalistic criteria where the identification of forensic evidence is central even when the case is not strictly provable. Where cases cannot be so constructed, or where the weight of evidence is not sufficient, the case is quickly filtered out of the system. What the current system does is provide mechanisms and rationales for controlling demand and thereby for prioritizing work. Unfortunately, the way it operates is not only contrary to the Children Act, it leaves children vulnerable and exposed.

References

ALDRIDGE, M. (1994) *Making Social Work News*, London, Routledge.

AUDIT COMMISSION (1994) *Seen But Not Heard: Coordinating Child Health and Social Services for Children in Need*, London, HMSO.

BARCLAY, P. (1995) *Joseph Rowntree Foundation Inquiry into Income and Wealth, Volume One*, York, Joseph Rowntree Foundation.

BOTTOMS, A.E. (1977) 'Reflections of the renaissance of dangerousness', *Howard Journal of Penology and Crime Prevention*, **16**, 2, pp. 70–96.

DENMAN, G. and THORPE, D. (1993) *Family Participation and Patterns of Intervention in Child Protection in Gwent* (A Research Report for the Area Child Protection Committee, Gwent, Lancaster) Department of Applied Social Science, Lancaster University.

DEPARTMENT OF HEALTH (1991) *Child Abuse: A Study of Inquiry Reports 1980–1989*, London, HMSO.

DEPARTMENT OF HEALTH (1994) *Children Act Report 1993*, London, HMSO.

DARTINGTON SOCIAL RESEARCH UNIT (1995) *Child Protection: Messages from Research*, London, HMSO.

DEPARTMENT OF HEALTH AND SOCIAL SECURITY (1974) *Non-Accidental Injury to Children*, (LASSL Local Authority Circular, (74), (13)).

DEPARTMENT OF HEALTH AND SOCIAL SECURITY (1976) *Non-Accidental Injury to Children: The Police and Case Conferences*, (LASSL Local Authority Circular, (76), (26)).

DEPARTMENT OF HEALTH AND SOCIAL SECURITY (1982) *Child Abuse: A Study of Inquiry Reports 1973–1981*, London, HMSO.

DEPARTMENT OF HEALTH AND SOCIAL SECURITY (1985a) *Review of Child Care Law: Report to Ministers of an Interdepartmental Working Party*, London, HMSO.

DEPARTMENT OF HEALTH AND SOCIAL SECURITY (1985b) *Social Work Decisions in Child Care: Recent Research Findings and Their Implications*, London, HMSO.

DINGWALL, R. (1989) 'Some problems about predicting child abuse and neglect', in STEVENSON, O. (ed.) *Child Abuse: Public Policy and Professional Practice*, Hemel Hempstead, Harvester-Wheatsheaf.

DONZELOT, J. (1988) 'The promotion of the social', *Economy and Society*, **17**, 3, pp. 395–427.

FRANKLIN, B. (ed.) (1986) *The Rights of Children*, Oxford, Basil Blackwell.

FRANKLIN, B. (ed.) (1995) *A Comparative Handbook of Children's Rights*, London, Routledge.

FRANKLIN, B. and PARTON, N. (eds) (1991) *Social Work, the Media and Public Relations*, London, Routledge.

FREEMAN, M.D.A. (1983) *The Rights and Wrongs of Children*, London, Francis Pinter.

GEACH, H. and SZWED, E. (eds) (1983) *Providing Civil Justice for Children*, London, Arnold.

GIBBONS, J. (1993) Personal communication.

GIBBONS, J., CONROY, S. and BELL, C. (1995) *Operating the Child of Protection System*, London, HMSO.

HALLET, C. and BIRCHALL, E. (1992) *Co-ordination and Child Protection: A Review of the Literature*, London, HMSO.

HILLS, J. (1995) *Joseph Rowntree Foundation. Inquiry into Income and Wealth, Volume Two*, York, Joseph Rowntree Foundation.

HOME OFFICE, DEPARTMENT OF HEALTH, DEPARTMENT OF EDUCATION AND SCIENCE, WELSH OFFICE (1991) *Working Together Under the Children Act 1989: A Guide to Arrangements for Inter-agency Co-operation for the Protection of Children from Abuse*, London, HMSO.

HOME OFFICE in conjunction with the DEPARTMENT OF HEALTH (1992) *Memorandum of Good Practice on Video Recording Interviews with Child Witnesses for Criminal Proceedings*, London, HMSO.

Households Below Average Income 1979–1990/91 (1993) London, HMSO.

LEVITAS, R. (ed.) (1986) *The Ideology of the New Right*, Oxford, Polity Press.

LINDSEY, D. (1994) *The Welfare of Children*, Oxford, Oxford University Press.

LONDON BOROUGH OF BRENT (1985) *A Child in Trust: Report of the Panel of Inquiry Investigating the Circumstances Surrounding the Death of Jasmine Beckford*, London, London Borough of Brent.

LONDON BOROUGH OF GREENWICH (1987) *A Child in Mind: Protection of Children in a Responsible Society, Report of the Commission of Inquiry into the Circumstances Surrounding the Death of Kimberley Carlile*, London, London Borough of Greenwich.

LONDON BOROUGH OF LAMBETH (1987) *Whose Child? The Report of the Panel Appointed to Inquire into the Death of Tyra Henry*, London, London Borough of Lambeth.

MORRIS, A., GILLER, H., SZWED, E. and GEACH, H. (1980) *Justice for Children*, London, Macmillan.

PARKER, R. (ed.) (1980) *Caring for Separated Children: Plans, Procedures and Priorities. A Report by a Working Party Established by the National Children's Bureau*, London, Macmillan.

PARTON, C. (1990) 'Women, gender oppression and child abuse' in The Violence Against Children Study Group, *Taking Child Abuse Seriously*, London, Unwin Hyman.

PARTON, N. (1985) *The Politics of Child Abuse*, London, Macmillan.

PARTON, N. (1991) *Governing the Family: Child Care, Child Protection and the State*, London, Macmillan.

ROSE, N. and MILLER, P. (1992) 'Political power beyond the state: Problematics of government', *British Journal of Sociology*, **43**, 25, pp. 173–205.

SECRETARY OF STATE FOR SOCIAL SERVICES (1974) *Report of the Inquiry into the Care and Supervision Provided in Relation to Maria Colwell*, London, HMSO.

SECRETARY OF STATE FOR SOCIAL SERVICES (1988) *Report of the Inquiry into Child Abuse in Cleveland Command 412*, London, HMSO.

Nigel Parton

Seebohm Report (1968) *Report of the Committee on Local Authority and Allied Personal Social Services Command 3703*, London, HMSO.

Social Services Committee (1984) *Children in Care* (HC 360), London, HMSO.

Taylor, L., Lacey, R. and Bracken, D. (1980) *In Whose Best Interests?* London, Cobden Trust/Mind.

Unsworth, C. (1987) *The Politics of Mental Health Legislation*, Oxford, Oxford University Press.

Wattam, C. (1992) *Making a Case in Child Protection*, London, NSPCC/Longman.

5 Back to the Future? Youth Crime, Youth Justice and the Rediscovery of 'Authoritarian Populism'

Tim Newburn[1]

Much contemporary academic discourse on the operation of the youth justice system or on the punishment of young offenders reads as if we are now more punitive and less concerned about the welfare of child offenders than at any time in the recent past. We have, however, only to look back a little over a century to see a time when children were not only punished by imprisonment but, on occasion, were subjected to transportation and even the death penalty. In fact, it is really only in the last 150 years that there have been discernible differences in the ways in which adult and child offenders have been treated by the criminal justice system.

Though great strides have undoubtedly been made in the treatment of young offenders over the past century or so, this remains highly contested terrain. This chapter considers developments in the 1980s and 1990s, a particularly interesting period in the history of juvenile justice. During the 1980s, the Thatcher administrations — for whom punitive 'law and order' policies were a central electoral strategy — adopted a series of policies which had the effect of reducing both recorded juvenile crime rates and the juvenile prison population. The 1990s, however, have seen a return of unbridled 'authoritarian populism' in juvenile justice, together with a renewed faith in the efficacy of prison for younger and younger children. A closer examination of these trends, and what might lie beneath them, is the subject of this chapter.

Punishment Versus Welfare in Juvenile Justice

From the late nineteenth century onwards a growing social reform movement sought to protect children from danger and exploitation and in the context of punishment to separate them from adults. Indeed, one commentator has suggested that the 'acceptance of Mary Carpenter's belief that children should not be dealt with as men [sic], but as children, was a seminal point in the evolution of the modern child' (May, 1973, p. 42). The first ten years of the twentieth century saw the establishment of the juvenile court and of 'borstal' institutions.

The seminal piece of legislation enshrining the principles that juveniles were to be treated separately from adults, and that they should be dealt with in a way that promoted their welfare, was the Children and Young Persons Act 1933 (amongst other things it prohibited capital punishment for those under the age of eighteen). Recorded juvenile crime, however, rose largely unabated during the 1930s and 1940s and, as Windlesham (1993, p. 69) has argued, from this point on 'the twin claws of the pincer that was to hold the development of penal policy fast in its grip were the remorseless increase in the incidence of crime, and the overcrowding in the prisons.'

The 1948 Criminal Justice Act contained provision (not activated until 1952) for new detention centre orders which were designed to maximize hard work and minimize amusement in a manner not unlike the 'short, sharp, shock' experiment in the 1980s and some of the more colourful suggestions made by Home Secretaries in the 1990s. At the end of the 1950s the Ingleby Committee, which had been set up to consider the operation of the juvenile court, was concerned about the conflict that it felt existed between the *judicial* and *welfare* functions of the juvenile court. This, it suggested, resulted in 'a child being charged with a petty theft or other wrongful act for which most people would say that no great penalty should be imposed, and the case apparently ending in a disproportionate sentence', and it recommended that the age of criminal responsibility be raised from 8 to 12 'with the possibility of it becoming 13 or 14' (Morris and Giller, 1987, p. 80). Although the major recommendations of the Ingleby Committee did not become law — the Children and Young Persons Act 1963, by way of compromise, raised the age of criminal responsibility to 10, for example — it did put the future of juvenile justice on the political agenda.

The 1960s saw a sustained series of campaigns over the treatment of juvenile offenders. The product was the Children and Young Persons Act 1969 which, had it ever been implemented in full, might have brought about a significant degree of depoliticization of the juvenile justice system, and the prioritization of 'welfare' over 'punishment' in interventions with young people. There was, however, a change of government before the Act was implemented and, although it is perhaps difficult to imagine having experienced Thatcherism, the Heath government of the early 1970s represented a new form of fairly harsh conservatism (Hall, Critcher, Jefferson, Clarke and Roberts, 1978).

Morris and Giller (1987, p. 111) argued that the juvenile justice policy at the end of the 1970s 'bore little resemblance to that proposed in the 1969 Act'. In particular, they suggest, the police and the Magistrates' Association had been successful in establishing their model of 'juvenile delinquency' as the dominant one in operation in the juvenile justice system. The 1970s had witnessed a series of 'moral panics' about the behaviour of young people in one form or another — whether in the guise of young persistent offenders, football hooligans, drug takers or victims of purveyors of obscenity and indecency (Newburn, 1991) — and by the early 1980s the law and order campaigns stoked in the general election of 1979 had gathered considerable force. By this point, the Magistrates' Association was pressing ever harder for short detention centre orders, a demand that was echoed by William Whitelaw, the Shadow Home Secretary, who called for the introduction of 'short, sharp, shock' treatment (Harwin, 1982).

The 'Successful Revolution'?

The Conservative Manifesto of 1979 promised to strengthen sentencing powers with respect to juveniles and young adults. The subsequent White Paper, *Young Offenders*, published in 1980 included proposals for the reintroduction of a limited number of detention centres with 'tougher' regimes, the 'experiment' beginning in two centres — Send (for 17–21-year-olds) and New Hall (for 14–16-year-olds) — in 1980. William Whitelaw, announcing the reform of detention centres, said that in the new regimes, 'life will be conducted at a brisk tempo. Much greater emphasis will be put on hard and constructive activities, on discipline and tidiness, on self-respect and respect for those in authority . . . These will be no holiday camps and those who attend them will not ever want to go back' (quoted in Home Office, 1984). The experiments, however, were fairly quickly found to be failures. The Home Office Young Offender Psychology Unit which evaluated these initiatives concluded: 'Apparently, the announcement of the policy did not affect crime rates generally: there was no interruption in trends in crime among young people generally not in the catchment areas of the two pilot project regimes especially.'

Despite this, Whitelaw's successor Leon Brittan remained steadfast in his public support of these new detention centre regimes and, indeed, announced in the Commons that the regimes were to be extended to all detention centres. The Thatcherite rhetoric remained tough: the streets were once again to be made safe, and the police were to be given new powers to sustain their fight against crime. However, the legislation emanating from the Home Office — at least as far as juveniles were concerned — contained countervailing tendencies. Central to the Criminal Justice Act 1982 was the aim of limiting the use of custody for young offenders; it shortened the detention centre sentence (its minimum and maximum lengths were reduced from three and six months to twenty-one days and four months respectively). Imprisonment for under-21s was abolished and the end of the road for borstals was signalled with the new order for 'Youth Custody' (the institutions becoming known as Youth Custody Centres). The Youth Custody Order was a determinate sentence whose length was fixed by the sentencing court (though with the possibility of remission and parole). The minimum Youth Custody sentence was four months one day, and magistrates and juvenile courts could impose sentences between the minimum and six months. The government's intention was that the shorter (though 'sharper') sentence, together with a requirement that sentencers should only impose a custodial sentence if they were satisfied that no other alternative was possible, would reduce the number of juveniles held in custody (discussed in

Figure 5.1: Males aged 14–16 sentenced to custody 1971–1990

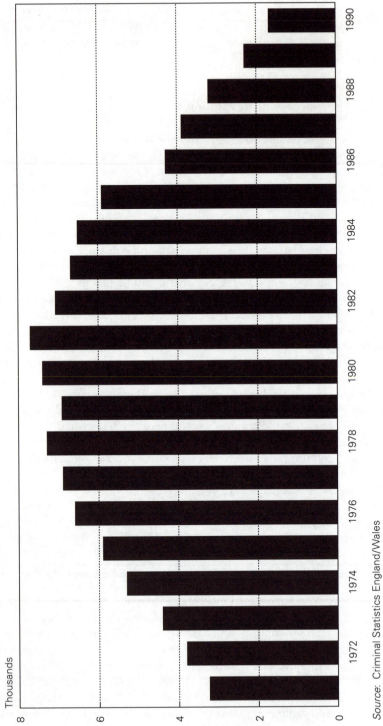

Source: Criminal Statistics England/Wales

Young Offenders, 1980, para. 46). There was considerable scepticism in some quarters, however, at the extent to which the government really was committed to the use of community-based alternatives to imprisonment, and there were fears that custodial institutions would become ever more central in juvenile justice (Allen, 1991).

Taken together, the 1980 White Paper and the 1982 Act represent a fairly fundamental attack on the welfarist principles that underpinned the Children and Young Persons Act. Gelsthorpe and Morris (1994, p. 972) have argued that they 'represented a move away from treatment and lack of personal responsibility to notions of punishment and individual and parental responsibility'. They also represented a move away from executive (social workers) to judicial decision making, and from the 'child in need' to the juvenile criminal — what Tutt (1981) called the 'rediscovery of the delinquent.'

Unlikely as it may seem against this background, a significant and sustained decline in the use of custody for juveniles is exactly what happened during the 1980s (see Figure 5.1). As Rutherford (1986, p. 5) commented, the paradox is that 'the decade of "law and order" was also the decade of what has been called "the successful revolution" in juvenile justice.'

One former Home Office minister has described this transformation as 'one of the most remarkable post-war achievements of deliberate legislative enactment' (Windlesham, 1993), and, seen against the backdrop of 'evolution, revolution and counter-revolution' in juvenile justice (Morris and Giller, 1987) described above, it is impossible to deny that it is indeed a remarkable achievement. The extent to which this 'revolution' may be attributed to deliberate legislative enactment is, however, somewhat more debatable. In some respects the Home Office could take credit for aspects of the transformation: the combination of aspects of the 1982 Criminal Justice Act, together with the Intermediate Treatment initiative announced not long after may have had some impact. On the other hand, there are a number of important structural changes which were at least equally, if not more, important.

In the first instance, although it cannot explain the full extent of the fall in numbers, there were significant demographic changes during the 1980s. There was, for example, a 17 per cent decline in the number of males in the 14–16 age group between 1981–88. Furthermore, in the same period, the number of young people sentenced also decreased by about 38 per cent (Allen, 1991). It may be that the 1982 Criminal Justice Act 'served as a catalyst in that it presented both opportunities but also a challenge' (Rutherford, 1989, p. 28), but crucial was the fact that this 'challenge was taken up by practitioners at the local level.' The success of the general policy of 'diverting' juveniles from prosecution meant that there were far fewer candidates for custodial sentences. This policy arose partly as a result of the insight from labelling theory — that involvement in the criminal justice process may, on occasion, reinforce rather than deter further offending (Taylor, Walton and Young, 1973).

One of the keys to diversion was the increased use of cautioning by the police. The 1980 White Paper had accepted that 'juvenile offenders who can

be diverted from the criminal justice system at an early stage in their offending are less likely to reoffend than those who become involved in judicial proceedings' (Home Office and Department of Health, 1980, para. 3.8). The police
clearly have great discretion in dealing with offenders, particularly so with juvenile offenders and, indeed, successive research studies have shown that there
are marked variations in the use of cautioning between police forces (Tutt and
Giller, 1983; Laycock and Tarling, 1985; Evans and Wilkinson, 1990). A series
of Home Office circulars (in 1978, 1985 and 1990) encouraged the police to
use their power to caution. The 14/1985 Circular issued to chief constables
included criteria to be applied by the police with the aim of increasing the
likelihood of diversion from prosecution. The 1990 Circular included national
standards and also, though it suggested they should be used sparingly, recognized the possible use of 'multiple cautions': it countenanced 'offenders being
cautioned more than once, provided the nature and circumstances of the most
recent offence warrant it.'

Alongside the increase in the use of cautioning there were also changes
in the use of non-custodial penalties — diversion once again, this time from
custody rather than prosecution.[2] This was part of the development of a
more general 'bifurcatory' policy in which, in theory, custodial sentences were
reserved for the violent, the dangerous and the recidivist, and non-custodial
sentences were increasingly to be used for the more run-of-the-mill juvenile
offenders. This dichotomization of offenders was characteristic of much penal
policy in the 1980s and reflected in part an increasing governmental recognition of the general failure of the criminal justice system to impact significantly
upon crime. This coincided with the end of the 'rehabilitative ideal' (Allen,
1981). Research which questioned the effectiveness of rehabilitation (Brody,
1976; Lipton *et al.*, 1975) led to diminishing faith in the efficacy of treatment
and training. The consequence was a renewed search for alternative means of
dealing with, or managing, young offenders in the community.

The 1982 Act introduced new requirements that could be attached to
supervision orders (Graham and Moxon, 1986). The following year, the DHSS
issued a circular in which it announced that £15 million was to be provided
to support intensive Intermediate Treatment (IT) programmes as an alternative to custody. The intention behind such intensive community-based supervision was to encourage further diversion from custody of young people at
risk of imprisonment. Monitoring of the subsequent development of schemes
by National Association for the Care and Resettlement of Offenders (NACRO)
suggests that this initiative may have had a significant impact on the custodial
sentencing of juveniles (NACRO, 1987).

In addition to announcing the funding, the Department of Health also
recommended that work with serious and persistent juvenile offenders should
be coordinated by inter-agency committees. Subsequently, such multi-agency
juvenile justice committees or panels were formed, often involving sentencers
as well as representatives of other relevant agencies involved in work with
young offenders. One of the consequences of this, it has been argued (NACRO,

1989), has been to provide a first step towards a more integrated system of juvenile justice (Allen, 1991). Pitts (1992) has even suggested that 'the IT initiative appears to have been the most successful innovation in the criminal justice system in the post-war period' (p. 182).

In addition to the decline in the numbers of juveniles sentenced to custody during the latter part of the 1980s, there was also a shift in the use of detention centre and borstal sentences. In the aftermath of the 1982 Act, magistrates took the opportunity to use their new powers to send juveniles to borstal and were much less attracted to the new 'short, sharp, shock' detention centre regimes. In fact the experiment was, largely, a failure; evaluation by the Home Office's Young Offender Psychology Unit concluded that the new regimes seemed to be no more effective than the previous ones. More than half of those sent to detention centres had been reconvicted within a year, irrespective of the type of regime in the centre at which they served their sentence (Home Office, 1984). Moreover, as Pitts (1995, p. iv) observes, magistrates tended to ignore the short, sharp, shock, 'in favour of a long, numb one'. Despite this, the 'short, sharp, shock' experiment was, briefly, extended to all detention centres, though aspects of the regime were modified. 'The political damage was limited', suggests Windlesham (1993), 'but it is hard to avoid the verdict that sound penal administration was made to serve the needs of a defective icon of political ideology' (p. 161).

In the longer term, the government decided to abolish the separate Detention Centre sentence. The Criminal Justice Act 1988 included a new sentence of 'detention in a young offender institution', and separate Detention Centres ceased to exist, being amalgamated with youth custody centres to become Young Offender Institutions (YOIs). Courts were given the power to decide on the length of sentence though the location where the sentence was to be served was to be determined by the Home Office. Detention in a YOI is available for people aged 15 and above.

So successful was this general policy of diversion perceived to be that the government began to explore the possibility of extending the gains made with the younger age group to 17-year-olds. Indeed, as early as 1988 in the Green Paper *Punishment, Custody and the Community*, the Home Office signalled its intention to transfer the lessons learnt in juvenile justice to policies in relation to offenders more generally, though it recognized that modifications would need to be made (Home Office, 1988, paras, 2.17–19). It did, however, emphasize the reasons for seeking to restrict the use of custodial sentences for young offenders:

> . . . most young offenders grow out of crime as they become more mature and responsible. They need encouragement and help to become law abiding. Even a short period of custody is quite likely to confirm them as criminals, particularly as they acquire new criminal skills from the more sophisticated offenders. They see themselves labelled as criminals and behave accordingly. (para. 2.23)

The 1991 Criminal Justice Act, in tandem with the Children Act 1989 which was part of the same general development (Faulkner, 1992), continued the by now well-established, twin-track approach of punishment and welfare. The Children Act gave statutory recognition to the need to avoid prosecution. The Criminal Justice Act 1991 changed the name of the Juvenile Court to the Youth Court and extended its jurisdiction to include 17-year-olds. The 1991 Act and subsequent Home Office Circular (30/1992), explaining the changes brought about by the legislation, reminded sentencers of s44 of the Children and Young Persons Act 1933 which states that 'all courts must have regard to the welfare of children and young people who appear before them.' The Act extended this consideration to 17-year-olds. The legislation also gave magistrates new sentencing powers within the overall framework created by the 1991 Act (including unit fines, community sentences and custody) along with a new scheme of post-custody supervision. The Act reduced the maximum term of detention in a YOI to 12 months, and brought 17-year-olds within the ambit of s53 of the Children and Young Persons Act 1933 which gives the Crown Court the power to order longer terms of detention in respect of certain 'grave crimes'. Finally, again reinforcing lessons learnt from developments in practice over the past decade, the 1991 Act signalled the importance of inter-agency and joint working by giving Chief Probation Officers and Directors of Social Services joint responsibility for making local arrangements to provide services to the Youth Court.

As Pitts (1995, p. iv) notes, whilst it may seem 'paradoxical that a radical law and order government presided over this unprecedented programme of penal reform, it is best seen as a product of political pragmatism.' Nonetheless, it is important to reiterate the point that the Thatcher administrations of the 1980s presided over a sustained decline in the juvenile prison population, and a significant decline in the number of known offenders aged 10–16. At least within the Home Office much of this was interpreted as 'success' and the general approach was to be extended to 17-year-olds, with talk of attempting the same strategy with young adults — 18–21-year-olds — in the near future. Five years on, however, and many of the gains that had actually been made in the 1980s have been lost. 'Authoritarian populism', highly visible in relation to discourse about Detention Centres yet notably absent in much of the rest of Tory juvenile justice policy in the 1980s, is once again very much the order of the day.

The Return of Authoritarian Populism

From 1991 onwards there was a noticeable increase in official concern about juvenile offending. Such concern, though to an extent ever-present in our society (Pearson, 1983), was fuelled by one or two very specific factors in the early 1990s. The first of these was the well-publicized urban disturbances of 1991. Though they were not on the scale or, indeed, similar in their causes or style to the riots of the early 1980s, the disturbances at Blackbird Leys (Oxford), Ely (Cardiff) and on the Meadowell estate in Tyneside focused attention on young men in large-scale violent confrontations with the police. In many cases, these were a consequence of attempts by the police to put a stop to the very public displays of 'joyriding' so popular with young men and with the journalists who increasingly turned up to capture their activities for posterity (Campbell, 1993).

'The 1991 riot season was', as Bea Campbell (1993) puts it, 'detonated in Ely.' In August 1991, Ely on the outskirts of Cardiff was the scene of a significant confrontation between young men and the police. The riot was sparked by a dispute between two local shopkeepers, and the perceived heavy-handed policing of a local campaign against one (an Asian) shopkeeper. In the event there were three days of disturbances, a large number of arrests, and acres of newsprint. Next was Blackbird Leys in Oxford. The focus here was cars rather than race. The estate was home to frequent, and popular, public displays of *hotting*, or joyriding high performance cars. Although this had apparently been going on for some time, in August 1991 the police decided to put an end to it. This was easier said than done, and the next few weeks saw highly public (spectators frequently brought deckchairs with them) police attempts to out-manoeuvre and outdrive the local hotting stars. Once again, the end result was a series of large-scale public order disturbances, scores of arrests, some exciting television, and the venting of moral outrage in the press. After Thames Valley came Northumbria. In and around the Meadowell estate the primary police concern was 'ramraiding' — using cars as battering rams to break through shop fronts in order to raid the premises. Like the hotters from Blackbird Leys, scanners were used to monitor police radio communications and, consequently, to avoid interception. There was a concerted police operation against ramraiding and car crime generally on the estate. On one occasion, two young men who were travelling in a stolen Renault turbo were involved in a high-speed chase with the police and crashed at 200 kph, both dying instantly. Within days the estate exploded.

What these three sets of public disturbances did was allow long-standing concerns about young or very young offenders to be dusted down, given a slightly modern gloss, and paraded in front of the cameras. It was increasingly suggested that the greatest scourge of inner-city life was the criminal who was too young for the criminal justice system to do anything about. Without entering into full-scale conspiracy theories, this was a convenient moment for the rise of such a panic, with numerous chief constables concerned about levels of funding for their forces, and a Home Secretary keen to re-establish his populist credentials.

From mid-1991 onwards, stories started to appear in the press about youngsters who, it was believed, were so involved in crime that they accounted for a significant proportion of juvenile crime in the areas in which they lived. Furthermore, it was suggested that the police and courts were powerless to deal with these offenders. The issue was taken up in a speech to the Federated Ranks of the Metropolitan Police in October 1992 by the then Home Secretary,

Kenneth Clarke. A small number of children, he suggested, 'are committing a large number of crimes. There is a case for increasing court powers to lock up, educate and train them for their own and everyone else's interest. We will certainly be taking a long hard look at the options which are available to the courts in dealing with serious offenders of this age. If court powers need to be strengthened or new institutions created, then they will be.'

By this stage it was open season in the press. The *Daily Mail* on 10 September 1992 under the headline, 'One-boy crime wave,' began its story, 'He was only 11 when his life of crime began with the theft of chocolate bars from a corner shop . . . within two years he had become a one-boy crime wave.' The previous day, the *Sun* had reported the case of a young boy of 13 it claimed had committed 225 thefts and been arrested 14 times. The *Daily Express* (9 September 1992) summed up the police view with the headline, 'Mini-gangster is beyond our control.' The *Daily Star* (30 November 1992) following its report of a case involving an 11-year-old offender, headlined its editorial, 'We've got too soft,' and went on: 'CHILDREN are supposed to be little innocents — not crooks in short trousers. But much of Britain is now facing a truly frightening explosion of kiddie crime. As we reveal today, too many youngsters are turning into hardened hoods almost as soon as they've climbed out of their prams.'

Although public concern about the level of juvenile crime and the perceived ineffectiveness of the criminal justice system to deal with the problem remained high in the following months, it is possible that the concern would not have turned to panic were it not for the tragic events of February 1993 and their highly publicized aftermath. The abduction and murder of a young child would have affected public consciousness in any event; the fact that within a short period two 10-year-old boys were arrested on suspicion of having committed the offences concerned, caused profound shock to a whole nation, and provided the strongest possible evidence to an already worried public that there was something new and terrifying about juvenile crime.

The following month, Kenneth Clarke announced that the government proposed to introduce legislation that would make a new disposal available to the courts. These 'secure training orders' were to be aimed at 'that comparatively small group of very persistent juvenile offenders whose repeated offending makes them a menace to the community' (Hansard 2 March 1993, col. 139). The new order would apply to 12–15-year-olds (later amended to 12–14-year-olds) who had been convicted of three imprisonable offences, and who had proved 'unwilling or unable to comply with the requirements of supervision in the community while on remand or under sentence.' The order was to be a custodial one and would be served in a 'secure training unit' which, he suggested, would provide 'high standards of care and discipline'. Regimes would include provision for education and training for inmates; after release, individuals would be subject to 'rigorous, consistent and firmly delivered' supervision until their supervising social worker or probation officer felt that he or she was no longer a threat to society.

Somewhat earlier, in the autumn of 1992, the House of Commons Home

Affairs Committee (HAC) had announced that it would be enquiring into issues affecting juvenile offenders and the particular problems of persistent offenders. In explaining its reasons for doing so the Committee said: 'We decided on this enquiry both because of public concern about the level of juvenile crime in particular, and because of the apparent inability of the criminal justice system to deal adequately with it' (HAC, 1993).

Given what has been said above about recent trends in juvenile crime — a relatively sharp decline in recorded juvenile crime during the 1980s and early 1990s — it is worth briefly considering what the Home Affairs Committee made of the fact that there existed significant 'public concern about the level of juvenile crime'. The Committee received much evidence which backed up the picture presented by official criminal statistics of a general decline of *recorded* juvenile crime. The word 'recorded' is important here, for a number of witnesses made much of the fact that the same period may well have seen a significant rise in the use of informal warnings by the police (sometimes referred to as informal cautions), and that because such warnings are not recorded, they may account, at least in part, for some of the dissonance between what official statistics suggested and what the public and politicians felt.

In addition, evidence was presented by the Association of Chief Police Officers (ACPO) which challenged the view that there had been a decline in juvenile offending during the 1980s. They argued that, given the decline in the juvenile population, the increase in crime more generally, and the generally reduced rate of detection, the period from 1980 to 1990 had in fact witnessed a 54 per cent rise in juvenile crime. Indeed, they were given some support from the Shadow Home Secretary and one of the Shadow Home Affairs Ministers who also suggested that it was 'difficult to believe Home Office claims that offending by young people has actually gone down across the country' (HAC, 1993, para. 7). The Home Affairs Committee in seeking an explanation for this apparent disagreement suggested that it was in part due to the fact that the official criminal statistics referred to numbers of offenders whereas ACPO were referring to the number of offences. As ACPO then said, whilst it did not challenge the proposition that the number of known juvenile offenders had fallen, that is not the same as saying 'that the amount of crime committed by juveniles has not increased.' The Home Affairs Committee (1993) was, not unnaturally, unable to resolve the issue, but it did suggest that:

> . . . one possible explanation for the apparent discrepancy between ACPOs picture of greater juvenile offending and the decline in the number of juvenile offenders is a growth in the numbers of *persistent* offenders . . . If there is a small but growing number of juvenile offenders responsible for many offences (some of which they may be convicted or cautioned for and some of which may go undetected) it is possible to reconcile the indisputable fact that the number (and rate, to a lesser extent) of known juvenile offenders has fallen over

time with the more speculative assertion that the number of offences committed by juveniles has risen. (para. 15)

Having identified this possibility, the Home Affairs Committee then went on to consider the issue of persistent offending and received a generally uniform picture from the majority of agencies. ACPO, for example, talked of a 'small hard core who have absolutely no fears whatsoever of the criminal justice system', and continued, 'society is entitled to expect a degree of protection from the ravages of the persistent juvenile offender.' Although the other witnesses were not quite so certain in their descriptions, there were few who took exception to the idea that there existed a small group of offenders that might, as the Home Affairs Committee put it, be described as 'persistent juvenile trouble makers'. The Committee went on, 'the Association of Chief Officers of Probation (ACOP) told us that there might be, for example, 10–12 such individuals in Hampshire, while NAPO suggested that there were 12–20 in Newcastle. This may only be, as ACOP said, "a very, very small handful", but there is clearly a significant group of individuals country-wide who cause a disproportionate amount of the crime attributed to young people.'

There was little chance that public concern about 'serious' juvenile offenders would lessen, for in November 1993 the trial of the two youngsters accused of James Bulger's murder took place at Preston Crown Court amidst massive national and international media interest (the press coverage of this trial is dealt with in detail in Chapter 9 in this volume). Despite a change of Home Secretary, there was no change of tack in juvenile justice policy. At the Conservative Party Conference just before the trial in Preston the new Home Secretary, Michael Howard, announced his 'law and order' package. The description is not a loose one, for the approach taken by Howard flew directly in the face of all the major trends in criminal justice since the late 1980s. The government were by this stage under pressure from a Labour Party which appeared to be persuading voters that it could be just as 'tough on crime' as the traditional party of law and order claimed to be, whilst simultaneously implementing social policies that, as in Tony Blair's famous soundbite, would make them 'tough on the causes of crime' as well. The choice that Howard made in seeking to bolster his Party's and his own fortunes was to return to the strident tones reminiscent of Mrs Thatcher's 'authoritarian populism' (Hall, 1983).

The measures that Howard announced were punitive, involving a reassertion of the central position of custody in a range of sanctions he interpreted as having deterrence as their primary aim. Most famously, he announced that previous approaches which involved attempts to limit prison numbers were henceforward to be eschewed. The new package of measures would be likely to result in an increase in prison numbers, an increase which he appeared to welcome: 'I do not flinch from that. We shall no longer judge the success of our system of justice by a fall in our prison population . . . Let us be clear. *Prison works*. It ensures that we are protected from murderers, muggers and rapists — and it makes many who are tempted to commit crime think twice' (quoted in Gibson, Cavadino, Rutherford, Ashworth and Harding, 1994, p. 83; emphasis added).

The government's response to the 'problem' of persistent offending by juveniles was to include clauses in the Criminal Justice and Public Order Bill which provided for the introduction of a new 'secure training order'. Five new secure training centres were to be built, each housing approximately forty inmates. The new sentences would be determinate sentences, of a maximum of two years, half of which would be served in custody and half under supervision in the community. Section 19 of what eventually became the Criminal Justice and Public Order Act 1994 also allowed for the new institutions to be managed by public, voluntary or private organizations, though such was the antipathy towards the new provisions by public and voluntary organizations that it was 'clearly envisaged that in practice they will be built and operated by the private sector' (NACRO, 1994).

There has been widespread criticism of, and resistance to, the new provisions for dealing with 12–14-year-olds. Arrangements are still being made for the construction of the first of the new secure training centres, planning permission having been refused on more than one occasion. The resistance to secure training centres has, however, mainly come from professionals working with young offenders, rather than opposition politicians. By and large the secure training order has met with relatively little political hostility within parliament, and other elements of the 1994 Criminal Justice and Public Order Act have received far more attention and sustained criticism. The 'punitive solution' to the issue of persistent offending by young people, whilst running counter to much of what had been learnt in youth justice in the 1980s, is set to proceed.

One might think that reintroducing custody for 12–14-year-olds would be enough even for a populist like Michael Howard. However, this is clearly not the case. Stimulated at least in part by Tony Blair's own brand of penal pragmatism, the Prime Minister and his Home Secretary have launched several initiatives to win back the law and order territory they are perceived to have lost. In February 1995, thanks to a Prison Service document that was leaked, we were informed that the government was keen on the idea of introducing American-style 'boot camps' for young offenders. Both the Director General of the Prison Service and the Home Secretary had visited America to inspect the high impact incarceration programmes being run on Rikers Island and in other parts of the country (see reports in the *Times*, 6 February 1995; and the *Daily Telegraph*, 10 August 1995).

Familiar battle lines were drawn once again, with critics of the Home Secretary's (still unannounced proposals) pointing to the similarities between British boot camps and the failed short, sharp shock experiments of the 1980s. In August 1995 a further leak suggested that the regime at Thorn Cross — the proposed site for the first of the boot camps — would be somewhat different than had been envisaged. The scheme was only to apply to low-risk prisoners, it would be voluntary, and there would be greater emphasis on vocational training than on US-style harsh military exercise.

If anyone took this as an indication that the Home Secretary no longer perceived his popularity to be linked to how austere he could make prisons for young offenders sound they would soon have been disabused by the latest proposal to be made public (once again via a leak). In August 1995, it became apparent that there had been correspondence between the Home Secretary and the Defence Secretary, Michael Portillo, exploring the possibility of using the Military Corrective Training Centre at Colchester for young offenders ('Tearaways face life on fatigues,' *Daily Telegraph*, 25 August 1995). Using the 'glasshouse' for young miscreants is, of course, a logical move for a Home Secretary whose postbag is no doubt full of pleas for the return of military service for young people. It appears, though, that the Ministry of Defence is not looking particularly kindly on Mr Howard's suggestion, though in an era of penal policy where the soundbite is more important than the strategy, perhaps he has already achieved his central aim.

Conclusion

The recent history of youth justice policy makes very depressing reading. Secure training centres, boot camps, the glasshouse all smack more of the nineteenth than the twentieth century. However, as I hope I have illustrated, the politics of youth justice are rather curious. Although the first Thatcher administration was elected on an unashamedly law and order ticket, and espoused a set of values that were solidly in line with the spirit of that manifesto, the 1980s were a time of optimism, albeit limited optimism, in youth justice. The use of custody declined; indeed, as evidenced by the decline in recorded juvenile crime, the use of the criminal justice system appeared to be declining.

All this changed, and changed extraordinarily quickly in the 1990s. Lessons were learned in the 1980s, and some were put into practice. However, the politicization of criminal justice ensured that they would quickly be undermined. This wholesale politicization of criminal justice — perhaps the most lasting legacy of Thatcherism in this area — maximizes the likelihood that long-term benefits will continually be sacrificed on the alter of short-term expediency. With the front bench Home Affairs spokesmen (and they *are* generally men) of both major parties battling to 'out-tough' each other, there appears little prospect of coherent and forward-thinking policy making. Sadly, the prospects of there being new criminal justice legislation in the near future that is a product of coherent thought and long-term planning is slim. Short-term electoral advantage (whether imagined or real) is once again the driving force in criminal justice policy making.

Notes

1 I am grateful to Ann Hagell for her helpful and supportive comments on the first draft of this paper.

2   This is not to ignore the quite extended debate that has taken place about the possibility that some of these changes — increased use of cautioning and non-custodial
penalties, for example — may have resulted in a degree of 'net-widening', i.e.,
bringing into the criminal justice process children who would not otherwise have
been there (cf. Ditchfield, 1976; Farrington and Bennett, 1981; Farrington, 1992).

References

ALLEN, F. (1981) *The Decline of the Rehabilitative Ideas*, New Haven, Yale University
Press.

ALLEN, R. (1991) 'Out of jail: The reduction in the use of penal custody for male
juveniles 1981–88', *Howard Journal*, **30**, 1.

BRODY, S.R. (1976) *The Effectiveness of Sentencing*, Home Office Research Study No 35,
London, HMSO.

CAMPBELL, B. (1993) *Goliath: Britain's Dangerous Places*, London, Methuen.

DITCHFIELD, J. (1976) *Police Cautioning in England and Wales*, Home Office Research
Study No. 37, London, HMSO.

EVANS, R. and WILKINSON, C. (1990) 'Variations in police cautioning policy and practice
in England and Wales', *Howard Journal of Criminal Justice*, **29**.

FARRINGTON, D.P. (1992) 'Trends in English juvenile delinquency and their explanation',
International Journal of Comparative and Applied Criminal Justice, **16**, 2.

FARRINGTON, D. and BENNETT, T. (1981) 'Police cautioning of juveniles in London',
British Journal of Criminology, **21**, pp. 123–35.

FAULKNER, D.E.R. (1992) 'Magistrates in the Youth Court', *The Magistrate*, September.

GELSTHORPE, L. and MORRIS, A. (1994) 'Juvenile justice 1945–1992', in MAGUIRE, M.,
MORGAN, R. and REINER, R. (eds) *The Oxford Handbook of Criminology*, Oxford,
Oxford University Press.

GIBSON, B., CAVADINO, P., RUTHERFORD, A., ASHWORTH, A. and HARDING, J. (1994) *Criminal
Justice in Transition*, Winchester, Waterside Press.

GRAHAM, J. and MOXON, D. (1986) 'Some trends in juvenile justice', *Home Office Research
Bulletin*, **22**, pp. 10–13.

HALL, S. (1983) 'The great moving right show', in HALL, S. and JACQUES, M. (eds) *The
Politics of Thatcherism*, London, Lawrence and Wishart.

HALL, S., CRITCHER, C., JEFFERSON, T., CLARKE, J. and ROBERTS, B. (1978) *Policing the
Crisis: Mugging, the State and Law and Order*, London, Macmillan.

HARWIN, J. (1982) 'The battle for the delinquent', in JONES, C. and STEVENSON, J. (eds)
The Yearbook of Social Policy in Britain, 1980–81, London, Routledge and Kegan
Paul.

HOME AFFAIRS COMMITTEE (1993) *Juvenile Offenders*, Sixth Report, London, HMSO.

HOME OFFICE (1984) *Tougher Regimes in Detention Centres: Report of an Evaluation
by the Young Offender Psychology Unit*, London, HMSO.

HOME OFFICE (1988) *Punishment, Custody and the Community*, Cm 424, London, HMSO.

LAYCOCK, G. and TARLING, R. (1985) 'Police force cautioning policy and practice in
England and Wales', *Howard Journal of Criminal Justice*, **24**.

LIPTON, D., MARTINSON, R. and WILKS, J. (1975) *Effectiveness of Treatment Evaluation
Studies*, New York, Praeger.

MAY, M. (1973) 'Innocence and experience: The evolution of the concept of juvenile
delinquency in the mid-nineteenth century', *Victorian Studies*, **17**, 1.

Morris, A. and Giller, H. (1987) *Understanding Juvenile Justice*, Beckenham, Croom Helm.

NACRO (1987) *Diverting Juveniles from Custody: Findings from the Fourth Census of the Projects Funded under the DHSS Intermediate Treatment Initiative*, London, NACRO Juvenile Crime Section.

NACRO (1989) *Progress through Partnership*, London, NACRO.

NACRO (1994) *The Criminal Justice and Public Order Bill and Young Offenders*, London, NACRO, May.

Newburn, T. (1991) *Permission and Regulation: Law and Morals in Post-war Britain*, London/New York, Routledge.

Pearson, G. (1983) *Hooligan: A History of Respectable Fears*, London, Macmillan.

Pitts, J. (1992) 'Juvenile justice policy in England and Wales', in Coleman, J.C. and Warren-Adamson, C. (eds) *Youth Policy in the 1990s*, London, Routledge.

Pitts, J. (1995) 'Scare in the community: Britain in a moral panic. Part one: Youth Crime', *Community Care*, 4–10 May.

Rutherford, A. (1986) *Growing Out of Crime: Society and Young People in Trouble*, Harmondsworth, Penguin.

Rutherford, A. (1989) 'The mood and temper of penal policy: Curious happenings in England during the 1980s', *Youth and Policy*, **27**.

Taylor, I., Walton, P. and Young, J. (1973) *The New Criminology: For a Social Theory of Deviance*, London, Routledge and Kegan Paul.

Tutt, N. (1981) 'A decade of policy', *British Journal of Criminology*, **21**, 4.

Tutt, N. and Giller, H. (1983) 'Manifesto for management — the elimination of custody', *Justice of the Peace*, **151**, pp. 200–2.

Windlesham, Lord (1993) *Responses to Crime (vol 2): Penal Policy in the Making*, Oxford, Oxford University Press.

6   Gillick and After: Children and Sex in the 1980s and 1990s

Jane Pilcher

The campaign waged by Victoria Gillick in the 1980s against the provision of contraception to girls under the age of 16 made her into a household name. Despite losing her case in a House of Lords decision in 1985, Mrs Gillick has continued to campaign against what she would see as the contamination of children's innocence and the erosion of parental rights through children's increased access to sexual knowledge and advice. In addition to her continuing objections to the provision of contraceptive services to the under-16s (for example, in 1989, 1992, and 1994[1]), Mrs Gillick has publicly complained about or criticized various sex education materials,[2] describing one as 'state funded pornography' (The *Guardian*, 25 March 1994). Clearly, a full decade after the House of Lords ruling, Mrs Gillick has not withdrawn from her campaign. Her ongoing agitations are a firm indication of the extent to which the issue of children and sex remains a highly contentious one in contemporary Britain.

Throughout the 1980s and 1990s, there have been a series of 'moral eruptions' (Weeks, 1991), especially amongst the New Right, on the issue of children and sex. These include the Gillick case itself, local authorities 'promoting homosexuality to children at the ratepayers' expense' (which led to Section 28 of the Local Government Act 1988), the content of sex education more generally and, most recently, the issue of children and computer pornography (Home Affairs Committee, 1994).

Focusing primarily on the Gillick case, it is the argument of this chapter that such 'moral eruptions' are highly revealing, both of conceptions of childhood dominant in British society and aspects of New Right politics. The chapter begins by locating the issue of children and sex within New Right concerns more generally and then gives a descriptive account of the Gillick litigation. The main part of the chapter examines the 1985 House of Lords Gillick judgment in terms of the conceptions of childhood that it contains. The legacies of Gillick are then assessed, first, for the narrow concern of the original litigation (that is, contraception for the under-16s) and second, for children's autonomy rights more generally. Here, particular attention is paid to the issue of school sex education since, in this 'moral eruption', New Right conceptions of children and sex have held fast against any advances thought by many to have been achieved through Gillick for children's autonomy rights.

As noted elsewhere in this volume (see O'Connell Davidson and Sanchez Taylor), Western ideologies around sexuality and childhood mean that the pairing of 'children' with 'sex' is morally inappropriate: children are asexual, innocent and pure (see Jackson, 1982; Ennew, 1986). Therefore, evidence of childhood sexuality revealed by, for example, their actual sexual activities and corresponding needs for contraceptive services, their interest in and use of computer-based pornography, and their responses to programmes of school sex education, undermine ideas about what childhood should 'properly' be. This perspective on children and sex is expressed particularly strongly by the moral authoritarian right in British politics. The New Right's interest in child-hood can be located in the broader context of their concerns, especially that of re-establishing the primacy of the private sphere ('the family', organized along patriarchal lines in terms of both gender and generation) over the pub-lic sphere (the state, especially at the level of local government, and medical, teaching and social work professionals).

The various 'moral eruptions' of the 1980s and 1990s on the issue of chil-dren and sex are comprised, to varying degrees, of discourses which centre on *parental* rights to control their children's access to sexual knowledge and/or advice, in the face of 'interference' from others — especially medical and ped-agogic 'others'. For example, in school sex education, recent legislative changes influenced by the activities of moral authoritarian conservatives have clearly prioritized the rights of parents over those of children and of teachers (Thomson, 1994; Department for Education [DFE], 1993), whilst concerns about control-ling children's access to computer pornography are expressed in terms of the computer illiteracy of parents in the face of children's computer competency (Home Affairs Committee, 1994; see also Holland, this volume). As is illus-trated below, discourses of parental rights were also central to the Gillick case, a 'moral eruption' of the 1980s which, in the 1990s, continues to have rami-fications for children's access to sexual knowledge and advice and for their autonomy rights more generally.

The Gillick Case

Debates on the issue of the provision of contraception to girls who are under the legal age of consent for sexual intercourse can be traced back at least to a decade before Gillick initiated her legal action. Following the 1973 National Health Service (Reorganization) Act, the Department of Health and Social Security (DHSS) issued a memorandum of guidance on family planning ser-vices to health authorities in May 1974 (All England Law Reports [AELR], 1985; Durham, 1991). In December 1980, the DHSS issued a revised version of the earlier guidance, which contained a section (Section G) on family planning services for young people. This guidance to health authorities stated, amongst other matters:

i) that family planning clinic sessions should be available for 'people of all ages', but that efforts might be made to make separate, less formal arrangements for 'young people';

ii) that where medical professionals are approached by 'persons under the age of 16' for advice on family planning, 'special care is needed not to undermine parental responsibility and family stability';

iii) that when consulted by persons under the age of 16, medical professionals 'will always seek to persuade the child to involve the parent or guardian . . . and will proceed from the assumption that it would be most unusual to provide advice about contraception without parental consent', other than in 'exceptional cases';

iv) that, nevertheless, the principle of confidentiality between patients and doctors should not be abandoned for 'children under 16';

v) that 'the nature of counselling must be a matter for the doctor or other professional worker concerned and that the decision whether or not to prescribe contraception must be for the clinical judgement of a doctor'.

In short, the guidance condoned the practice of providing contraceptive advice and services to young people below the age of consent to sexual intercourse, principally on the grounds of doctor–patient confidentiality and the need to protect young people from the risk of pregnancy, sexually transmitted diseases and other 'consequences' which may threaten 'stable family life' (AELR, 1985, pp. 405–6).

The DHSS memorandum of guidance on the provision of family planning services to young people caused some debate and led to campaigns by conservative moral lobbyists, including Victoria Gillick, against its suggestion that advice on and prescriptions for contraception could be given regardless of age (Durham, 1991). Partly in response to such campaigns, the government instigated reviews of the policy on the underage prescription of contraception, but ultimately cited patient confidentiality as a reason why the practice supported by the DHSS guidance could be condoned (Durham, 1991). Following the issue of the revised guidelines in 1980, Mrs Gillick made known her objections to her local health authority. She formally forbade any of its medical staff to give her underage daughters any contraceptive or abortion advice or treatment without her prior consent. In 1982, dissatisfied with the response she had received from her health authority (that medical treatment was a matter for a doctor's clinical judgment), Mrs Gillick began legal proceedings against the health authority and the DHSS. She sought to establish, firstly, that the DHSS Circular was unlawful in that it advised medical professionals to cause or encourage unlawful (that is, underage) sexual intercourse, or to be an accessory to unlawful sexual intercourse, contrary to the relevant sections of the 1956 Sexual Offences Act. Secondly, Mrs Gillick sought to establish that medical staff of the health authority could not give advice on or treatment for contraception to any of her underage children without her consent; to do so would be unlawful in that it would be inconsistent with her parental rights (AELR, 1985). Mrs Gillick was supported in her campaign by Conservative Members of Parliament, as well as by various extra-parliamentary groupings (Durham, 1991).

The case brought by Mrs Gillick against her health authority and the DHSS went to court, but the ruling, in 1983, was not in her favour. The judgment was that, firstly, medical professionals who prescribed contraceptives to girls under the age of 16, in accordance with the DHSS guidance, would not be committing any offence under the 1956 Sexual Offences Act. Secondly, that a parent's interest in his or her child did not amount to a 'right' but rather to a responsibility or duty, so that advising on or prescribing contraceptives to a girl under the age of 16 without her parents' consent did not amount to unlawful interference with parental rights.[3] Dissatisfied with the ruling, Mrs Gillick took her case to the Court of Appeal, which, in 1984, overturned the decision of the earlier court. The DHSS guidelines on the provision of contraceptive services to young people were now ruled to be illegal and were subsequently suspended (AELR, 1985).

In addition to the suspension of the DHSS guidelines, there were several other immediate effects of the Appeal Court's ruling. The Family Planning Information Service withdrew two of its leaflets which advised young people about sex and contraception because they contained statements to the effect that anyone could attend a family planning clinic and receive confidential advice and treatment (*Times Educational Supplement* [*TES*], 15 March 1985). The day after the Appeal Court found in favour of Mrs Gillick, the DHSS issued a Circular to local medical and education authorities which stated that 'a doctor or any other professional' providing advice or treatment on contraception or abortion to a person under 16 without 'parental consent or that of the court is not lawful' (*TES*, 15 March 1985). As the newspaper article in which this was reported pointed out, 'any other professional' could be taken to mean teachers, health visitors and anyone else involved in sex education in schools. Moreover, following the Appeal Court's ruling and the subsequent issuing of the DHSS Circular, those in both the medical and teaching professions were confused as to what might be constituted as 'advice'. As I argue later, confusion (especially amongst doctors, teachers, and young people themselves) about what is and is not lawful in the advising of young people about sexual matters is one of the lasting legacies of the Gillick case.

The importance of a 'parental rights' discourse to the Gillick case is evident from the phrasing of the legal action which Mrs Gillick initiated in 1982 and in the initial judgment against her. Following the 1984 Appeal Court ruling in her favour, those involved in advising young people about sexual matters, as well as academic commentators, recognized the extent to which parental rights had been upheld over and above the rights of all other parties. David (1986), writing prior to the later House of Lords ruling on the Gillick case, noted that the case had been persistently presented as a parental rights (and especially a *mother's* rights) issue and that there had been little discussion of the rights of young people. A *TES* article reported reactions to the Appeal Court ruling under the headline 'Parents' Power to Say No' (15 March 1985). Spokespersons for the Health Visitors Association and the National Union of Teachers both recognized that the Appeal Court ruling in favour of Mrs Gillick meant that parental rights had been extended. The Gillick case was also recognized to hold portents for the future. Commentators predicted (with foresight, as is shown later) that the case had ramifications for parental authority in areas other than that of providing contraceptive advice and/or services to young people (*TES*, 15 March 1985; David, 1986).

On behalf of the DHSS, the then Secretary of State for Health, Kenneth Clarke, appealed to the House of Lords in an attempt to reverse the 1984 judgment of the Appeal Court. As Durham (1991) argues, this action by the Thatcher administration is a revealing indication of the complexity of New Right politics. Clearly, there existed a degree of independence between the Thatcher administration and the intra- and extra-parliamentary 'moral lobby'. The appeal by the DHSS can also be recognized as an early example of the tensions between what Thomson (1993) has called discourses of 'sexual moralism' and those of 'public health pragmatism' on the issue of young people and sex. In 1985, the House of Lords overturned the decision of the Appeal Court and found in favour of the DHSS, a decision which led to the reinstatement of the memorandum of guidance on family planning services. This was the end of the legal struggles between Mrs Gillick, her local health authority and the DHSS, but, as noted earlier, Mrs Gillick has continued to campaign on the issue and, indeed, on the issue of children and sex more generally.

The 1985 Gillick Judgment

The House of Lords judgment in favour of the DHSS and against Mrs Gillick was the result of a majority, rather than a unanimous, decision: three out of five judges found for the DHSS and two for Mrs Gillick. An analysis of the reasoning by which the five Lords reached their individual verdicts is revealing about conceptions of children and childhood predominant in British society, not least those held by this influential body of persons.

There was agreement amongst the five Law Lords on the central issue at hand. In the words of Lord Fraser, the central issue was whether a doctor could lawfully prescribe contraception for a girl under 16 years of age without the consent of her parents, or as Lord Templeman put it, 'who has the right to decide whether an unmarried girl under the age of 16 may practice contraception?' (AELR, 1985, p. 431). The three key parties to such a decision, as identified by the Lords in their deliberations on the matter, were the parents, the doctor and the girl herself. Where Lords Fraser, Scarman and Bridge (who found against Mrs Gillick) disagreed with Lords Brandon and Templeman (who found in favour of Mrs Gillick) was over the legality of the rights of the various parties to make such a decision.

In reaching his judgment, Lord Brandon specifically argued against the DHSS's claim that it had a statutory duty to provide contraceptive services to girls under the age of 16 because the wording of the relevant provision refers to 'persons' and does not specify an age. Lord Brandon agreed that the relevant provision does not define 'persons' but, in his opinion, 'persons' did not include girls under the age of 16. The main element of Lord Brandon's decision centred around his interpretation of the criminal law governing the sexual relations of girls under the age of 16. For Lord Brandon, the Sexual Offences Act 1956 shows that parliament regards sexual intercourse between a man and a girl under the age of 16 as a serious criminal offence on the part of the man. It 'necessarily' follows from this that persons promoting, encouraging or facilitating sexual intercourse between a man and a girl under the age of 16 may themselves be committing a criminal offence. It was the opinion of Lord Brandon that to give a girl aged under 16 advice about contraception, to examine her with a view to her using contraception and to prescribe contraceptive treatment for her all 'necessarily' involve promoting, encouraging or facilitating a criminal offence. Since the provision of contraceptive facilities to girls under the age of 16 is unlawful in all circumstances, it was his ruling that the issue of parental consent and knowledge is immaterial: 'making contraception available to girls under the age of 16 is unlawful, whether their parents know of and consent to it or not' (AELR, 1985, p. 431).

The main thrust of Lord Brandon's decision in favour of Mrs Gillick and against the DHSS thus centred around his interpretation of the scope of the 1956 Sexual Offences Act. Although his opinion that girls under the age of 16 are not 'persons' is revealing about his conception of children and of childhood, the issue of children's capacities and rights formed only a marginal component of Lord Brandon's judgment. The same cannot be said for the second Lord who found in favour of Mrs Gillick. In the judgment of Lord Templeman, the issue of children's capacities and powers of decision making were a central element and, as will shortly be demonstrated, was thus more in keeping with the manner by which the Lords reached their majority verdict against Mrs Gillick. For Lord Templeman, a girl under the age of 16 does not possess the right in law to decide for herself to practice contraception. He cited the 1956 Sexual Offences Act as evidence that parliament does not regard girls under the age of 16 as being 'sufficiently mature' to consent to sexual intercourse. For Lord Templeman, it follows from this that 'such a girl cannot therefore be regarded as sufficiently mature to be allowed to decide for herself that she will practise contraception for the purpose of frequent or regular or casual sexual intercourse' (AELR, 1985, p. 431). Having concluded that a girl under the age of 16 lacks the capacity to consent to contraceptive advice and treatment in her own right, Lord Templeman then went on to consider the respective rights and duties of parents and doctors in the provision of contraceptive facilities to girls under the age of 16. In his opinion, the law does allow parents and doctors to decide that contraceptive facilities should be available to girls under the age of 16, when there is agreement between them that this course of action is in the best interests of the girl. However, difficulties arise where the parent(s) and the doctor differ. In considering the respective rights and duties of parents and doctors when there is disagreement as to the best course of action, Lord Templeman also found it necessary to consider whether girls under the age of 16 have the capacity to consent to medical treatment *per se*.

The vocabulary employed by Lord Templeman in his deliberations in this respect is highly revealing about the conceptions of children and of childhood which informed his eventual decision in favour of Mrs Gillick. Throughout the relevant passages of his judgment, Lord Templeman referred to 'infants', by which he meant all those under the legal age of majority of 18.[4] For Lord Templeman, parents have the right in law to decide on behalf of 'the infant' on all matters which the infant is not competent to decide. Where a patient is an 'infant', the medical profession accepts that a parent has the right to consent to treatment on behalf of that 'infant'. Lord Templeman also allowed for the practice of doctors carrying out 'some forms of treatment' with the consent of the 'infant patient' and against the opposition of the parents. He argued that, 'The effect of consent of the infant depends on the nature of the treatment and the age and understanding of the infant' (AELR, 1985, p. 432). For Lord Templeman, however, a girl under 16 is not of an age or understanding to consent to treatment when that treatment is contraceptive in nature. His view that girls under 16 lack the competency to decide to practise sex and contraception, he argued, is supported in law by the 1956 Sexual Offences Act. Lord Templeman further contended that doctors are 'not entitled to decide whether a girl under the age of 16 shall be provided with contraceptive facilities if a parent who is in charge of the girl is ready and willing to make that decision in exercise of parental rights' (AELR, 1985, p. 435). In Lord Templeman's opinion, doctors cannot lawfully advise on or prescribe contraceptives to girls under the age of 16 without parental knowledge or consent. To do so would amount to 'an unlawful interference with the rights of the parent' and could only be condoned where the parent had abandoned their child or had abused their parental powers or was otherwise unavailable for whatever reason. The practice of 'secretly' providing contraceptive services to the under 16s encourages participation in sexual intercourse, Lord Templeman argued, and thereby 'offends basic principles of morality and religion which ought not to be sabotaged in stealth by kind permission of the national health service' (AELR, 1985, p. 433).

Thus, although Lords Brandon and Templeman both found in favour of Mrs Gillick and against the DHSS, it is clear that they did not follow the exact same line of argument to reach their decision. Lords Brandon and Templeman disagreed over the legality of ever providing contraceptive services to girls under 16 and on the respective rights of parents and doctors to consent to contraceptive services for those under the age of 16. For Lord Brandon, the issue of parental consent was immaterial because making contraception available to girls under 16 was, in all circumstances, unlawful. In contrast, for Lord Templeman, parents and doctors who together agreed that it was in a girl's

best interest to receive contraceptive advice and treatment, would not be acting unlawfully. It would be an unlawful interference with parental rights, however, if a doctor alone and without the knowledge and consent of a parent,
provided contraceptive services to a girl who was under the age of 16. Thus
for Lord Brandon, the law prohibited both children and their parents from
consenting to contraceptive services for the under-16s, and medical professionals from providing such services. In Lord Templeman's opinion, the law
did not allow children alone to consent to contraceptive services or doctors
alone to provide them, but it did allow parents and doctors together to consent
to such services on behalf of the interests of the under-16s.

So far in this examination of the judgments that formed the 1985 Gillick
case, several key themes have emerged which are revealing about conceptions
of children and of childhood held by members of the highest legal body in
Britain. The first of these is the idea that children are not 'persons' and therefore
do not have the rights of 'personhood' (or citizenship) enjoyed by persons,
that is by adults; specifically the right to contraceptive services provided by
the DHSS. The second is the issue of the incompetency and immaturity of children, on which the denial of their personhood is based. Lord Brandon did not
explain his reasoning for classifying children as non-persons, but his colleague,
Lord Templeman, was more forthcoming in his explanation of why children
do not possess the same rights of personhood as adults. For Lord Templeman,
children do not possess lawful rights to self-determination, at least in relation
to sex and contraception, because they lack sufficient competency and maturity to consent to such activities. At the chronological age of 16, however, girls
can lawfully be regarded as having attained the capacity to consent to both sex
and contraception. The third theme, evident in Lord Templeman's deliberations, is that it is the parents of the under 16s who have the strongest rights,
over and above those of doctors and, especially, of the under-16s themselves.

The conceptions of children, childhood and the extent of parental rights
over the under-16s revealed by an examination of the deliberations of Lords
Brandon and Templeman, can be contrasted with those held by the three Law
Lords whose majority decision against Mrs Gillick now forms the basis of the
law governing the provision of contraceptive services to girls under 16, and
which has been held to have ramifications for children's autonomy rights above
and beyond this particular issue.[5] An initial point made by Lord Fraser was that
none of the statutory provisions governing contraceptive advice and treatment
place any limit on the age of persons who may seek such advice and treatment.
He then went on to identify three strands of the argument that was under his
consideration. These were, first, whether a girl under 16 years old has the legal
capacity to give valid consent to contraceptive advice and treatment, second,
whether giving such advice and treatment to a girl under 16 infringes the parents' rights and, third, whether a doctor who gives such advice and treatment
to a girl under 16 without her parents' consent incurs criminal liability.

In his deliberations on the first point, Lord Fraser reviewed various provisions (including the 1969 Family Law Reform Act and the 1944 Education Act)

before concluding that, taken together, such provisions do not suggest that a child under the age of 16 lacks the capacity to consent to medical treatment, including contraceptive advice and treatment. Lord Fraser said that he was 'not disposed to hold now . . . that a girl aged less than 16 lacks the power to give valid consent to contraceptive services and treatment, merely on account of her age' (AELR, 1985, p. 409). Lord Fraser's interpretation of the law on this point contained a proviso which, in subsequent years, has assumed great importance in debates concerning children's rights to self-determination (see below). The proviso was that the consent of a child is only valid if that child has 'sufficient understanding' of what is proposed and is capable of expressing his or her own wishes.

In Lord Fraser's deliberations on the second element of the argument under his consideration, he made an initial point that parental rights exist for the benefit of the child, rather than for the parent. He further argued that it is in the 'ordinary experience of mankind' (*sic*) for a parent gradually to relax their control over a child as that child matures and according to that child's developing understanding and intelligence, rather than to remain in complete control over the child until the age of majority is reached. For Lord Fraser, once the idea of 'absolute' parental authority is dismissed in this way, the solution to the issue of the provision of contraceptive services to the under-16s is dependent upon a judgment of what is best for the welfare of a particular child. In making this judgment, Lord Fraser suggests that doctors may, in some cases, be better placed than parents. In such cases, the doctor would be justified in proceeding to provide contraceptive services without parental consent or knowledge, provided that the doctor was satisfied that a number of criteria applied to the particular case at hand. The criteria identified by Lord Fraser are:

i)   that the girl (although under 16 years of age) will understand the doctor's advice;
ii) that the doctor cannot persuade the girl to inform her parents that she is seeking contraceptive advice;
iii) that the girl is very likely to begin or continue having sexual intercourse with or without contraceptive treatment;
iv) that unless she receives contraceptive advice or treatment, her physical and/or mental health are likely to suffer;
v)   that her best interests require the doctor to give her contraceptive advice and/or treatment without parental consent. (AELR, 1985, p. 413)

These criteria on which a doctor must be satisfied before providing contraceptive services to a girl under 16 without parental knowledge or consent were important in framing Lord Fraser's ruling on the third strand of legal argument under his consideration: whether a doctor giving contraceptive advice or treatment to an underage girl without her parents' consent incurs a criminal liability. For Lord Fraser, a doctor who, in providing contraceptive services to an underage patient, does so in the honest belief that he or she is acting in the best interests of that patient, is 'unlikely' to be committing an offence under the 1956 Sexual Offences Act. Further, Lord Fraser ruled that, as long as the doctor was satisfied that the girl in question has the capacity to understand any advice given, 'there will be no question of his (*sic*) giving contraceptive advice to very young girls' (AELR, 1985, p. 414). For these reasons, Lord Fraser did not consider that the DHSS guidance interfered with parents' rights.

In his own deliberations, Lord Scarman made interpretations of the law comparable with those of Lord Fraser and, indeed, ultimately reached the same conclusion. For Lord Scarman, as for Lord Fraser, the statutory powers governing family planning services do not express any limitation as to the age of those eligible for advice or treatment. Nor did Lord Scarman find in law 'any encouragement' or 'any compelling reason' for holding that parliament has accepted that a child under 16 cannot consent to medical treatment. As for parental rights, Lord Scarman's opinion was that the law has never treated such rights as 'sovereign', and that the exercise of such rights are governed by the paramount consideration of the welfare of the child and exist only as long as they are needed for the protection of the child. Moreover, he made the specific point (contra Lord Brandon) that the law has never treated children other than as 'person[s] with capacities and rights recognised by law'. Lord Scarman concluded that,

> as a matter of law the parental right to determine whether or not their minor child below the age of 16 will have medical treatment terminates if and when the child achieves a sufficient understanding and intelligence to enable him [*sic*] to understand fully what is proposed. (AELR, 1985, p. 423)

Consequently, Lord Scarman was satisfied that the DHSS guidance did not involve the infringement of parental rights. As to the question of whether doctors who provide contraceptive services to girls under the age of 16 violate the criminal law, Lord Scarman concurred with Lord Fraser: 'If the prescription is the bona fide exercise of [a doctor's] clinical judgement as to what is best for his [*sic*] patient's health, he has nothing to fear from the criminal law . . .' (AELR, 1985, p. 425).

Having examined the deliberations of both the pro- and anti-Gillick Lords, the main contrasts in the conceptions of children and of childhood they contain are clear. One area of difference was whether children can be regarded as 'persons'. For Lords Brandon and Templeman, children under the age of 16 are not 'persons' in that they do not have 'sufficient maturity' or understanding to be self-determining, especially in relation to sex and contraception. In contrast to the conception of children as non-persons held by Lords Brandon and Templeman, Lords Fraser and Scarman disregarded the importance of chronology in determining who has 'personhood'. Instead, they suggested that what matters is whether a child, who is chronologically a minor in law, has 'sufficient understanding and intelligence' to make self-determining choices. A second area of difference between the pro- and anti-Gillick Lords was over who has the strongest 'rights' claims in childhood. For Lord Templeman, if not for Lord Brandon, parental rights over the under-16s (or even the under-18s) are absolute and exist over and above doctors' rights, and especially, children's own rights. In contrast, for Lords Scarman and Fraser, parental rights are not absolute or 'sovereign'. Rather, they decline in proportion with the growing maturity, understanding and intelligence of the child. Therefore a minor in law can reach 'an age of discretion' in law if she or he attains sufficient understanding and intelligence before reaching the chronological age of majority. It is suggested by the deliberations of Lords Scarman and Fraser, then, that children have potential rights claims over and above those of parents. In the words of Lord Scarman,

> The law relating to parent and child is concerned with the problems of the growth and maturity of the human personality. If the law should impose on the process of 'growing up' fixed limits where nature knows only a continuous process, the price would be artificiality and a lack of realism in an area where the law must be sensitive to human development and social change. (AELR, 1985, p. 421)

Although it might be suggested that conceptions of children and of childhood contained within the 1985 House of Lords Gillick judgment are peculiar to the five Lords whose deliberations formed the judgment, it is my argument that the ideas about children, childhood, parents and parenthood present within the 1985 decision have a wider resonance. In particular, the views held by Lords Brandon and Templeman on the immaturity and incompetency of children and of the necessary features of childhood defined in opposition to adulthood, can be recognized as key components in the construction of childhood which is dominant in contemporary Britain, that is, one which is in accordance with what Archard (1993) has called 'the caretaker thesis'. This proposes that children cannot be seen or treated as self-determining because they have not developed the capacity to make their own rational, autonomous decisions. Consequently, 'caretakers' (adults, but especially parents) should make decisions for them. In contrast, the views held by Lords Fraser and Scarman on the capacities of children and the nature and extent of parental rights, are in line with the conceptions of children and of the potentialities of childhood held by child liberationists (see Archard, 1993). Given that it is the 'caretaker' rather than the 'liberationist' perspective which dominates conceptions of childhood in contemporary Britain, the fact that the judgments of the anti-Gillick Lords held sway and subsequently determined the legal position governing the provision of contraceptive services to the under-16s is remarkable. Yet, even more remarkable is the way in which the 1985 House of Lords decision has been held to have ramifications for children's autonomy rights beyond the rather narrow issue of their access to contraceptive services.

Legacies of the Gillick Judgment

The 1985 House of Lords decision in the Gillick case represented the end of Victoria Gillick's legal actions to change the law on the provision of contraceptive services to the under-16s. Although the final judgment went against her, and the DHSS memorandum to which she objected was reinstated, there is an outcome of the case in which she and her supporters may find some compensation. Evidence strongly suggests that a high level of confusion surrounds the provision of contraceptive advice to the under-16s. Various surveys have reported that teachers, doctors and young people remain unclear as to what is and what is not legal in this area (see Allen, 1991; reports in the *Guardian*, 10 July 1992, 19 November 1993, 20 November 1993; the *Times*, 18 September 1994). The issuing, some seven years after the Gillick Judgment, of guidelines to medical professionals on confidentiality and 'people under 16' (British Medical Association *et al.*, 1993) may well be a rather belated attempt to improve a situation of confusion which the Gillick case exacerbated (Editorial, the *Guardian*, 20 November 1993).[6] The BMA guidelines draw upon the wording of the DHSS memorandum that was the original subject of contention and also explicitly refer to the 1985 Gillick Judgment itself. In the light of the government's commitment to meet *The Health of the Nation* targets on rates of pregnancy amongst the under-16s, this broader political context may lead to further attempts to reduce confusion amongst all those involved in the sex education of young people: 'public health pragmatism' may yet win out against 'sexual moralism' (Thomson, 1993).

A more tangible legacy of the Gillick Judgment is the way in which, as a consequence of the interpretations of the law made by a majority of the Lords in 1985, it is now widely regarded as a benchmark case in establishing the competency and autonomy of children in a variety of areas. Douglas (1992), for example, describes the 1985 Gillick Judgment as 'a landmark' decision which has had a 'tremendous influence', whilst Lyon and Parton (1995, p. 43) state that it has resulted in a fundamental undermining of the 'traditional notion of parental rights to govern children'. The Children's Legal Centre (1993) suggests that the Gillick Judgment established a range of rights for young people. These include the right to consent to medical treatment (not just treatment for contraception), the right to make choices about their religion, the right to change their name, and the right to seek confidential advice and counselling (see also Bainham, 1988; Eekelaar, 1986, 1991). All such rights, however, are subject to a young person being what has come to be known as 'Gillick competent' (Douglas, 1992), that is, whether they have sufficient competence to understand fully what is being proposed.

The Gillick Judgment is also seen to have directly influenced an important piece of legislation dealing with children, the 1989 Children Act. Lyon and Parton (1995) argue that certain provisions of this Act drew explicitly on the notion of 'Gillick competency', including those relating to a child's right to terminate the appointment of a guardian and to refuse to undergo medical or psychiatric examinations as directed by a court under, for example, a supervision order (see also Bainham, 1990; Douglas, 1992).

In several respects, then, the 1985 Gillick Judgment can, and has been, interpreted as a legal precedent which has resulted in a reduction of 'parent power' and a corresponding extension of 'children's power'. The notion of the 'Gillick competent' child has entered legal discourse in a whole range of areas, an outcome which Mrs Gillick herself undoubtedly neither anticipated nor welcomed. Yet, the positive legacy of Gillick for extending children's autonomy rights should not be overstated. To begin with, the intentions of the Law Lords in making their 1985 judgment have themselves been the subject of debate (see references in Lyon and Parton, 1995). Moreover, whilst in theory the Gillick Judgment enshrined the notion of the 'Gillick competent' child, the issue of what constitutes competency has, in practice, been difficult to establish. Furthermore, legal decisions concerned with children's autonomy have not always followed the Gillick principle. Lyon and Parton (1995) examine judicial interpretations of certain provisions of the Children Act 1989, and conclude that many of its 'so-called Gillick provisions', conferring rights upon children, are 'in reality merely conferring strong rights claims for the child's voice to be heard' (p. 543). In other words, although children's rights to have their expressed wishes heard have been upheld under the 1989 Act, their rights to self-determination have often been overruled 'in their own best interests', as this is defined by adults rather than by children themselves.

Douglas (1992) makes a further point that the 1989 Act reasserts parental rights against the state's right to intervene in family life. Consequently, the Act, along with a series of other legal decisions, may be interpreted as attempts to return to 'parent power' and so undermine the principle of the 'Gillick competent' child (see also Winter and Connolly, this volume; Freeman, 1995). This trend is also evident in education. The many legislative changes in education introduced by the various Conservative governments in the 1980s and 1990s have all 'disregarded' the principles contained within the 1985 Gillick Judgment (Jeffs, 1995). Indeed, in the realm of sex education, the post-1985 changes contradict principles many thought had been established by the Gillick case.

Direct links between the Gillick case and school sex education were first made in the 1984 DHSS Circular, issued to health authorities and to local education authorities after the Court of Appeal found in favour of Mrs Gillick and ruled that the provision of contraceptive advice and treatment to girls under 16 without parental consent was illegal. As noted earlier, this Circular advised that 'a doctor or any other professional' acting in this way would be engaging in unlawful behaviour (*TES*, 15 March 1985). Even after the final ruling by the House of Lords in 1985, those involved in school sex education still faced difficulties in advising pupils under the age of 16 about sex and contraception. In September 1987, following the Education (No. 2) Act 1986, the Department of Education and Science (DES) issued Circular 11/87 which advised local education authorities on sex education in schools (DES, 1987). The Circular had a subsection devoted to the issue of advising pupils under 16, which made specific reference to the 1985 Gillick Judgment. However, rather than promoting the concept of the 'Gillick competent child', the Circular stated that the judgment related only to the nature and context of medical advice and treatment in the supply and use of contraceptive devices and that such circumstances 'have no parallel in school education'. The Circular explicitly warned teachers that 'giving an individual pupil advice [on contraception] without parental knowledge or consent would be an inappropriate exercise of a teacher's professional responsibilities, and could, depending on the circumstances, amount to a criminal offence' (DES, 1987, para. 25). These guidelines on the legality of teachers advising pupils under the age of 16 about contraception remained in force until superseded by Circular 5/94, in May 1994 (DFE, 1994). Draft versions of Circular 5/94 retained specific warnings to teachers, and repeated the earlier guidance that to advise pupils under 16 on contraception without parental knowledge and consent would be professionally 'inappropriate' and 'could' amount to a criminal offence. After expressions of concern by teachers' unions and welfare organizations, the Education Secretary John Patten indicated that he would look again at the guidelines (the *Times*, 11 April 1994). However, a *Guardian* editorial three weeks later (3 May 1994) criticized Patten for issuing 'threatening advice' to teachers in the draft guidelines and argued that, like health workers, teachers should be protected from prosecution. In the face of such pressures, the final version of the Circular did omit explicit references to teachers committing criminal offences, but nevertheless left teachers in a difficult position. The new guidelines reminded teachers that 'particular care' must be exercised when advising pupils under 16 about contraception. The 'general rule' to be followed is that advising on such matters without parental knowledge and consent would be an 'inappropriate exercise of a teacher's professional responsibilities'. Rather than explicitly warning teachers about engaging in criminal behaviour, the Circular (which, at the time of writing, remains in force) conveys a more ambiguous but nonetheless threatening message:

> Teachers are not health professionals, and the legal position of a teacher giving advice in such circumstances has never been tested in court. (DFE, 1994, para. 39)

The concept of the 'Gillick competent child' is completely absent from the guidelines on the legality of teachers providing contraceptive advice to the under-16s. When placed in the broader legislative context of which the Circular is a part, this absence is not surprising. Circular 5/94 as a whole stresses the role and rights of *parents* and must be understood as part of the Education Act 1993, particularly section 241. This established the right of parents to withdraw their children from any or all parts of a school's programme of sex education (other than those elements which are required by the National Curriculum Science Order; see DFE, 1994, para. 36), irrespective of the wishes of the child itself.

Although the Gillick Judgment of 1985 should be recognized as highly significant for the issue of children's rights of autonomy, its legacy can be regarded neither as absolute nor unitary. Aside from the confusion that is still prevalent amongst doctors, teachers and young people themselves as to what is and what is not legal, key areas of legislation affecting children's lives have been interpreted in such a way that the principles established by the Gillick Judgment are either side-stepped or completely ignored. Mrs Gillick may despair at the way in which her name has entered the legal discourse, but she can find comfort in the limited extent to which the 'Gillick competent child' exists in practice. As Eekelaar (1986, p. 180) notes, that five of the nine judges who at various stages gave a decision in the Gillick litigation, did so in favour of Gillick, is illustrative of the ambiguity in current perceptions of the proper scope of children's autonomy interests. This ambiguity is especially evident around the issue of children and sex.

Acknowledgments

The research on which this chapter draws was supported by a grant from the Research Committee of the Social Science Faculty of the University of Leicester. I would also like to thank the British Medical Association and the Brook Advisory Centre for their help in providing information used in this chapter.

Notes

1 See letter to the *Times*, 24 March 1989; *Childright*, March 1992; letter to the *British Medical Journal*, 29 January 1994.
2 See the *Times*, 24 January 1990, 31 October 1990. Victoria Gillick's moral concerns extend over a wide range and are complexly interwoven. See Coward, 1989; Durham, 1991.
3 Following this decision, over 200 MPs petitioned Ministers to review the DHSS guidelines, so as to require consultation with parents before contraceptive services were provided to the under-16s (the *Times*, 11 November 1983, cited in Eekelaar, 1986).
4 Here, Lord Templeman is following the legal definition of the term. Contemporary, everyday understandings of 'infant' (babies or very small children) correspond more with its Latin derivation, *infans*, meaning 'unable to speak'.
5 Here I will examine only the deliberations of Lords Fraser and Scarman, since that of Lord Bridge, although in agreement with his aforementioned colleagues, was concerned principally with the issue of the court's jurisdiction over the conduct of administrative authorities such as the DHSS.

6   Aside from the confusion it caused, Gillick has also been identified as a causal factor of the increased rates of teenage pregnancy which occurred in the 1980s (Brook
Advisory Centres, 1994/5, 1995).

References

ALL ENGLAND LAW REPORTS (1985) 'Gillick v West Norfolk and Wisbech Area Health
Authority and another', **3**, pp. 402–37.

ALLEN, I. (1991) *Family Planning and Pregnancy Counselling Projects for Young People*, London, Policy Studies Institute.

ARCHARD, D. (1993) *Children, Rights and Childhood*, London, Routledge.

BAINHAM, A. (1988) *Children, Parents and the State*, London, Sweet and Maxwell.

BAINHAM, A. (1990) 'The Children Act 1989: Adolescence and children's rights', *Family
Law*, **20**, pp. 311–14.

BRITISH MEDICAL ASSOCIATION *et al.* (1993) *Confidentiality and People Under 16*, London, BMA.

BROOK ADVISORY CENTRES (1994/5) *Annual Report*, London, Brook Advisory Centres.

BROOK ADVISORY CENTRES (1995) 'Teenage pregnancy — Key facts', August 1995, London, Brook Advisory Centres.

CHILDREN'S LEGAL CENTRE (1993) 'At what age can I . . . ?', *Childright*, No. 93, January/
February 1993.

COWARD, R. (1989) 'Mother of morality', *New Statesman and Society*, 31 March, pp. 14–
15.

DAVID, M. (1986) 'Moral and maternal: The family in the right', in LEVITAS, R. (ed.) *The
Ideology of the New Right*, Cambridge, Polity Press.

DEPARTMENT FOR EDUCATION (1994) *Education Act 1993: Sex Education in Schools*,
Circular 5/94, London, Department for Education.

DEPARTMENT OF EDUCATION AND SCIENCE (1987) *Sex Education at School*, Circular 11/87,
London, Department of Education and Science.

DOUGLAS, G. (1992) 'The retreat from Gillick', *Modern Law Review*, **55**, pp. 569–76.

DURHAM, M. (1991) *Sex and Politics: The Family and Morality in the Thatcher Years*,
London, Macmillan.

EEKELAAR, J. (1986) 'The emergence of children's rights', *Oxford Journal of Legal Studies*,
6, 2, pp. 161–82.

EEKELAAR, J. (1991) 'Parental responsibility: State of nature or nature of the state', *The
Journal of Social Welfare and Family Law*, pp. 37–50.

ENNEW, J. (1986) *The Sexual Exploitation of Children*, Cambridge, Polity Press.

FREEMAN, M. (1995) 'Children's rights in a land of rites', in FRANKLIN, B. (ed.) *The
Handbook of Children's Rights*, London, Routledge.

HOME AFFAIRS COMMITTEE (1994) *Computer Pornography*, HCP 126, House of Commons,
London, HMSO.

JACKSON, S. (1982) *Childhood and Sexuality*, Oxford, Basil Blackwell.

JEFFS, T. (1995) 'Children's educational rights in a new ERA?' in FRANKLIN, B. (ed.) *The
Handbook of Children's Rights*, London, Routledge.

LYON, C. and PARTON, N. (1995) 'Children's rights and the Children Act 1989', in FRANKLIN,
B. (ed.) *The Handbook of Children's Rights*, London, Routledge.

THOMSON, R. (1993) 'Unholy alliances: The recent politics of sex education', in BRISTOW,

J. and Wilson, A. (eds) *Activating Theory: Lesbian, Gay and Bisexual Politics*, London, Lawrence and Wishart.

Thomson, R. (1994) 'Moral rhetoric and public health pragmatism: The recent politics of sex education', *Feminist Review*, No. 48, pp. 40–60.

Weeks, J. (1991) 'Pretended family relationships', in Clark, D. (ed.) *Marriage, Domestic Life and Social Change*, London, Routledge.

7 Growing Pains: The Developing Children's Rights Movement in the UK

Annie Franklin and Bob Franklin

It is much easier to join the Scottish National Party (SNP) or the Vegetarian Society than the Children's Rights Movement. The two former organizations have headquarters to which prospective members can send their application forms along with the appropriate membership fee. In return they will receive the organization's written constitution which: articulates a set of consensually agreed aims and objectives; offers an agreed procedure for making changes to those objectives; establishes the rules governing the conduct of the organization's affairs, and; articulates the various power relationships between individual members, constituent organizations and the local and regional branches which constitute the larger group. Joining the SNP or the Vegetarian Society, moreover, is an act which publicly expresses commitment to a clearly articulated ideology, or set of moral values and principles, which informs the activities of the group and provides them with a degree of organizational cohesion.

The Children's Rights Movement differs radically from this organizational pattern. It is a 'social movement' which, like the student movement, the green movement, the women's movement and the equivalent children's rights movement in America (Edelman, 1977; Gross and Gross, 1977), must be differentiated from a number of related phenomena such as spontaneous acts of protest, organized single issue interest groups, voluntary organizations, political organizations such as parties, and wholly cultural movements such as religious sects. The distinctive features of a social movement are: its emphasis on occasional mass mobilization; its flexible organizational structure; its tendency to operate, at least in part, outside established institutional frameworks, and; its objective of bringing about social change (or preserving aspects of the political order) as a central aim (Scott, 1992, p. 132).

The Children's Rights Movement approximates Scott's model. The movement has no headquarters, membership fee, constitution or agreed aims, objectives or ideology. It is an extremely heterogeneous movement which represents a very loose and shifting coalition of constituent organizations and individuals which subscribe to a broad set of values and seek to achieve a wide and occasionally divergent range of policy goals and objectives. Its members are children and young people, social, welfare and legal professionals, politicians and academics and teachers. The diversity of the Movement is evident. The *UK Agenda For Children*, drafted by the Children's Rights Development Unit (CRDU) and criticizing the British government's progress in implementing the United Nations Convention on the Rights of the Child, listed 180 organizations which supported the *UK Agenda* and which may each be considered constituents of the Children's Rights Movement. The A to Z of the list begins with A Voice For The Child in Care, includes the Advisory Centre for Education, Barnardos, Child Poverty Action Group, EPOCH, Family Rights Group, Kids Club Network, NCH Action for Children, the Refugee Legal Centre, Save The Children Fund, Who Cares? Scotland and Woodcraft Folk and concludes with the Youth Council for Northern Ireland and Youthaid (CRDU [Children's Rights Development Unit], 1994, pp. xvi–xvii).

Perhaps the only central or core belief uniting this wide-ranging community is their commitment to the general principle, which has informed much post-war child welfare legislation, that in decisions concerning children the prime need is to promote the 'best interests of the child'. But even this apparently un-contentious principle prompts immediate difficulties. Conceptually, rights may be incompatible with interests. Adults' desire and ability to determine what is in a child's best interests and to direct children accordingly, may leave children with no rights at all (Eekelaar, 1994, p. 42).

The difficulties in analysing the Children's Rights Movement, which are generated by this organizational and ideological plurality, are compounded by the inherent complexity and uncertainties surrounding the meaning of the terms 'children' and 'rights'. So far as the former is concerned, a succession of historians and sociologists have illustrated convincingly that the divergent 'childhoods' which different 'children' experience are social constructions expressing the distinctive gender, class, ethnic or historical location of particular children (Aries, 1962; Laslett, 1965; Holt, 1975): a variety of popular images of childhood are the consequence (Holland, 1992). As for the latter, a wide range of rights have been claimed by and for children including the basic human right to life, health services, education and an acceptable standard of living (UN Convention articles 1, 24, 28, 27) as well as more radical claims for the right to vote, work and own property (Farson, 1977; Franklin, 1986, 1992). This is a very mixed bag, in terms of the variety of rights which are being claimed, the difficulties inherent in enforcing them, the resources necessary to meet them and the social and political consequences upon granting them.

In this chapter we outline some of the central ideas and major debates concerning children's rights which have recently characterized this ideologically and programmatically diverse movement. We also detail some of the Movement's proposals and policy prescriptions designed to empower children and enable them to achieve their rights entitlements. But first, we offer a brief account of the history of the movement and the factors influencing its growth.

From Participation to Protection and Almost Back Again:
Developmental Phases in the Children's Rights Movement

The Children's Rights Movement enjoys a rich and substantial heritage. Its modern beginnings can be traced to the later part of the nineteenth century, although earlier writers expressed libertarian aspirations for children. In 1797, for example, the Newcastle born pamphleteer and socialist, Thomas Spence, published a tract entitled *The Rights of Infants* in which he argued in favour of giving children and their mothers the right to vote (Spence, 1797; Rudkin, 1927, p. 217). This pre-empted, by almost two centuries, Firestone's observation that it is impossible to 'speak of the liberation of women without also discussing the liberation of children and vice versa' (Firestone, 1972). An early article discussing 'The Rights of Children' also appeared in *Knickerbocker* (Slogvolk, 1852) in 1852, while in France, Jean Valles established a society for the protection of the rights of children in the aftermath of the Paris Commune; his novel *L'Enfant* was dedicated to all oppressed children (Zeldin, 1973). The Movement has also been characterized by children's political activism. Martin Hoyles, for example, recalls the 1888 Matchgirls' strike against low pay, victimization and dangerous conditions (Hoyles, 1989, p. 66).

School provided perhaps the obvious forum for this activism, especially at the turn of the twentieth century. In 1911 there was a national wave of children's school strikes in sixty towns and cities; 1914 witnessed the start of the three year strike by children, led by Violet Potter, in support of two socialist teachers who were sacked by the managers of Burston School in Norfolk (Hoyles, 1989, pp. 79–84). The child saving Movement witnessed the development of juvenile justice, compulsory education and the prominence of adults in the Children's Rights Movement. The first Declaration of the Rights of the Child, drafted by Eglantine Jebb the Founder of The Save the Children International Fund in 1924, was concerned with the needs and rights of children in the aftermath of the so called 'Great War'. The focus of the Declaration was on providing food for the hungry, nursing for the sick and support for orphans and waifs; a successive Declaration was made in 1959 and the UN Convention on the Rights of the Child was agreed in 1989 (Newell, 1991, pp. xv–xvi).

More recently, the Children's Rights Movement has developed through three discernible phases. Each phase has been characterized by the activities of a distinctive set of key actors, seeking to achieve a different type of rights provision, intended to be exercised in alternative social arenas. The boundaries of these three phases are not clearly drawn and some overlap is evident across them.

The first phase runs across the decade of the 1970s. It was characterized by claims for libertarian participation rights for children; especially, but not wholly in education. Conventional schools were judged oppressive institutions with many similarities to prisons. Keith Paton's pamphlet, *The Great Brain Robbery* (1971), sported a bright yellow cover with Dennis the Menace announcing that, 'all over the world school has an anti-educational effect on children'.

At the same time A.S. Neill was writing about the various participation rights enjoyed by children at Summerhill, his free school in Suffolk. American academic and educational philosopher John Holt was proposing the abolition of the age of suffrage, the extension of a whole range of participatory rights to children and the need for children to *Escape from Childhood* (Holt, 1975). Education was the arena in which this drama of rights was enacted; school was the villain of the piece. Illich's (1973) injunction to de-school society seemed on all progressive lips.

This libertarian mood spawned a number of magazines, produced by children with titles such as *Braindamage, Blazer* and, in Hackney, *Miscarriage.* Most were low on production values and life expectancy but, 'their very existence was a challenge, an assertion of pupils' rights to address each other publicly and to speak aloud those things which are normally giggled over or muttered' (Holland, 1992, p. 88).

By 1972, children's claims for rights in education generated two national political organizations; the explicitly political Schools Action Union (SAU) which was eventually controlled by Maoists and the more trade union style National Union of School Students (NUSS) within the NUS. SAU organized a number of strikes around issues such as corporal punishment, uniforms and racism; the *Times* estimated the number of children strikers on a protest march on 17 May 1972 at 2,500 (Hoyles, 1989, p. 85). Press reporting denied the children's political motive, alleging the strikes merely offered an excuse for truanting. The same motive was imputed to the 4,000 children and young people at the Youth Trade Union Rights Campaign (YTURC) March at Liverpool pierhead on 25 April 1985 to protest against government plans to make the Youth Training Schemes compulsory (Franklin, 1986, pp. 47–8).

The International Year of the Child (IYC) in 1979 marked a watershed for the Children's Rights Movement. The focus of activity shifted from education rights to the social and welfare arena; the objective was to win rights to protect children rather than participation rights to facilitate their involvement in decision making. The Movement also became colonized by adults who, in future, would make rights claims on behalf of children. There is of course a logic here. If children are judged to be weak, vulnerable and in need of protection how can they exercise autonomy rights and make decisions? Freeman is clear about the shift that IYC initiates. 'The International Year of the Child', he argues, 'does not belong to the tradition of child liberation. Its values, its whole ethos, harked back to an earlier era of concern for children' (Freeman, 1983, p. 24).

This second phase harks back to the child saving Movement of the early part of the twentieth century with its concern to protect children, individual children, rather than with upholding the rights of children in general. In IYC there were good reasons to focus on protecting children. Internationally, fifteen million children under five died during IYC. Four hundred million children under the age of six did not have access to health services and one hundred million children suffered from malnutrition (Freeman, 1983, p. 24). Domestically, the tragic deaths of Jasmine Beckford, Kimberley Carlile and Tyra Henry,

97

reported in a blaze of sensationalist media coverage, served to underline and reinforce the new paramountcy on protection rights. Throughout the 1980s the media were crucial to the development of the Children's Rights Movement by placing child protection issues on the public agenda. The extensive media attention to the Cleveland affair offered further illustration of the need to protect children; even, or perhaps especially, in the family setting. Esther Rantzen's *Childwatch* television programme attracted substantial audiences and triggered the inauguration of ChildLine in 1986.

IYC prompted two further developments which were to prove highly consequential, although their impact was to be more crucial to the third phase of the Children's Rights Movement's recent history. First, on the eve of IYC, the Polish government proposed the drafting of the UN Convention on the Rights of the Child to establish an internationally agreed minimum set of rights for children and secure individual governments' compliance with them. Second, the Children's Legal Centre was established in IYC to campaign and advise children about their rights. The Centre's lobbying and educational work has been significant in seeking protection rights for children while also advocating the libertarian case for participation rights. Regrettably the Centre closed in February 1995 after a distinguished record of child advocacy but reopened at a new base at Essex University, from where it operates a telephone help line for children and publishes it journal *Childright*.

A third phase of the Movement for children's rights can be dated from the late 1980s. Adults continued to be the key actors within the Movement and the social and welfare arena continued to be the focus for rights campaigning, but this phase was marked by a renewed emphasis on the need for participation rights. The shift was a consequence of necessity rather than choice. It became clear during the 1980s that the protection of children from the adult and systems abuse which they suffered, required the active participation of children in certain aspects of decision making. The empowerment of children was the crucial ingredient in their protection; the acquisition of participation rights was the handmaiden of the protectionist agenda. This realization explains why it is only in the social and welfare spheres that claims for participation rights are being made by, and for, children. Any discussion of participation rights in education, for example, is confined to those of parents. It is also the reason why initiatives such as Article 12 and the Children's Rights Commissioner (see below) are so important; they try to generalize the requirement for participation rights beyond the arena of social and welfare policy.

This third phase can be dated more precisely. Its arrival was signalled by the Children Act and the UN Convention on the Rights of the Child, both in 1989. The Children Act carefully straddles the divide between protectionist and participatory rights. Its guiding principle is that 'the child's welfare is paramount' but the legislation also supports the principle that where possible and appropriate the 'ascertainable wishes and feelings of the child concerned' should inform decisions (Children Act, 1989, Sect 1(3)(a)). In truth the judiciary have interpreted this latter requirement conservatively, falling back on paternalistic assumptions of children's incompetence (Lyon and Parton, 1995, pp. 40–53). For its part, the UN Convention advocates a wide range of rights which for reasons of convenience, as well as agitprop purposes, have been labelled the 'three P's': rights to provision, protection and participation (Franklin, 1995, p. 16).

No Slick Slogans! The Ideology of the Children's Rights Movement

In an essay published in 1973, children's rights were described as 'a slogan in search of a definition' (Rodham, 1973, p. 487). In the subsequent quarter of a century a good deal of theoretical and conceptual analysis, as well as the provisions of the UN Convention and other children's rights charters, have mapped out and explored much of the rights terrain. But despite such endeavours, the territory of children's rights remains hotly contested. The Movement's various constituent groups are committed to quite distinctive value positions. The discussion below outlines: firstly, the different moral and policy positions concerning rights adopted by different groups; secondly, the debate between those who argue for participation rights for children and others who wish to limit children's rights claims to protection rights and; finally, the reformulation of rights as entitlements to provision, protection and participation contained in the UN Convention on the Rights of the Child.

Ideological Pluralism and the Children's Rights Movement

Michael Wald's classification of the different types of claims which are made under the general rubric of children's rights, illustrates well the various positions concerning rights which continue to characterize the ideas of the Children's Rights Movement (Wald, 1972, pp. 255–82). Wald distinguishes four distinctive categories of rights claims which he calls rights against the world (pp. 260–1), rights to protection from inadequate care (pp. 261–5), rights to fuller adult legal status (pp. 265–270) and, finally, rights versus parents (pp. 270–4).

The first category is concerned with rights to 'freedom from poverty, to adequate health care, to adequate housing and a safe community' (Wald, 1972, p. 260). Wald believes these 'are the most important rights that could be given to children' since they 'lie at the heart of the child's well being' (1972, p. 260). They are essentially welfare rights although they are not easily formulated as rights against anyone; they are, rather, rights against everyone. Hence Wald's label 'rights against the world'. These rights are typically found in declarations and charters of Children's rights although they are central to the activities of groups such as UNICEF, Child Poverty Action Group (CPAG), Children's Rights Development Unit (CRDU), Shelter, Simon Community, Anti Slavery International and many others.

Rights to protection encompass the claim that the state should actively protect children from harm by adults; especially their parents. The essential concern is to protect children from sexual and physical abuse, inadequate care, and physical or emotional neglect. But Wald (1972) argues that protection rights in this category may include adult controls on violence on television as well as prohibitions on children eating junk food (p. 264). It should be clear from these latter two illustrations that rights to protection do not involve any changes to the status of children or offer them any greater autonomy or independence from parents or other adults; indeed one consequence of protection rights may in some, but certainly not all cases, be to diminish autonomy rights. Groups within the Children's Rights Movement with specific commitments to protection rights include the Family Rights Group, End Physical Punishment of Children (EPOCH), ChildLine, NCH Action for Children, and Parents for Safe Food.

Wald's third category, rights to fuller adult status, embraces the right to vote, to work, to drive, to drink alcohol, to express themselves freely and read literature without censorship; rights which are currently enjoyed solely by adults. Those who argue that children should enjoy such rights believe that age is an arbitrary and inadequate criterion to use to assess rights competence. Children, moreover, should not be subject to compulsory education, 'a form of coercion that would be unconstitutional if attempted with adults' (Wald, 1972, p. 265). Extending these adult rights to children and young people would substantively enhance their autonomy.

Finally, rights versus parents, which are 'perhaps the most controversial and complex' (Wald, 1972, p. 270). This category of rights suggests that children should enjoy greater independence from parents prior to achieving the socially agreed of majority. Conceding such rights would allow children autonomy over decisions such as 'whether to have an abortion, to receive drug, alcohol or medical care, to go to a certain school or participate in religious exercises, to use contraceptives or to enter a mental hospital' (Wald, 1972, p. 273). The intention of rights versus parents, as with rights to fuller adult status, is to tilt the balance between children's autonomy and their reliance on adult decision making in favour of the former. Groups with particular commitments to elements of these latter two rights categories include The Children's Legal Centre, Who Cares? Scotland, Advice Advocacy and Representation Services for Children, Article 12, as well as major children's charities such as Save the Children Fund whose work in its UK and Europe department is premised on a commitment to increasing children's participation rights.

On closer inspection, however, Wald's fourfold classification tends to collapse. The 'rights versus parents' category is simply one aspect of the claim that children should have 'fuller adult rights'. Similarly, 'rights against the world' or 'welfare rights' are one element of 'rights to protection'. Wald's four rights categories dissolve into the simpler distinction between the 'nurturance' and 'self-determination' orientations (Rogers and Wrightsman, 1978, p. 61), which has recently become known as the distinction between protection and libertarian rights.

The debate about whether children require rights to participation as well as protection is alive and well within the Children's Rights Movement. Children's need for protectionist rights to adequate food, shelter and clothing is uncontested, although parents who collect benefits on behalf of their children to guarantee such needs are met, are likely to be labelled 'scroungers' by a 'scrounge-phobic' press and community (Golding and Middleton, 1982). There is, however, a good deal less consensus for the view that children require and are capable for exercising participation rights.

Opponents suggest that children lack rationality and the capacity to make reasoned and informed decisions. This incompetence is compounded by children's modest experience, which makes it highly probable that they will make mistakes. The paternalist concludes that we should not abandon children to the freedom of their own incompetencies; the results will inevitably be harmful (Scarre, 1980, 1989). Other less sceptical voices suggest a 'compromise' which offers a limited extension of rights to specific children (Archard, 1993).

Libertarians protest on a number of grounds. First, children do make rational decisions about a variety of matters. Some may be relatively trivial decisions about whether to play football or Nintendo. Others may be more consequential; deciding whether a particular adult is trustworthy, for example. Second, the probability of making mistakes should not debar anyone from making their own decisions. Such an assumption confuses the right to do something with doing the right thing. There is also a tautology here. If children are excluded from decision making because they might make mistakes, how do they ever get started? This is Catch 22. Third, mistakes are not necessarily a bad thing but provide opportunities for learning which children should be encouraged to grasp; and with alacrity. Fourth, adults are often poor decision-makers; history illustrates the point well and it is important to avoid double standards. Fifth, allocating rights according to the age principle is incoherent and arbitrary, with different age requirements for adult rights applying in different spheres. In the UK, this means an individual is criminally responsible at 10, sexually adult at 16 but denied political rights of suffrage until 18. Sixth, rights should be allocated according to competencies not age. Presumably paternalists do not wish to exclude children from participation because they are children but because they are assumed to be incompetent in certain relevant respects. Applied consistently, the principle that allocates rights according to competence would exclude everyone who lacked the relevant competencies; adults as well as children. There are subsidiary concerns here. What would serve as criteria of competence for participation and who would adjudicate whether particular individuals met such criteria? Seventh, advocates of participation rights suggest that exclusion on the age principle is unfair because children can do nothing to alter the circumstances which exclude them. Children cannot age prematurely and thereby secure rights. Finally, denying participation rights to everyone under 18 assumes a homogeneity among children which the plurality of their intellectual and emotional needs, skills, competencies and achievements undermines. Consigning all children to the category of 'non-adults' denies that different children possess different competencies and thereby should enjoy distinctive rights entitlements when they are able to exercise them.

Advocates of both participation and protection rights coexist within the Children's Rights Movement; the opposition between the two positions should not be overstated. Children are claiming and require an expansion of both kinds of rights. Protecting children and establishing their right to participate in decision making can be complementary; certainly this has been the adult experience.

The UN Convention and the Three Ps

The UN Convention on the Rights of the Child is significant for the Children's Rights Movement for at least three reasons. First, it establishes a raft of civil, economic, social and cultural rights which children around the world require as a minimum. Second, it designates an independent body — the UN Committee on the Rights of the Child — to monitor and assess different governments' progress in achieving compliance with the UN Convention and implementing its proposals. Third, it has become a focus for the activities of the Children's Rights Movement and enjoys very wide spread support for the rights claims embodied in its various provisions. The Convention offers no slick slogans to silence all dissenting voices but it has won a remarkable consensus behind its aims and objectives, which has unified the Children's Rights Movement. Joan Lestor, Labour's designated Minister for Children in the run up to the 1992 General Election believed it had established for the first time, 'a universally agreed set of rights for children' and also 'stimulated debate within the developed world about a meaningful interpretation and implementation of those rights' (Lestor, 1995, p. 101). The moral and political significance of the Convention is not easily overstressed; especially when more than 160 governments have ratified their compliance with its provisions. One observer has argued for the incorporation of the Convention into English law so that a breach of the Convention would constitute, 'an infringement of English law with all the implications this would have' (Freeman, 1995, p. 82). In many ways, the Convention has become somewhat akin to a manifesto for the Children's Rights Movement. Certainly its proposals seem to possess an ability to unite and unify disparate groups which no previous document has enjoyed.

The 54 articles of the UN Convention catalogue a wide range of rights entitlements including the most basic right to life, the right to adequate health care, food, clean water and shelter, rights to protection against sexual abuse, neglect and exploitation, rights to education, privacy and freedom of association, expression and thought, which are grouped under three broad categories and labelled the 'three Ps'; the rights to provision, protection and participation. Three articles have come to be considered especially significant. Article 2 affirms the principle of non-discrimination. The Convention's provisions apply to all children without regard to 'race, colour, sex, language, religion, political or other opinion, national, ethnic or social origin, property, disability, birth or other status.' Article 3 confirms the principle that 'in all actions concerning children . . . the best interests of the child shall be a primary consideration.' Finally, Article 12 'assures to the child who is capable of forming his or her own views, the right to express those views freely in all matters affecting the child, the views of the child being given due weight in accordance with the age and maturity of the child.' In claiming this right for children, the Convention went beyond its predecessors and established for the first time children's right to a say in decisions affecting their lives. Article 12 enjoys substantial symbolic significance because it converts the child into a 'principal' in the Convention (Pais, 1992, p. 75). It also leans toward the libertarian philosophy so characteristic of the Children's Rights Movement in the 1970s.

The word, however, should not be mistaken for the deed. The UN's success in securing the compliance of individual governments with the Convention is equivocal. The British case is illustrative. The British government's hostility to the UN Convention is longstanding. When the Polish government initially suggested a Convention on Children's Rights in the International Year of the Child in 1979, the British government was the only one to reject the idea and suggest it was unnecessary. Britain eventually ratified the Convention in December 1991 but demanded the maximum three reservations concerning: regulation of wages; rights of separated children to be reunited with their family; custodial placements of children with adults. When governments have ratified the Convention, they are obliged to examine closely its implications for all aspects of law, policy and practice concerning children; propose measures to guarantee compliance; and, make a full report to the appropriate UN Committee overseeing implementation of the Convention within a two year period and subsequently every five years. The Government submitted *The UK's First Report to the UN Committee on the Rights of the Child* in February 1994 (Department of Health, 1994, p. 131).

Many voluntary groups and charities working with children, however, were very unhappy with what appeared to be the government's lack of concern for children's rights issues. The Children's Rights Development Unit (CRDU), established in March 1992 for three years, funded by the large charitable trusts such as Gulbenkian and key child welfare organizations such as Save the Children, with a specific brief to ensure the fullest possible implementation of the Convention, claimed the UK's report to the UN Committee was 'complacent' (Lansdown, 1995, p. 108). It was, moreover, 'dishonest by omission, highlighting particular laws and statistics that indicate compliance, without adequate recognition of gaps, inconsistencies and blatant breaches' (CRDU, 1994, p. xi). Given its founding brief to monitor and publicize the implementation of the Convention, the CRDU felt obliged to set the record straight by undertaking 'with very few resources . . . the exercise which should be carried out by government' (CRDU, 1994, p. xii).

The resultant document entitled *The UK Agenda for Children* claims that, 'there is a very clear dissonance between a professed commitment to children's welfare and the effective implementation of that commitment' (CRDU, 1994, p. xiii); an imaginative euphemism for government hypocrisy. The *UK Agenda* is a damning indictment of the British government's indifference to children's rights issues and its unwillingness to comply with the minimum rights requirements demanded of signatories to the UN Convention on the Rights of the Child. The *UK Agenda* contains fourteen authoritative reports focused on a particular area of children's rights including:

- Personal freedoms
- Care of children
- Physical and personal integrity
- An adequate standard of living
- Health and health care services
- Environment
- Education
- Play and leisure
- Youth justice
- Child labour
- Immigration and nationality
- Children and violent conflict — Northern Ireland
- Abduction
- International obligations to promote children's rights

Each report concludes by offering a concise summary and action points to secure British government compliance with the Convention. The *UK Agenda's* overall conclusion is all too depressing; 'it is clear that whether for reasons of poverty, ethnicity, disability, sexuality, immigration status or geography, many children are denied fundamental rights in the Convention' (CRDU, 1994, p. xiii).

The CRDU's allegation that the government had failed to show 'any serious attempt at implementation' of the Convention, was endorsed by the highly critical and admonishing response of the UN Committee which received the British government's *First Report* in January 1995. The UN Committee's eight page report contains a mere three paragraphs focusing on positive aspects of Britain's implementation of the Convention, but sixteen paragraphs devoted to critical commentary and a further twenty-three detailing recommendations for change. The report claimed the British government breached the spirit of the Convention. The Committee claimed that Article 3 of the Convention which requires that laws should be framed in the 'best interests of the child', appears to have been disregarded in significant areas such as health, education and social security. The report criticized the high numbers of children living in poverty and expressed concern about numbers of teenage pregnancies, rising divorce rates, cuts in state benefits and the prevalence of children sleeping and begging on the street; building secure training units for young offenders would be in clear breach of the Convention. The UN recommended laws to proscribe the physical punishment of children in families and at privately funded schools. More broadly, the report argued for measures to end health inequalities between children from different social and ethnic backgrounds and to alleviate homelessness (*Childright*, January 1995). In short, the UK Committee gave the government a bloody nose. The government seemed to believe that children's rights — always understood as rights to provision and protection rather than participation — was a problem which only developing countries needed to address. It appears to have been shocked by the UN Committee's response to its submission. Officials at the Department of Health are reported to have been given instructions not to attend meetings where children's rights would be discussed: the government has 'taken its bat home'.

From Ideology to Policy; Article 12 and the Children's Rights Commissioner

The UN Convention on the Rights of the Child straddles the division we have tried to establish between ideology and policy within the Children's Rights Movement. The various provisions of the Convention, more than any other single document, articulate the moral and political beliefs of the movement, but they also signal very clear, if basic, policy prescriptions as well as providing a yardstick of good practice against which to measure the effectiveness of extant policies relating to children. The close connection between ideology and policy is perhaps nowhere more clearly evident than in the emergence of the Article 12 group.

Article 12

This newly formed group takes its name from the Convention provision concerned to ensure, 'the child's right to express an opinion and to have that opinion taken into account, in any matter or procedure affecting the child' (UN Convention on the Rights of the Child, Article 12). The group's focus is upon children's participation and promoting the rights contained in the UN Convention. It is, moreover, a group which aims to be child led and to encourage children to speak for themselves without any mediation by adults.

The idea for Article 12 emerged from the consultation which the CRDU undertook with children and young people while drafting the *UK Agenda*. A recurrent theme of the consultation was that adults do not listen, respect, take seriously, or value what children and young people have to say. Furthermore, all adults, whether parents, teachers, social workers, journalists, politicians or policy-makers were judged to be guilty of this dismissive attitude and behaviour. Children and young people perceived 'childhood' as a phase in which they suffered low status, were subordinated in power relationships and exercised precious little influence on the decisions crucial to their own lives and well-being. Unsurprisingly, many of the young people consulted spoke strongly in favour of an organization which could act as a voice for children and young people.

Some of the young people proposed a conference to explore the idea. The event was hosted by Channel 4 in 1994; motives were at least in part utilitarian. The television company was interested to discover those issues that were problematic and a source of concern to children and young people because it was planning a new series of programmes, subsequently titled *Look Who's Talking*, targeted at children. A steering group was established, drawing members from the conference participants, with the aim of developing a new organization for children, led by children. Two principles informed the structure of the steering group. First, members were to be drawn from the broadest (social, gender, ethnic) possible spectrum to ensure representativeness. Second, it was agreed that membership of the steering group and the organization should be restricted to people under 18 years of age.

Article 12 aims to give a voice to children and young people, articulate their concerns and promote their rights detailed, and in part established, by the UN Convention on the Rights of the Child. There is an emphasis on working within an equal opportunities framework. But the steering group has had to confront a number of quite distinctive problems in addition to those which routinely dog the powerless in society. Commitments to school work and possible restriction at home, mean they can only meet at limited times. It is, moreover, difficult for members based far apart to network and remain in contact between meetings; adults pay telephone bills. Meetings are costly to organize but young people have little direct access to resources. There are additionally a plethora of legal and practical obstacles to young people establishing an organization. A group of children under 18 may not readily find themselves acceptable to the accrediting bodies and will certainly experience difficulties in convincing a bank to let them open an account. But the members of Article 12 intend to be self-organizing, to maintain control of their organization and to prove their capabilities. There is, of course, a discernible tension and dilemma here. It is almost impossible for Article 12 to achieve these ambitions for children's autonomy without accepting support from adults and adult organizations with the consequent benefits which derive from the latter's preferential access to resources and the legitimacy which society confers uniquely on adults.

In order to try to resolve this dilemma, a number of organizations, which can readily be identified as part of the Children's Rights Movement, have offered support 'without strings' to enable Article 12 to develop through its early stages. Article 12 was supported initially by a youth worker from the Children's Rights Development Unit (CRDU) but, since the ending of the CRDU in March 1995, Save the Children has funded the worker in a freelance capacity to continue supporting the group. The National Children's Bureau have offered Article

12 office space in London and the Children's Society have expressed an interest in helping the group's future development.

The very difficult work necessary to establish a new organization and place it on a working footing is currently being undertaken. The intention is to create a central office — in London — with regional and local affiliated groups throughout the country. The organization intends to employ staff although whether these workers will be under 18, has yet to be agreed.

Article 12 must also draft a constitution establishing working procedures and principles as well as a detailed organizational structure; a turgid process which has defeated a great many adult groups. Article 12's strength lies in the clarity of its major aims and objectives, especially offering advice on empowerment to children and young people; conducting relevant research; raising public and organizational awareness of children's issues; and publishing research outcomes and literature concerning children's rights. There is a steering group, but establishing individual membership, local groups and formal systems are high priorities for the new organization. Broad membership will need to be developed over the next couple of years and the judgment of the group's success or failure will have to wait.

These are still very early days for Article 12. The self-organized Children's Rights Movement of the 1970s was ridiculed by the media and those in authority and finally collapsed, discredited; some would say unfairly. The same risks lie in wait for any new group established to prove children's competencies and worth. Additionally, there are very real practical problems to confront, not least the fact that the period in which young people have enough freedom to take an active part in such a group is limited to a very few years, so the group's turnover will always be high, creating difficulties with sustaining membership, momentum and continuity. But if the Children's Rights Movement is to develop beyond the activities of well-meaning adults and the sometimes tokenistic involvement of children, it is crucial that Article 12, or a similar group expressing children's autonomous concern to promote their rights, is successful. The problems are evident; the possibilities even more so.

The Children's Rights Commissioner

The desirability of establishing a Children's Rights Commissioner, intended to be an advocate for children, who would promote and protect children's rights is an idea which enjoys a considerable pedigree in the British setting; it was first suggested by the National Council for Civil Liberties (NCCL, now Liberty) in the early 1970s. After much campaigning, a clause proposing the establishment of such a Commissioner was drafted for inclusion into the Children's Bill (1975). Regrettably, the proposal fell at the Committee stage (Rodgers, 1979, p. 276). Subsequently, the idea of a Commissioner for Children has been developed in the setting of the local, rather than the national, state through the appointment of Children's Rights Officers (CROs) in more than twenty local authorities throughout the UK (Ellis and Franklin, 1995, pp. 89–100).

As their name suggests, Children's Rights Officers' general brief is to protect and promote the rights of children and young people in need. Their client group is usually restricted to those children looked after by the local authority and, consequently, Children's Rights Officers are mostly located in social services departments. They enjoy both an ombudswork and policy remit. The ombudswork brief involves trying to help to resolve the concerns, complaints and grievances of particular children, perhaps about their relationship with a member of staff in a residential home, or the placing of an advertisement seeking foster parents in a national newspaper without seeking the child's prior permission. Their policy remit is largely limited to issues which are susceptible to local decision making. In Leeds, for example, the CRO was instrumental in helping children to contest and reverse the social services policy decision to close their residential home without consulting them before making the decision of closure (Ellis and Franklin, 1995, pp. 93–4). CROs have only a limited capacity to act in national arenas, but they have established an association, designed primarily to offer members mutual support and a forum for discussion of common problems and opportunities, which may eventually be able to represent their experiences in national policy debates concerning children.

The broader aim of establishing a national Commissioner has recently enjoyed something of a popular revival. This renewed enthusiasm has undoubtedly been prompted, at least in part, by the Norwegian experience of ombudswork with children, recorded in Flekkoy's excellent study *A Voice for Children* (Flekkoy, 1991, p. 249), as well as the appointment of similar officers in Israel, New Zealand and Costa Rica. Joan Lestor (1995) believes the role of a Minister and Commissioner for children would be complementary:

> The Minister would help draw up policy, the Commissioner would be consulted on it and would monitor its impact and effectiveness. The Minister would work within government as a catalyst for change and a policy coordinator. The Commissioner would be free to criticise from the outside and would have additional responsibilities and powers, for example, to conduct formal investigations on issues of significant and symbolic importance. Both . . . would actively seek the views of children and young people. They would also be charged with monitoring effective service provision at central and local government level and by other service providers to identify any groups of children whose needs are not being met. This would be a close working relationship. (p. 106)

The study by Rosenbaum and Newell (1991), *Taking Children Seriously: A proposal for a Children's Rights Commissioner*, funded by Calouste Gulbenkian Foundation, offers the most detailed examination and forceful advocacy of this idea. They suggest that it is children's particular vulnerability to ill treatment; the lack of coordination across government departments in provision of services for children; children's complete lack of political rights; the need to ensure long-term government compliance with the UN Convention on the Rights of the Child, which make the case for establishing the office of Commissioner so necessary.

Particularly close attention is paid to the various ways in which the Commissioner should seek to involve children and young people in the enterprise. The Commissioner should: organize local or national discussion forums for young people; establish advisory groups of children to discuss policy and priority for the Commissioner's work; establish a network of regional advisory groups; form specialist advisory groups — children in care and adopted children — to advise the Commissioner; maintain close contacts with national and local organizations of children and young people; request feedback from children via media; establish children's opinions on particular issues via survey research, and; take note of children's opinions contained in letters and 'phone calls to the commissioner.

While this study offered very practical proposals for establishing a Commissioner, however, it was not implemented by government. In truth, the Conservative government of the day was known to be highly unsympathetic to the idea of a Commissioner and consequently a campaign was initiated to try to build support for implementing the proposal and creating a Commissioner for Children's Rights.

The Steering Committee of the Campaign for a Children's Rights Commissioner was established in October 1991 following the launch of *Taking Children Seriously* (Rosenbaum and Newell, 1991). The membership of the Steering Committee has changed on several occasions, but has always been representative of supporting organizations, including: A Voice for the Child in Care, ChildCare Northern Ireland, Children in Wales, Children's Rights Development Unit, Guide Association, National Children's Bureau, National Society for the Prevention of Cruelty to Children (NSPCC), Royal College of Nursing, Save the Children and the Scottish Child Law Centre. The aim of the Campaign Steering Committee has always been straightforward: to win support for the establishment of an office of a Children's Rights Commissioner. Its objectives, however, have needed to reflect the political climate in which the Committee was operating. Winning and expanding political support has always been crucial to the enterprise since the funding necessary to establish the Commissioner post must come directly from government. Early soundings suggested that both labour and the liberal democrats were generally supportive of the proposal. The initial work of the Steering Committee, therefore, focused on attempting to consolidate parties' willingness to express support for the idea into a firm manifesto commitment. The Steering Committee was working to a fairly short-term deadline given the constitutional requirement for a General Election in 1992 at the very latest. But the signals were positive that if there was a change of government, as many expected, the proposal for a Children's Rights Commissioner would be implemented. Activities focused on meeting key politicians in both parties to lobby for a definite manifesto commitment to the proposal.

Public support for the new post would also be crucial, as Flekkoy shows it had been in Norway (Flekkoy, 1995, p. 186). Consequently, the Steering Committee considered various ways of raising public awareness of the advantages and benefits which would undoubtedly accrue from appointing a Commissioner and worked hard to gain support from a very wide range of bodies in order to establish the legitimacy and respectability of the proposal. An agit-prop campaign was mounted. A short leaflet explaining the ideas behind the Commissioner proposal was targeted at the general reader and suggested various ways in which the public might offer support to the campaign. Letters were sent to hundreds of organizations, formally seeking their support for the establishment of a Commissioner. It was hoped that in considering their support for the proposal, organizations would begin to see how they might relate to the Office of a Commissioner and recognize the potential which such an office promised. The Steering Committee felt it was important to extend support for the proposal beyond the specialist child welfare field and eventually secured endorsement from such diverse bodies as the Association of Metropolitan Authorities, The Law Society, the Royal College of Physicians, the Union of Moslem Organizations, the London Homelessness Forum, Community Service Volunteers and the Campaign for State Education, amongst others.

When the Conservative Party were returned to office in the General Election of April 1992, the Campaign Steering Committee had to review its future. The Conservative Party had never supported the idea; the clear party line was that since the Conservative government had introduced the Children Act, no other institutional mechanism was required to achieve children's rights.

A broad meeting of supporting organizations was held to consider the way forward. It was agreed that a Steering Committee should continue to meet to keep the idea alive, but that any attempt to persuade the government to shift its position would inevitably prove fruitless. The group planned a 'softly softly' campaign designed to sustain the interest of the public, politicians and others, in the proposal. The Steering Committee would also be ready to revive full and energetic campaigning activities when the time was more propitious for achieving its desired outcomes, probably in the run up to a new General Election.

The Steering Committee continues to meet regularly and to build support for the proposal. Since March 1995, it has enjoyed additional support from the Children's Rights Office which emerged phoenix-like from the ashes of the CRDU, and is, again, funded from trusts and children's charities. The Office has a full-time worker who campaigns for the establishment of a Commissioner. The Steering Committee continues to meet regularly to plan the campaign. Interest has been sustained through occasional seminars discussing ombudswork in other countries and by following political developments in all three main parties; the Labour Party has now given a formal commitment to establishing the office of Children's Rights Commissioner if they are elected.

The Steering Committee focused particular attention on the UN Committee's report on the UK government's performance in implementing the UN Convention on the Rights of the Child. It seemed clear that the establishment of a Commissioner would have been a constructive way to make progress here and might have served to convince the UN Committee that the UK took its responsibilities seriously. The UN Committee hopes that there may be a Children's Rights Commissioner for the UK before the millennium when the UN Committee next reports; depending on the outcome of the next General Election.

The Children's Rights Movement: A Summary

The Children's Rights Movement has always been characterized by diversity in terms of the range of its constituent organizations, the plurality of its moral and ideological commitments as well as the broad compass of its policy ambitions. The UN Convention on the Rights of the Child has proved highly successful in unifying the Movement; it has offered a rallying point. The UN Convention has provided a manifesto articulating a moral and political agenda which has won the support of the majority of member groups; it also offers a programme of policy proposals designed to empower children and young people. The future of children's rights, as well as of the Movement to achieve them, is uncertain in the current political climate with its emphasis on retreating from any progressive policy suggestion. But the hope must surely be that in ten years time there will be a fourth phase in the development of the Children's Rights Movement. In this next phase, children will be the key political actors, seeking to establish their rights to protection but also their rights to participate in a range of settings which extend beyond the social and welfare arenas; no matter how important. For Thatcher's children, such a prospect was unthinkable; Major's children can entertain only marginally greater hopes for optimism. But children's claims for rights have proved morally sound, politically persistent and stubbornly resilient to government indifference and hostility; the future is open.

References

Archard, D. (1993) *Children; Rights and Childhood*, London, Routledge.

Aries, P. (1962) *Centuries of Childhood*, London, Jonathan Cape.

Article 12, (undated) Development Plan April 1995–March 1998 (unpublished).

Children's Rights Development Unit (1994) *UK Agenda for Children*, London, CRDU.

Department of Health (1994) *The UK's First Report to the UN Committee on the Rights of the Child*, London, HMSO.

Edelman, P. (1977) 'The Children's Rights Movement', in Gross, B. and Gross, R. (eds) *The Children's Rights Movement: Overcoming The Oppression of the Young*, New York, Anchor, pp. 203–6.

Eekelaar, J. (1994) 'The interests of the child and the child's wishes: The role of dynamic self-determination', *International Journal of Law and the Family*, **8**, pp. 42–61.

ELLIS. S. and FRANKLIN, A. (1995) 'Children's Rights Officers', in FRANKLIN B. (ed.) *The Handbook of Children's Rights: Comparative Policy and Practice*, London, Routledge, pp. 89–100.

FARSON, R. (1977) 'Birthrights', in GROSS, B. and GROSS, R. (eds) *The Children's Rights Movement: Overcoming the Oppression of the Young*, New York, Anchor.

FIRESTONE, S. (1972) 'Down with childhood', in FIRESTONE, S. *Dialectic of Sex*, London, Bantam Books, pp. 72–105.

FLEKKOY, M. (1991) *A Voice For Children: Speaking Out as their Ombudsman*, London, UNICEF and Jessica Kingsley.

FLEKKOY, M. (1995) 'The Scandinavian experience of children's rights', in FRANKLIN, B. (ed.) *The Handbook of Children's Rights: Comparative Policy and Practice*, London, Routledge, pp. 163–76.

FRANKLIN, B. (1986) *The Rights Of Children*, Oxford, Blackwells.

FRANKLIN, B. (1992) 'Votes for children', *Childright*, April, no. 85, pp. 10–15.

FRANKLIN, B. (1995) 'The case for children's rights: A progress report', in FRANKLIN, B. (ed.) *The Handbook of Children's Rights: Comparative Policy and Practice*, London, Routledge, pp. 3–25.

FREEMAN, M. (1983) *The Rights and Wrongs of Children*, London and Dover, Frances Pinter.

FREEMAN, M. (1995) 'Children's rights in a land of rites', in FRANKLIN, B. (ed.) *The Handbook of Children's Rights: Comparative Policy and Practice*, London, Routledge, pp. 70–89.

GOLDING, P. and MIDDLETON, S. (1982) *Images of Welfare: Press and Public Attitudes to Poverty*, London, Martin Robertson.

GROSS, B. and GROSS R. (eds) (1977) 'Introduction', in GROSS, B. and GROSS, R. *The Children's Rights Movement: Overcoming the Oppression of the Young*, New York, Anchor, pp. 1–12.

HOLLAND, P. (1992) *What is a Child: Popular Images of Childhood*, London, Virago.

HOLT, J. (1975) *Escape From Childhood*, London, Penguin.

HOYLES, M. (1989) *The Politics of Childhood*, London, Journeyman.

ILLICH, I. (1973) *De Schooling Society*, Penguin.

LANSDOWN, G. (1995) 'The Children's Rights Development Unit', in FRANKLIN, B. (ed.) *The Handbook of Children's Rights: Comparative Policy and Practice*, London, Routledge, pp. 107–19.

LASLETT, P. (1965) *The World We have Lost*, London, Methuen.

LESTOR, J. (1995) 'A Minister for Children', in FRANKLIN, B. (ed.) *The Handbook of Children's Rights: Comparative Policy and Practice*, London, Routledge, pp. 100–7.

LYON, T. and PARTON, N. (1995) 'Children's rights and the Children Act 1989', in FRANKLIN, B. (ed.) *The Handbook of Children's Rights: Comparative Policy and Practice*, London, Routledge, pp. 40–56.

NEWELL, P. (1991) *The UN Convention and Children's Rights in the UK*, London, National Children's Bureau.

PAIS, M. (1992) 'The United Nations Convention on the Rights of the Child', *Bulletin on Human Rights*, pp. 75–6.

PATON, K. (1971) *The Great Brain Robbery*, Manchester, Moss Side Press Ltd.

RODHAM, H. (1973) 'Children under the law', *Harvard Educational Review*, **43**, pp. 479–93.

RODGERS, R. (1979) 'A new ombudsman — defender of children's rights', *Where?* no. 152, pp. 267–71.

ROGERS, C. and WRIGHTSMAN, L. (1978) 'Attitudes towards children's rights: Nurturance or self-determination', *Journal of Social Issues,* **34**, 2.

ROSENBAUM, M. and NEWELL, P. (1991) *Taking Children's Rights Seriously; A Proposal for a Children's Rights Commissioner,* London, Calouste Gulbenkian Foundation.

RUDKIN, O. (1927) *Thomas Spence and His Connections,* London, George Allen and Unwin.

SCARRE, G. (1980) 'Children and paternalism', *Philosophy,* **55**, pp. 117–31.

SCARRE, G. (1989) *Children, Parents and Politics,* Cambridge, Cambridge University Press.

SCOTT, A. (1992) 'Political culture and social movements', in ALLEN, J., BRAHAM, P. and LEWIS, P. (eds) *Political and Economic Forms of Modernity,* Cambridge, Polity Press, pp. 129–60.

SLOGVOLK (1852) 'The rights of children', *Knickerbocker,* no. 36, pp. 489–90.

SPENCE, T. (1797) *The Rights of Infants,* London, Thomas Spence.

UN COMMITTEE ON THE RIGHTS OF THE CHILD (1995) *Response to the UK's First Report to the UN Committee on the Rights of the Child,* reprinted in *Childright,* vol. 114, March, pp. 3–7.

'UN COMMITTEE CRITICISE UK "RIGHTS OF CHILD" REPORT' (1995) *Childright,* vol. 114, pp. 3–5, March.

WALD, M. (1972) 'Children's rights: A framework for analysis', *University of California Davis Law Review,* **12**, pp. 252–82.

ZELDIN, T. (1973) *France 1848–1945,* Oxford, Oxford University Press.

8   The Politics of Child Poverty 1979–1995

Carey Oppenheim and Ruth Lister

Introduction

> We Conservatives believe in the family. It is the most important insti-
> tution in society . . . The family is under threat from the left. They hate
> it because it is a bastion against the dominant state. (Rt Hon Peter
> Lilley MP, Speech to the Conservative Party Conference, October 1992)

The Conservative Party defines itself as the party of 'the family'. But this identification has become particularly problematic at a time when the 'family' is in
disarray and when government policy has, in many ways, disadvantaged families. This chapter explores the tensions in New Right ideology on the family,
poverty and childhood and the ways in which these are reflected in many of
the policies directed towards children and families. It focuses on three areas
of policy: child benefit, the Social Security Act 1986 and, in particular, the Child
Support Act. It concludes by comparing the rhetoric and policy with the material
reality of children's lives and contemporary expectations of childhood. Children themselves, it argues, are all too often absent from the political theatre of
family policy.

New Right Rhetoric on Family, Poverty and Childhood

The starting point of this chapter is 1979. However, it is important to stress the
long-standing marginalization of children in political discourse. For example,
the ambivalence about state support for the costs of children and the neglect
of the distribution of income within the family long pre-date the Thatcher era
(Lister, 1991a). Moreover, since 1979 there have been differences of emphasis
with a softening of some (though by no means all) of the hard edges of market
individualism under Major (Lister, 1995).

Two interpretations of conservatism — *laissez faire* individualism and
traditionalism (Hoover and Plant, 1989) — have jockeyed for dominance
throughout the 1980s and 1990s, and the tensions between these is reflected
in the rhetoric surrounding the 'family' and poverty. Children themselves are
largely ignored in the rhetoric and when they do appear they do so largely as
objects rather than subjects (Save the Children Fund [SCF], 1995).

One of the guiding principles of the New Right is the pursuit of freedom by reducing the role of what is seen as a 'coercive' state on economic and ideological grounds. The consequent dual emphasis on both the market and the 'family' as bastions of freedom has, however, been characterized by tensions between the two.

The New Right sees the 'family' as a counterpoint to or as a bastion, in the words of Social Security Minister Peter Lilley, against the state. The prevailing assumptions about the 'family' in New Right thinking are familiar: it represents the foundation of society as a whole, the seat of traditional Conservative values; it is indivisible, hiding differences of interest or power between individual family members; it is traditional in terms of family type[1] and the division of labour;[2] and it is the site of responsibility, in particular, parental responsibility.

Parental responsibility has been a recurring theme in Conservative rhetoric and policy and is perhaps best epitomized by the Child Support Act.

> There are some things government cannot escape doing. It must decide who is responsible for the support of children — the parents or the taxpayer. The question cannot be evaded. We believe that both parents should be responsible for their children. And that responsibility continues even if they sadly split up. The taxpayer should only be involved if parents do not have the means to support their own children. The Child Support Agency was established to implement that principle. (Rt Hon Peter Lilley MP, Speech at Birmingham Cathedral, 20 June 1994)

Here parents and taxpayers are set up as mutually exclusive categories and children are seen to be the responsibility of taxpayers *only if* parents do not have enough money. In practice, all taxpayers contribute to the welfare of *all* children and not just children in poverty, for example, through the payment of child benefit. The rhetoric, however, shifts the *perception* of the boundary between state and family provision. The shifting of this line (be it in perception or practice) has led to a growing privatization of the responsibility for bringing up and supporting children. The quotation also highlights the ambivalent relationship of the state to the family (Finch, 1989), where parental, and in particular fathers', financial obligations towards their children have to be enforced by extensive state action, a notion which sits uncomfortably with the minimalist state of *laissez faire* Conservatism.

There is another tension which runs through New Right thinking — the emphasis on the '*family*' within traditional conservatism and the '*individual*' within neo-liberal *laissez faire* economics. When the rhetoric of the market is uppermost it is individuals as consumers and economic actors, who are seen as the primary unit. The emphasis on individual enterprise in the market place as almost the defining feature of success may conflict with other areas of life such as family obligations. The limitations of a totally market-dominated view of society are expressed clearly by John Gray (1993):

> Vital as the market is as an expression of individual freedom, it is only one dimension of society in which individuals make choices and exercise responsibility. People also live in families and belong to churches and other voluntary associations in which market exchange is inappropriate or peripheral. (p. 63)

The clash between the economic imperative and the tasks of sustaining relationships, in particular caring for children, is illustrated by an important dilemma in New Right thinking about whether a lone parent's obligation to work or to care for her children should be primary (Gilder, quoted in Roche, 1992).

In the view of the New Right, the welfare state's role is to ensure a minimum level of subsistence but not to promote justice or equality. It is up to the market to provide rising living standards for the poor (Hoover and Plant, 1989, p. 52). John Moore MP, the Secretary of State for Social Security, argued in his now renowned speech in 1989, that absolute poverty had come to an end and that relative poverty was no more than a synonym for inequality. He rejected what he termed as 'arbitrary and exaggerated estimates of the number of people said to be living in "poverty"' and cast doubt on the validity of the measurement of poverty and thus its prevalent meaning.

Targeting (or means-testing) those in poverty has been the central strategy of limiting public expenditure and of changing the climate of welfare to promote self-help (Moore, 1987).[3] There is a strong emphasis on personal responsibility for poverty. Poverty has come to be redefined as 'dependence'. For the British New Right, heavily influenced by American social policy (Novak, 1987) and in particular by Charles Murray (1984), 'dependence' is epitomized by long-term reliance on state benefits and those 'dependants' constitute the so-called 'underclass'.[4] For Murray, the 'underclass' is defined by *behaviour* — high rates of illegitimacy, crime and drop-out from the labour market. The welfare state is seen as generating the very problems it is designed to solve. At its most reductionist, poverty is defined as dependency which is a behavioural problem induced by the welfare state itself.

This change in definition clearly leads to differing solutions. Poverty cannot now be solved by money but by inducements to change behaviour. Part of this strategy involves re-introducing a distinction between the deserving and undeserving poor. Digby Anderson of the Social Affairs Unit, a right-wing think-tank, writes in the *Sunday Times*:

> A more common sense morality would distinguish between those in difficulty through no fault of their own . . . and those who contributed to their circumstances. For increasingly, low incomes are associated with behaviour, such as irresponsible sexual habits and unstable family formation, lack of commitment to work or training and failure to save or spend prudently . . . *it is time to bring back the notions of deserving and undeserving poor, to restore moral discrimination to social policy.* (29 July 1990, our emphasis)

The effect on children of policies designed to change the behaviour of parents is discussed in some recent writings. Novak *et al.* (1987) are relatively sanguine about the punitive impact on children of benefit sanctions directed at parents who do not fulfil their obligations. They suggest that failure to implement sanctions allows parents to use their children as hostages, condones continuing irresponsibility, possibly harming children even further, and makes exceptions that undermine the whole system (Novak *et al.*, 1987, p. 115). The essence of these ideas in a watered down form filters into the thinking behind the Child Support Act. Such ideas highlight how a redefinition of poverty as problematic behaviour particularly exposes children.

Another prominent strand in the rhetoric about poverty and social security is the rejection of 'rights' (Moore, 1987). Hoover and Plant point to an inherent tension between the market and social rights which remained hidden in the 1950s and 1960s while the economy was growing, but came to the surface with the pressures on public spending. They write:

> Any defence of a more limited role for government in the field of welfare must therefore seek to limit the role of rights claims in this field. (1989, p. 53)

This approach is indeed translated into policy; the clearest example is the introduction of the social fund (see p. 16) which was supposed to promote self-reliance and replaced rights with discretion.

The silence about children themselves is deafening.[5] They are notably absent in the rhetoric about the family and poverty, other than as the 'victims' of lone parenthood and family breakdown. Their star appearance is in the title of the government's child maintenance proposals: *'Children Come First'* (DSS, 1990). But, as we will see, the promise is not fulfilled. Save the Children Fund (SCF, 1995) have suggested a number of explanations for children's invisibility. First, children are treated as part of adult categories such as the family, household or economic grouping in both the collection of statistics and the formulation of policy; second, they are not seen as economically productive; third, they are seen as adults 'in apprenticeship', enjoying a standard and universal model of childhood, and; finally, they are seen primarily as passive rather than as autonomous. This analysis provides a number of windows through which to view the construction of children in the rhetoric about the family and poverty.

> Family policy has been used as a euphemism for children's policy in Western Europe. Although aimed at the family the target population of such policies has actually been the adults in their capacity as parents and policy has been directed towards influencing their behaviour and circumstances. (SCF, 1995, p. 41)

This highlights the ways in which family policy is wrongly equated with policies for children, moreover it describes precisely the thrust of the Child Support Act which is primarily directed at changing the behaviour of absent parents, largely fathers, rather than at mitigating poverty amongst children.

Neo-liberal rhetoric places great emphasis, as we have seen, on the individual as an economic being. Thus if children are perceived to be economically inactive they carry no weight, either in rhetoric or in policy. The pervasiveness of the economic model results in the elevation of the 'taxpayer' as the central arbiter of policy making. Many policy documents repeatedly call for changes in the name of the taxpayer, inevitably excluding children, since they do not pay tax. In fact, the portrayal of children as unproductive is inaccurate; aside from paid work (often in the informal sector) many children work within the home, paid or unpaid. There has been recent research on children as carers which shows how children in some circumstances are actively engaged in caring for a sick or disabled parent (Becker, 1995). This not only challenges the view of children as economically inactive but also the view of children as passive and not capable of bearing responsibility. The rhetoric, where it does address children, often sees them as the mere objects of parental authority and control (Patten, 1993; Howard, 1995).

One area where children *are* discussed is as the 'victims' of lone parenthood and family disruption. However, the debate about lone parenthood often appears to be motivated less by worries about its impact on the quality of childhood than by more instrumental concerns about how it affects children's chances of growing up to be economically productive, law-abiding and family-promoting citizens. Again strongly influenced by debates from the US, lone parents are now seen as undermining the traditional family, a threat to the social order and as a burden on the public purse — as 'dependants' on the state *par excellence* (Murray, 1984). In fact the relationship between lone parenthood and poor outcomes for children is complex and it is clear that poverty plays a crucial role (Burghes, 1994). The demonization of lone mothers and their children (who do not conform to an idealized model of universal childhood) is in effect to make them society's outcasts.

Income Maintenance Policies for Children

Income maintenance policies of the last decade and a half have undergone substantial change, highlighting many of the themes we have touched on. In this section we focus on three areas: child benefit, the Social Security Act 1986 and the Child Support Act.

Child benefit is the only financial support in the tax and benefit system which is directed towards all children. As such it is one important indicator of government commitment to the principle of universal support for all children. As Marina Warner (1989) writes:

> the point about universal benefits is that they affirm the value of such social tasks as having children, rearing them, or caring for relatives;

they make benefit themselves an expression of collective approval
for the endeavour, not begrudged handouts stigmatising the recipients
as beggars and failures. (pp. 4–5)

Phased in between 1977 and 1979 with all-party support, child benefit was
a replacement for family allowances and child tax allowances. Despite what
was then strong cross-party consensus, child benefit's role has been subject to
continuing debate. During the Fowler Reviews of Social Security in 1984–85
child benefit came under the spotlight with repeated leaks about its possible
means-testing and taxation. But it survived intact, in part because of the breadth
of support it held within the Conservative Party from the left and right and, in
particular, from the Conservative Women's Committee (Lister, 1991a).

The result was an explicit endorsement of society's responsibility towards
all children in the form of child benefit in the Green Paper on the Reform
of Social Security. This commitment was reaffirmed in the 1987 Conservative
Party Manifesto: 'child benefit will continue to be paid as now and direct to the
mother.' However, the promise turned out to be rather thin in practice. Child
benefit was frozen for three years in succession as part of a strategy of redir-
ecting financial support from universal support to means-tested benefits for
poorer families with children.

Despite the endorsement of the Green Paper, in the autumn of 1987 the
press suggested that an internal review of child benefit was taking place which
was considering a number of options such as means-testing, taxing it or mer-
ging it with the new family credit (Bennett, 1988). In the face of the government's growing unpopularity the policy changed and in April 1991 child benefit
was increased for the first child. In the 1991 Budget, the government made an
important commitment to increasing child benefit in line with inflation. In both
cases, one can detect the influence of John Major's personal commitment to
child benefit, first as Chancellor, then as Prime Minister (Lister, 1995).

Thus the rhetoric of encouraging the family to displace state support stands
alongside the implicit endorsement of some degree of collective responsibility for children. In reality the commitment ebbed and flowed throughout the
period, whilst means-tested benefits for poor families with children continued
to receive priority in policy decisions. The continued debate across the political spectrum about child benefit's universality, together with the reluctance
to finance it at an adequate level illustrates the difficulty of achieving a deep-
rooted legitimacy for a benefit for all children.

The Social Security Act 1986 (SSA) was the centrepiece of the Thatcher
government's social security strategy, implemented fully, together with a further Act, in 1988. It had a number of aims: to ensure that the social security
system was consistent with the government's overall objectives for the economy;
to direct resources to those in greatest need; to simplify the benefits structure;
to improve the administration of benefits; and, most important of all, to 'reinforce personal independence rather than extend the power of the state' (DHSS,

1985). The focus on providing support for those in 'genuine' need can be seen as part of the strategy of rendering the extent of poverty as minimal. If poverty is fairly minimal, the role of state provision can be equally minimal.

The SSA is wide-ranging — here we spell out its implications for families with children on low incomes. Families with children were a priority group for improvements within the context of a means-tested strategy. Family credit — a means-tested supplement to low wages — replaced family income supplement (FIS). When it was first proposed in the Green Paper, the government intended that it should be paid through the wage packet and thus in most cases to the male breadwinner. This drew on the view of the family as unitary, despite the evidence from studies of the distribution of income within the family that the money would be less likely to be spent on children as a result. The intention, therefore, was not primarily to benefit children but to provide a clear subsidy to wages in order to depress wage demands amongst the low paid (DHSS, 1985, p. 29). In practice, as a result of a joint lobbying initiative by the Child Poverty Action Group and the small employer associations, drawing on the support of Conservative women amongst others, this measure was defeated and family credit is now paid to the carer, in most cases the mother.

Family credit is considerably more generous than its predecessor. However, a number of changes make it less generous than it appears. Entitlement to free school meals is replaced by a cash sum which was merged into the overall payment. For those families receiving family credit and housing benefit, a large part of the cash compensation for the free school meals is lost as the family credit payment is counted as income for the purposes of housing benefit (McEvaddy, 1988). Many families with children receiving family credit, housing benefit and council tax benefit are caught in a severe poverty trap.[6] Families with children account for the bulk of those caught in severe poverty traps. Interestingly, family credit is an example of the extension of state involvement in subsidizing low wages, in contrast to the rhetoric of reducing welfare dependency, arguably creating a 'dependency culture' amongst low paying employers. So long as poor people are undertaking full-time paid work, and are thus removed from income support, the government is happy to subsidize this work through cheaper in-work benefits.

There was a degree of emphasis on the needs of children in the income support scheme (the replacement for supplementary benefit) with the introduction of both a family premium and one parent premium which were paid per family. However, some of these gains were offset by the introduction of the social fund. The fund replaced the old single payments scheme, which had provided entitlements to grants (for one-off needs such as furniture, clothing and household equipment) in defined circumstances, with a system of largely discretionary interest-free loans within a fixed budget and with no right of appeal. This change has particularly affected families with children who were heavily reliant on single payments. While the social fund is only a small component of the overall social security budget, it is one of the most overtly ideological of the 1986 Act's changes, directly concerned with reducing 'dependence' on the state and weakening the culture of 'welfare rights' (Lister, 1991b).

The social fund has resulted in a reduction in claimants' living standards with many falling below the income support level while they pay back loans. The reduction of costs has been paramount (Bennett, 1992). Research undertaken on behalf of the DSS by the Social Policy Research Unit provides a devastating critique of government policy: loans and community care grants are allocated randomly with no evidence of a consistent link with need; there is unmet need; and, some claimants are experiencing multiple debt (Huby and Dix, 1992). Research by children's charities has shown how badly families with children have been affected by the change (e.g., Barnardos, 1990). Many are forced to rely on family and friends, charity or high interest loans. Janet Finch and others suggest that people in fact tend to see 'kin as a last resort rather than a first' and are reluctant to seek help (Finch, 1989; Kempson, Bryson and Rowlingson, 1994). In the determination to reduce dependence on the state many claimants' 'dependency' has simply shifted to a different sphere but is often equally, or more, entrenched and debilitating.

It is worth noting in passing that young people have borne the brunt of some of the most severe reductions in benefit. Principal among a series of changes was the removal of entitlement to income support for 16- and 17-year-olds (Roll, 1988; Harris, 1989). The changes are driven by a desire to make parents take continuing responsibility for adult children, in effect raising the age of 'economic adulthood' (Finch, 1989) and once again, shifting the boundary between the state and family. Alongside the rise in unemployment and the deregulation of young people's wages, these social security changes have contributed to a substantial impoverishment of young people (MacLagan, 1993).

An analysis of the impact of the Social Security Act 1986 undertaken at the London School of Economics (Evans, Piachaud and Sutherland, 1994) found growing evidence of failure to meet genuine need. There does seem to have been a re-prioritization of groups within the means-tested scheme with families with children, sick and disabled people and the very elderly benefiting at the expense of the unemployed and, in particular, the young. However, the researchers found that within broad categories of gainers there were significant proportions of losers. The conclusion they draw is that the changes have 'churned' the incomes of the poor rather than targeted them. Importantly they found that the reforms appeared to make no difference to levels of poverty. In fact there was a slight increase in poverty under the new scheme if 30 per cent of average income is used as a threshold.

The introduction, implementation and subsequent reform of the **Child Support Act (CSA)** exemplifies many of the contradictions within the rhetoric about the family and poverty.

The CSA came into being in a context of rising concern about lone parenthood, reflecting both the financial and ideological preoccupations discussed earlier. In 1991 there were 1.3 million lone parent families (20 per cent of all families) a rise from 0.9m in 1981 (12 per cent of all families) (Haskey, 1994). A growing proportion of lone parents were reliant on income support — around 70 per cent in 1991 compared with 44 per cent reliant on supplementary benefit in 1981.

The CSA enshrines the principle of continuing financial parental responsibility through the establishment of a standard formula for the payment of child maintenance. The Child Support Agency traces absent parents, assesses, collects and enforces maintenance. Caring parents (usually women) are obliged to apply for maintenance if they are in receipt of income support or family credit and are required to name the father (unless they can prove 'good cause'). If they refuse to do so, a benefit penalty is applied. Alongside the maintenance changes, the government increased the maintenance disregard to £15 for recipients of family credit and changed the definition of full-time work for social security purposes from 24 to 16 hours so as to encourage lone parents off income support and into 'full-time' work. Crucially, lone parents and their children on income support do not benefit from the receipt of maintenance (unless they are lifted some way above income support) as the payment of maintenance reduces their income support, pound for pound.

Debates about the CSA echo many of the debates we have touched on. In the words of the former Social Security Secretary, Tony Newton MP, it: *'serves in a literal sense to bring home the responsibilities that family members owe to one another'* (Tony Newton, House of Commons, Hansard, col 178, 4 June 1991, our emphasis). This enforcement of responsibility is stated explicitly in relation to the power to deduct benefit from the caring parent who refuses to name the father. The clause:

> makes clear that a caring parent should also do what she can to help obtain maintenance from the absent parent. *It reminds her of her responsibility for her children* . . . (Lord Henley, 25 April 1991, House of Lords Hansard, col, 440, our emphasis)

The measure to deduct 5 per cent maintenance from an absent parent living on income support (with certain exceptions) draws on the same theme:

> The personal responsibility towards children is too important a principle to be ignored in such circumstances. (DSS, 1990, *Children Come First: The Government's Proposals on the Maintenance of Children*, Vol 1 HMSO)

Thus the enforcement of parental responsibility comes over and above the children's interests (see p. 117). Importantly, despite the presentation of parental responsibility as a universal obligation, in practice the legislation imposes its edicts only on those in poverty — for it is only people on benefit who have to comply with the provisions of the CSA. There is also, as Jane Millar has pointed out, a 'strongly didactic element' within *Children Come First*:

It is in the interests of children that they should be maintained by their parents. Maintenance provides them with a reliable source of income and *they learn about the responsibility which family members owe to each other.*

If the period of dependency on income support is reduced, then *children themselves are likely to gain a more positive attitude to work and independence.* (Millar, 1994, p. 71, our emphasis)

As in the rhetoric observed earlier, children are seen as objects and passive recipients of these values.

The CSA is, once again, about redrawing the boundaries between state and parental responsibility. Child Poverty Action Group (CPAG) has argued that:

the net effect of the formula would be to maintain women and children at income support levels from private rather than public means. (Garnham and Knights, 1994, p. 34)

The privatization of responsibility is seen most clearly in relation to the target for savings following the implementation of the Act. A savings target for the first year was set at £530 million of which £450 million would go to the Treasury, the remainder to lone parent families and their children (these savings have yet to be achieved). In the long term a target of £900 million per annum was set (Garnham and Knights, 1994). The control of public expenditure, rather than the improvement of children's living standards, is paramount.

The CSA also reinforces aspects of the traditional family model, in two ways. First, the formula contains an element for the carer of the children (long done away with in divorce proceedings). The government justifies this reinforcement of women's dependency on the father of their children as being part of the indirect costs of the care for children. However, it appears it is often resented by both the absent parent and the caring parent. Research has found that a large majority of lone mothers did not want maintenance to be paid in respect of themselves (Clarke, Craig and Glendinning, 1993). Secondly, the CSA is seen as a way of changing the behaviour of parents in the future, deterring them from separating, divorcing or entering lone parenthood (Evans, 1991).

The aim of reducing lone parents' 'dependency' on income support lies behind the changes to benefit rules, reflecting something of a shift towards seeing lone parents as 'workers' rather than 'mothers' (Millar, 1994).

Most women who want to provide a better standard of living for their children would far rather do so by going back to work than by staying on benefit. *We do not intend to try to weld them permanently*

> to income support. (Michael Jack MP, House of Commons Hansard,
> 4 June 1991, col. 244, our emphasis)

However, the fact that the government refrained from *requiring* lone parents to undertake paid work can be attributed to the self-styled 'Party of the Family's' residual concerns about forcing mothers into paid work (Lister, 1994). This illustrates the dilemma identified earlier within New Right thinking between the overriding obligation of parents to work and the task of caring for children (see p. 116).

Children are, of course, supposed to be at the heart of the legislation:

> The whole purpose of the Bill is, self-evidently, to benefit the child in
> that it provides for the assessment of the parents' financial liability for
> their children . . . The Bill is designed to advance the welfare of chil-
> dren. (Lord Chancellor, Lords Hansard, 25 April 1991, col. 409)

However, as we have seen, in a number of respects intention and reality are at odds. First, the bill was not conceived as part of an overall package aimed at reducing child poverty, unlike, for example, recent legislation in Australia (Millar and Whiteford, 1993; Whiteford, 1994). Secondly, the rationale for the legislation does not in fact put children at its centre, a flaw not remedied by the inclusion by the House of Lords of a clause on the welfare of the child. Instead the taxpayer comes first.

The conflict between the interests of the taxpayer and the child is re-flected in a number of ways. First, as we have noted, children of lone parents on income support gain almost nothing from the changes. Second, the benefit penalty is a clear case of where the punitive intent of the legislation directed towards the mother, in an effort both to enforce her responsibilities and to recoup money, has a detrimental effect on the children. Third, the initial failure of the maintenance assessment to take into account the costs of access to the child, which might be quite high in some cases, can mean loss of contact as the price of a higher maintenance payment. Fourth, many absent parents con-tribute benefits in kind (such as presents and holidays) particularly to mothers who are on income support (who would have to declare any formal mainten-ance) as a way of supporting children. Such informal help, clearly of benefit to children, is threatened by the changes which, by contrast, do not benefit the poorest children (Garnham and Knights, 1994). Fifth, although the receipt of maintenance may lift some families off income support, such families may find themselves worse off because of the loss of passported benefits such as free school meals. And finally, although the CSA calls for a balance to be struck between the interests of natural children and step children, in practice the lat-ter are disadvantaged. Some second families have reported that they are pay-ing out more in maintenance than they have left to look after their own children (Knights, 1994).

The CSA has rarely been out of the headlines since its introduction in 1993. The response to it has been particularly vocal among absent fathers. The

Network Against the Child Support Act (NACSA), an umbrella organization, has been one of the key lobby groups opposing the Act, highlighting the concerns of absent parents in particular. There are other groups such as the Campaign Against the Child Support Act linked to the Wages for Housework Campaign, Families Need Fathers and a host of local groups. While more established groups, such as the National Council for One Parent Families and Gingerbread, act on behalf of lone parents (largely mothers) and their children, it is notable that the press coverage has been dominated by the concerns of absent fathers. Newspapers have been peppered with headlines such as: 'Lilley tries to head off fathers fears on child support' (*Times*, 11 February 1993), 'Struggling CSA targets better off fathers' (*Guardian*, 13 September 1993), 'Absent fathers face four fold increase in maintenance (*Daily Telegraph*, 16 February 1993), 'Father forced to sell his home as payments soar' (*Daily Telegraph*, 6 October 1993), 'Payers angry at victimisation — the agency has created a nightmare world say fathers facing demands' (*Guardian*, 18 September 1993), 'CSA drove my gulf hostage son over the edge' (*Daily Mirror*, 4 January 1994). While this clearly does not constitute a media analysis, these headlines are typical. Across the political spectrum the response to the Agency has largely been viewed through the eyeglass of the absent, better off father.

While there are real difficulties for absent fathers in terms of often large and sudden increases in their bills, or dealing with past property settlements, or balancing the needs of second families with first families, there has been very little attention paid either to the experiences of low income absent parents or, in particular, to lone mothers and their children. This is partly because the legislation doesn't in fact affect them so overtly, but it is also that they are relatively weak actors in comparison with middle-class men. This imbalance is reflected in the reforms that have been made to the legislation. The most recent changes introduced in 1995 were revealingly greeted by the *Daily Express* as 'Victory for CSA fathers, Express praised for campaign to expose agency.' The changes largely benefit the absent parents and in particular the most affluent.[7]

The resistance to the legislation can be seen in the degree of noncompliance by absent parents. The National Audit Office reported a fivefold increase in unpaid maintenance between March 1994 and 1995 and a 'growing core' of uncollected debt (*Guardian*, 20 June 1995). This goes to the heart of the ambivalent relationship between the state and family pinpointed earlier. The enforcement of family responsibilities highlights the difficulty of extensive state involvement in the complex area of people's private lives (and the contrast, as noted previously, with the rhetoric of reducing the power of a 'coercive' state). The CSA is the embodiment of what Janet Finch has called a public enforcement of family obligation and an attempt to enforce a 'moral order' (Finch, 1989). The debate is suffused with morality: note the outrage on the part of 'responsible' middle-class fathers at the failure to tackle 'feckless' fathers. But, as Finch has noted, if obligations are not regarded as acceptable, people find ways of evading them — hence the high level of non-payment.

The Material Reality of Children's Lives

The trumpeting of the importance of 'the family' and of targeting help on those in 'genuine need' has been accompanied by a sharp growth in childhood poverty. There is no official definition of poverty in the UK; instead we use 50 per cent of average income after housing costs as a proxy for a relative poverty line (Oppenheim, 1993). Using this threshold, government figures show that in 1992–93 there were 4.3 million children living in poverty — a third of all children — compared to 1.4 million (10 per cent) in 1979 (see Table 8.1). The proportion of children in poverty has trebled. This increase is considerably greater than for the population as a whole.

Table 8.1: The number and proportion of children living on low incomes in 1979 and 1992–93 in the UK

	Below 50 per cent of average income*	
	1979	*1992–93*
Children	1.4m (10%)	4.3m (33%)
*All***	5.0m (9%)	14.1m (25%)

* Income is after housing costs
** 'All' includes children as well as adults
Source: DSS (1995) *Households Below Average Income: A Statistical Analysis, 1979–1992–93* and revised edition, London, HMSO.

The poorest section of the population have seen their real incomes either stagnate or fall. The bottom 10 per cent experienced no increase in their real incomes before housing costs and an 18 per cent fall after housing costs over the last 13–14 years, while the richest 10 per cent have experienced increases of 56 per cent before housing costs and 61 per cent after housing costs.[8] Figures for changes in real income by family type between 1979 and 1992–3, although subject to some uncertainty, show that certain groups in the poorest quintile have suffered large falls in their real income, including a fall of 14 per cent for couples with children. These figures could not be a clearer indictment of the view that the unfettered market will provide rising living standards for the poor. The DSS (1995a) concludes:

> Children's income position has been particularly affected by the increases in unemployment with children of both couples and singles not in full-time work substantially increasing their representation in the lower income groups. (p. 4)

The factors associated with lone parenthood are the other main trigger to the increase in child poverty. The Low Income Statistics produced by the Social Security Committee reveal the growing presence of children of lone parents at the poorest levels of income (see Table 8.2). Using income support as a threshold, the Social Security Committee concludes that 'lone parenthood is now the main reason for children appearing in [the] category of low income families.'

Table 8.2: Numbers of children in Britain in families living on or below
income support in 1992

All family types of which:	3,690,000
lone parent families	1,840,000
couples in full-time work	410,000
unemployed couples	1,075,000
other couples	365,000

Source: Social Security Committee (1995) *Low Income Statistics: Low
Income Families 1989–1992, First Report*, London, HMSO.

Children from black and minority ethnic groups are at grater risk of poverty than white children. While there are no figures published which look at childhood poverty and ethnic origin, new figures published by the DSS (1995b) show that all minority ethnic groups are far more likely to be reliant on means-tested benefits, suggesting that much higher numbers of children from those groups are living on meagre incomes (Oppenheim and Harker, 1996).

The oft-stated aim of meeting 'genuine need' is starkly at odds with the material and emotional difficulties for families with children who have to manage on income support (Kempson, Bryson and Rowlingson, 1994; Cohen, Coxall and Sadiq-Sangster, 1992; Oppenheim and Lister, 1996). In 1994, there were close to 3 million (2.98m) children under 16 living on income support in comparison with under a million (923,000) living on the equivalent provision, supplementary benefit, in 1979.[9] Income support provides a daily sum of £2.35 for a child aged under 11 excluding family premium and £3.85 including the premium (which is paid on a per family basis). The government has improved the real level of income support for some groups, for example by increasing the level of family premium above inflation and improving the level of child personal allowances. However, analysis by the Family Budget Unit at King's College, London, suggests that income support levels for families with children are still far too low to meet children's needs (Oldfield and Yu, 1993).

So far we have looked at the income poverty of children, but there is a growing amount of material which shows that broader indicators of childhood deprivation which encompass education, physical and emotional health, housing and well-being have worsened markedly over this period (Kumar, 1993; Wilkinson, 1994; Oppenheim, 1995). *The Index of Social Health* (Miringoff and Opdycke, 1993) which compares children's welfare among wealthy nations between 1970 and 1989 found that while children's social health in the UK and USA improved in the 1970s, it deteriorated substantially over the 1980s.

Here we have focused on the material deprivation of childhood. Recently there has been some discussion about the reduction in the amount of time parents have to spend with children — the 'parental time deficit' (Hewlett, 1993).[10] Hewlett links the 'parental time deficit' to the economic pressures faced by parents who are striving to provide an adequate income for their families. It is important to stress *parental* time, rather than the mother's time, as some commentators have used this argument to suggest that women should return to the home (Morgan, 1995). Two recent trends are relevant here: the sharpening of wage inequality with large rises in low paid work (Hills, 1995; Low Pay Unit, 1995) and the growing divide between the work rich and the work poor (Balls and Gregg, 1994). The latter identifies the tendency for new part-time jobs to go to women who are in couples where there is a partner who is also in paid work. Whilst both lone parents and unemployed couples have been largely excluded from any rises in employment.[11] In the UK there may well be a shortage of time for children in those families where both members of a couple are in paid work and especially where the couple have to work long hours to achieve an adequate wage. This issue highlights the conflict we identified earlier between the dominance of 'market' values, where the economic drive is paramount, and the fostering of caring relationships. Many parents — for which, read mothers — find themselves torn between financial pressures to maintain living standards and the care of their children (Hewitt and Leach, 1993).

The pressures on parents are heightened by the consumerization of childhood (see Patricia Holland's Chapter in this book). Children's needs, wants and expectations are increasingly shaped and defined by the market, which in turn creates persistent pressures on parents. Interestingly, children are not invisible when it comes to consumption, where they are perceived as economic actors by the private sector. Children are consulted about the marketing of goods for children — a rare area in which they are invited to influence decisions (SCF, 1995). Sue Middleton, Ashworth and Walker (1994) explore the power of advertising on children's consumer choices and the ways in which this acts as a financial pressure on parents. They find that children have a full and sophisticated understanding of advertising at a very young age:

> The all-pervasive nature of advertising in modern society is the source of many of the judgements which children make about what they and their peers must have in order to avoid (such) social exclusion . . . the combination of school peer and advertising pressures is inevitably translated by children into financial demands on their parents and/or other family members. (Middleton *et al.*, 1994, p. 148)

They conclude that advertising is a pressure which falls disproportionately on parents on low incomes. The contemporary equation of citizenship with consumption seems to be at its most 'corrupting' in relation to children. The exclusion of poorer children from full citizenship is becoming more pronounced, not just because of the overall growing divide between them and the rest of society, but also because childhood has become an increasingly costly business (Lister, 1990):

> the market's dream is to make every child expensive; children have become a consumer target, through their parents' pockets and their guilt. (Warner, 1989, p. 53)

Conclusion

The New Right rhetoric about the family, poverty and childhood is, as we have seen, riven with tensions. Central amongst these is the clash between the *laissez-faire* individualistic interpretation of Conservatism and the traditionalist one. The clarion calls of the 'family' and of 'meeting greatest need' have echoed through the Thatcher and Major years, yet the governments of this period have presided over an unrelenting rise in children's poverty.

The exposure of children to ever greater disadvantage is the result both of economic and social trends, such as the rise in unemployment and low wages and the increase in the number of lone parent families, as well as neo-liberal policies which have either failed to stem the rise in poverty or actively exacerbated it. The Social Security Act rejigged priorities, but did nothing more than churn the incomes of the poorest. The Child Support Act was not about tackling child poverty among lone parents, but about reinforcing parental responsibility and clawing back money for the Treasury.

Policies have shifted the perception as well as the reality of the boundary between state and family, a shift perhaps most clearly illustrated by the Child Support Act. The result is that childhood has in some senses been privatized. The emphasis has been on relinquishing society's responsibility for children, while at the same time making it more difficult for parents to fulfil their own responsibilities towards their children because of the growing economic pressures to which they are exposed. The fluid nature of the commitment to child benefit highlights the problems of retaining legitimacy for a universal benefit, given to all children by virtue of their childhood.

Children are inevitably peripheral in a politics which is dominated both by the concerns of the market, in which they can be but marginal players in their own right, and the indivisible 'family' in which they are subsumed. To the extent that they do appear in the debates it is as the instruments of wider policy concerns. Thus, the pursuit of ideological goals such as the enforcement of parental responsibility has in many cases overridden the needs of children themselves.

Future policy making needs to address children, their interests and concerns directly, enshrining the principles contained in the UN Convention on Children's Rights (Children's Rights Development Unit, 1994). Above all, it is crucial to reassert the importance of collective responsibility for the needs of children in helping to secure the material basis for childhood and in ensuring that children's life-chances are enhanced in the future.

Notes

1 While the traditional model of a married couple and children has predominated in the discussion (Willetts, 1991; Davies, 1993), more liberal notes have been sounded by politicians such as Virginia Bottomley (Community Care, 13 July 1994).

2   Calls for women to return to the home have emanated from the Institute for Economic Affairs (IEA) (Quest, 1994; Morgan, 1995); however, the importance of women as paid workers has also been recognized by government — witness the launch of the Decade of the Working Woman in the 1990s (Lister, 1995).

3   In fact means-testing undermines self-help as a growing number of people on the right are recognizing.

4   The term 'underclass' is controversial and in our view imprecise and unhelpful (see Lister, 1990; Oppenheim, 1989).

5   The Children Act is an important exception. This is one crucial piece of legislation where children have been seen as individuals in their own right (see Chapter 3, this volume).

6   The poverty trap is where a large part of any rise in earnings is lost through increased tax and reduced social security benefits (Hills, 1993).

7   The only gains for caring parents, usually lone mothers, are compensation for those on family credit who suffer a drop in the level of maintenance paid until their family credit is reassessed and a £5 weekly maintenance credit which allows the lone mother to keep up to £1,000 maintenance, payable on return to full-time work.

8   The figures are rather less stark if expenditure rather than income is used to measure living standards. A recent report by the Institute for Fiscal Studies shows that the expenditure of the poorest has increased since 1979 although by less than the average (see Goodman and Webb, 1995).

9   While supplementary benefit/income support has increased in real terms, accounting for some of the increase in the number of recipients, it has declined substantially as a proportion of average earnings.

10 We are conscious that such arguments can — and have — been used to justify demands for married women's exclusion from the workforce. It is important, therefore, to stress that what is at issue is the allocation of time between paid work and care for fathers as well as mothers, in the face of large-scale male absenteeism from unpaid care work.

11 The notion of parental time deficit is particularly shaped by the debate in the US. It may well be a more important issue in the US where the poverty of unemployment is translated into the poverty of low pay. Thus there will be more families with dual earners on low wages than in the UK, with important consequences for time spent with children.

References

BALDWIN, S. and FALKINGHAM, J. (ed.) (1994) *Social Security and Social Change: New Challenges to the Beveridge Model*, Hemel Hempstead, Harvester Wheatsheaf.

BALLS, E. and GREGG, P. (1993) *Work and Welfare: Tackling the Jobs Deficit*, Commission on Social Justice, No. 3, London, Institute for Public Policy Research.

BARNARDOS (1990) *Missing the Target*, London, Barnardos.

BECKER, S. (ed.) (1995) *Young Carers in Europe*, Loughborough, Loughborough University.

BENNETT, F. 'Foreword', in BROWN, J. (1988) *Child Benefit: Investing in the Future*, London, Child Poverty Action Group Ltd.

BENNETT, F. (1992) *Laying Bare the Lottery: The Social Fund Examined*, London, Child Poverty Action Group Ltd.

BURGHES, L. (1994) *Lone Parenthood and Family Disruption: The Outcomes for Children*, London, Family Policy Studies Centre.

CHILDREN'S RIGHTS DEVELOPMENT UNIT (1994) *UK Agenda for Children*, London, Children's Rights Development Unit.

CLARKE, K., CRAIG, G. and GLENDINNING, C. with THOMPSON, M. (1994) *Losing Support, Children and the Child Support Act*, London, Children's Society.

COHEN, R., COXALL, J. and SADIQ-SANGSTER, A. (1992) *Hardship Britain: Being Poor in the 1990s*, London, Child Poverty Action Group Ltd and Family Service Units.

COOTE, A., HARMAN, H and HEWITT, P. (1990) *The Family Way*, London, Institute for Public Policy Research.

DAVIES, J. (ed.) (1993) *The Family: Is It Just Another Lifestyle Choice?*, London, Institute of Economic Affairs.

DENNIS, N. and ERDOS, G. (1992) *Families without Fatherhood*, London, Institute of Economic Affairs.

DHSS (1985) *The Reform of Social Security, Volume 1*, Cmnd 9517, London, HMSO.

DSS (1990) *Children Come First: The Government's Proposals on the Maintenance of Children, Volume 1*, London, HMSO.

DSS (1995a) *Households below Average Income: A Statistical Analysis 1979–1992/3* and revised edition, London, HMSO.

DSS (1995b) *Family Resources Survey: Great Britain 1993/4*, London, HMSO.

EVANS, D. (1994) *Hansard*, 4 June, col. 215.

EVANS, M., PIACHAUD, D. and SUTHERLAND, H. (1994) *Designed for the Poor — Poorer by Design? The Effects of the 1986 Social Security Act on Family Incomes*, London, Suntory Toyota International Centre for Economics and Related Disciplines (STICERD), Welfare State Programme (WSP)/105.

FINCH, J. (1989) *Family Obligations and Social Change*, Cambridge, Polity Press.

GARNHAM, A. and KNIGHTS, E. (1994) *Putting the Treasury First: The Truth about Child Support*, London, Child Poverty Action Group Ltd.

GOODMAN, A. and WEBB, S. (1995) *The Distribution of UK Household Expenditure 1979–1992*, London, Institute for Fiscal Studies.

GRAY, J. (1993) *Beyond the New Right: Markets, Government and the New Common Environment*, London, Routledge.

HARRIS, N. (1989) *Social Security for Young People*, Aldershot, Avebury.

HASKEY, J. (1994) *Population Trends*, No **78**, Winter.

HEWITT, P. and LEACH, P. (1993) *Social Justice, Children and Families*, London, Institute for Public Policy Research.

HEWLETT, S.A. (1993) *Child Neglect in Rich Nations*, New York, UNICEF.

HILLS, J. (1993) *The Future of Welfare: A Guide to the Debate*, York, Joseph Rowntree Foundation.

HILLS, J. (1995) *Joseph Rowntree Inquiry into Income and Wealth, Volume 2*, York, Joseph Rowntree Foundation.

HOOVER, K. and PLANT, R. (1989) *Conservative Capitalism in Britain and the United States: A Critical Appraisal*, London, Routledge.

HOWARD, M. (1995) *Guardian*, 1 April.

HUBY, M. and DIX, G. (1992) *Evaluating the Social Fund: DSS Research Report No. 9*, London, HMSO.

Jones, G. and Wallace, C. (1992) *Youth, Families and Citizenship*, Milton Keynes, Open University Press.

Kempson, E., Bryson, A. and Rowlingson, K. (1994) *Hard Times? How Poor Families Make Ends Meet*, London, Policy Studies Institute.

Knights, E. (1994) 'The truth about child support: CPAG's monitoring of the Child Support Agency', *Benefits*, Issue 11, September/October.

Kumar, V. (1993) *Poverty and Inequality in the UK: The Effects on Children*, London, National Children's Bureau.

Le Grand, J. (1990) 'The state of welfare', in Hills, J. (ed.) *The State of Welfare: The Welfare State in Britain since 1974*, Oxford, Oxford University Press.

Lister, R. (1990) *The Exclusive Society, Citizenship and the Poor*, London, Child Poverty Action Group Ltd.

Lister, R. (1991a) 'The politics of child poverty: reflections on three decades.' Paper given at Social Policy Annual Conference.

Lister, R. (1991b) 'Social security in the 1980s', *Social Policy Administration*, **25**, 2, pp. 91–107.

Lister, R. (1994) 'The Child Support Act: Shifting family financial obligations in the UK', *Social Politics*, Summer.

Lister, R. (1995) 'Back to the family: Family policies and politics under the Major government', in Jones, H. and Millar, J. (eds) *The Politics of the Family*, Aldershot, Avebury.

Lister, R. (forthcoming) *Feminist Perspectives on Citizenship* (provisional title), London, Macmillan.

Low Pay Unit (1995) *Low Pay Review*, Issue **31**, January/February.

MacLagan, I. (1993) *Four Years' Severe Hardship*, London, Barnardos and Youthaid.

Marsland, D. (1986) 'Young people, the family and the state', in Anderson D. and Dawson G. (eds) *Family Portraits*, London, Social Affairs Unit.

McEvaddy, S. (1988) *One Good Meal a Day*, London, Child Poverty Action Group.

Middleton, S., Ashworth, K. and Walker, R. (1994) *Family Fortunes: Pressures on Parents and Children in the 1990s*, London, Child Poverty Action Group Ltd.

Millar, J. (1994) 'Lone parents and social security policy in the UK', in Baldwin, S. and Falkingham, J. (eds) *Social Security and Social Change: New Challenges to the Beveridge Model*, Hemel Hempstead, Harvester and Wheatsheaf.

Millar, J. and Whiteford, P. (1993) 'Child support in lone-parent families: Policies in Australia and the United Kingdom', *Child and Politics*, **21**, 1.

Miringoff, M. and Opdycke, S. (1993) *The Index of Social Health: Monitoring the Social Well-being of Children in Industrial Countries, A Report to UNICEF*, unpublished paper.

Moore, J. (1987) Speech to Conservative Political Centre Conference, 26 September.

Morgan, P. (1994) 'Double income, no kids: The case for a family wage', in Quest, C. (ed.) *Liberating Women from Modern Feminism*, London, Institute of Economic Affairs.

Morgan, P. (1995) *Farewell to the Family? Public Policy and Family Breakdown in Britain and the USA*, London, Institute of Economic Affairs.

Murray, C. (1984) *Losing Ground*, New York, Basic Books.

Murray, C. (1990) *The Emerging British Underclass*, London, Institute of Economic Affairs.

Novak, M. (1987) *The New Consensus on Family and Welfare*, London, American Enterprise Institute for Public Policy Research.

OLDFIELD, N. and YU, A. (1993) *The Cost of a Child: Living Standards for the 1990s*, London, Child Poverty Action Group Ltd.

O'NEILL, J. (1994) *The Missing Child in Liberal Theory: Towards a Covenant Theory of Family, Community, Welfare and the Civic State*, Toronto, University of Toronto Press in association with the Laidlaw Foundation.

OPPENHEIM, C. (1989) *Social Work Today*, 26 October.

OPPENHEIM, C. (1993) *Poverty the Facts*, London, Child Poverty Action Group Ltd.

OPPENHEIM, C. (1995) 'Must the child always suffer?', *Guardian*, 27 September.

OPPENHEIM, C. and HARKER, L. (1996) *Poverty: The Facts*, London, Child Poverty Action Group Ltd.

OPPENHEIM, C. and LISTER R. (1996) 'Poverty and family life', in ITZIN, C. (ed.) *Home Truths*, London, Routledge.

PAHL, J. (1989) *Money and Marriage*, London, Macmillan.

PATTEN, J. (1993) *Independent*, 7 October.

QUEST, C. (ed.) (1994) *Liberating Women from Modern Feminism*, London, Institute of Economic Affairs.

ROCHE, M. (1992) *Rethinking Citizenship*, Cambridge, Polity Press.

ROLL, J. (1988) *Young People at the Crossroads*, London, Family Policy Studies Centre.

SAVE THE CHILDREN FUND (1995) *Towards a Children's Agenda: New Challenges for Social Development*, London, Save the Children.

SOCIAL SECURITY COMMITTEE (1995) *Low Income Statistics: Low Income Families 1989–1992*, London, HMSO.

UTTING, D. (1995) *Family and Parenthood: Supporting Families, Preventing Breakdown*, York, Joseph Rowntree Foundation.

WARNER, M. (1989) *Into the Dangerous World*, London, Chatto.

WHITEFORD, P. (1994) 'Implementing child support: Are there lessons from Australia?', *Benefits*, Issue 11, September/October.

WILKINSON, R. (1994) *Unfair Shares: The Effects of Widening Income Differences on the Welfare of the Young*, London, Barnardos.

WILLETTS, D. (1991) *Happy Families? Four Points to a Conservative Family Policy*, London, Centre for Policy Studies.

9   Killing the Age of Innocence: Newspaper Reporting of the Death of James Bulger

Bob Franklin and Julian Petley

On 25 November 1993 the front page of the *Daily Star* featured pictures of two smiling young boys; the photos were captioned 'Killer Bobby Thompson — Boy A' and 'Killer Jon Venables — Boy B'. The headline below the photographs queried, 'How do you feel now you little bastards?' On its inside pages the paper reported the guilty verdicts which had been passed on the boys for the murder of James Bulger. There was a discernible irony in the newspaper's masthead slogan which appeared above its vulgar and vengeful headline; 'The Daily Star, The Newspaper that Cares.' The death of James Bulger and the subsequent trial of his killers prompted widespread moral outrage and triggered an exceptional and overwhelming flood of newspaper coverage. For the most part, press reporting of the case was highly sensational and vilified Venables and Thompson as 'monsters', 'freaks', 'animals' or simply as 'evil'. Even by the skewed standards of the British press, the 'normal' requirements of reporting were abandoned in favour of undiluted, vitriolic editorializing. The question 'How Could It Happen?' was asked over and over again, but the answers provided were generally unilluminating and revealed a good deal more about the values of the British press than the reasons for the killing.

The press corps was indeed in vengeful mood. Editorials expressed outrage, demanded retribution and offered a range of policy proposals designed to exact increasingly punitive measures from the criminal justice system. The 'demonizing' of Thompson and Venables was so relentless in the British press that one observer was prompted to describe it as, 'the kind of outbreak of moral condemnation that is usually reserved for the enemy in times of war' (King, 1995, p. 8; Jackson, 1994, p. 2). But journalists moved beyond their attack on Thompson and Venables to offer a new definition of the very nature of childhood; the 'innocent angels' of an earlier social construction of childhood were replaced by 'little demons'. As Marina Warner asserted in her 1994 Reith Lectures, 'the child has never been seen as such a menacing enemy as today. Never before have children been so saturated with all the power of projected monstrousness to excite repulsion — and even terror' (Warner, 1994, pp. 33–48; see also Warner, 1989, p. 43). It became clear that the extent and character of the coverage of the Bulger case signalled a phenomenon with a significance which extended beyond the tragic death of a particular child.

This chapter explores three aspects of that broader social significance. First, it analyses newspaper reporting of aspects of the Bulger case itself, to establish the ways in which newspapers report and construct events and thus set the agenda for broader public discussion. Second, it considers the various ways in which the Bulger case was related to these broader public discussions and how newspapers used the case to bring into focus more general contemporary worries and fears. Finally, press reporting of the Bulger case is compared with the death of a child in similar circumstances in Norway in 1994, as well as with the murder of 2-year-old George Burgess by two 8-year-old boys in Stockport in 1861. The comparisons reveal striking differences in press coverage which illuminate distinctive contemporary attitudes towards children within the different communities.

Reporting the Killing of Innocence

The extensive media reporting of the Bulger case illustrates the dramatic changes in news values and journalism's professional ethics as well as readers' appetites for certain kinds of news — which have transformed the editorial content of newspapers across the last two decades and which reflect the growth of what may be termed for convenience 'tabloid journalism'. While it is important, as Sparks reminds us, not to construct any myths about a golden age of journalism (Sparks, 1993, pp. 58–75), it is significant and interesting that the trial of Mary Bell for the murder of two young children in 1968 occasioned much less press coverage; journalists apparently found the story too distasteful. In the context of today's media scrums, it is both remarkable and instructive to recall that Mary Bell's parents were unable to sell their story to the national press. Sydney Foxcroft, the Newcastle-based stringer for the *Sun* and the *People*, listened to the Bells' story and claimed, 'I've never been so sickened in all my life. I rang through to the office in London afterwards and told them. They said they wouldn't touch it with a ten foot pole' (quoted in Grant, 1995, p. 12). But the intensive competition for readers and advertisers so evident in the tabloid newspaper market in recent years, appears to have dulled journalistic sensitivities and eroded their reluctance to print such stories. In Liverpool a quarter of a century later, journalists from around the globe descended in droves to report the Bulger case; the phenomenon of tabloid journalism is not restricted to Britain.

The story was highly attractive to journalists and contained all of the ingredients essential to a 'good story'. The murder of a child by other children is a rare event; there had been only twenty-seven such murders recorded in the previous 250 years. Criminal stories are perennially popular with readers, but here was a criminal saga not only concluding with a violent death, but in which both victim and perpetrators were very young children. The essential visual element which made the story so 'strong' for both the press and television was the availability of the security camera photographs in the shopping arcade. The hazy pictures of James Bulger and his abductors offered a haunting image of threatened childhood innocence and vulnerability (Young, 1996, pp. 111–145). The video pictures of Venables and Thompson leading James Bulger by the hand from the arcade tapped powerful emotional roots, but also created the opportunity to involve the public in resolving the mystery of the identity of the boy's assailants. In sum, the Bulger case involved many of the elements of more traditional stories about the physical or sexual abuse of children which journalists have come to cherish as highly newsworthy (Franklin and Parton, 1991, p. 47).

Some journalists are coolly analytical about the news value of such stories. 'Child abuse makes good copy,' one claimed. 'There is the trial which involves hundreds of column inches devoted to the details of the child's grisly end. This allows for both public conscience and appetite for horror to be satisfied at the same time. Then there is the ritual purification; the inquiry into what went wrong and the public execution of the guilty parties' (Hills, 1980, p. 19). On this occasion the guilty parties were Venables and Thompson. What are the most significant features of newspapers' coverage of the Bulger case to emerge from analysis of their editorial contents?

First, the extent of coverage was nothing less than phenomenal with both tabloid and broadsheet newspapers allocating a remarkably high news priority to the story. The *Daily Mail* carried twenty-four substantial stories on 25 November 1993, the day after the trial verdict was announced, with a further thirteen stories published during the following two days; a quite staggering total of 3,765 square inches of editorial across the threeday period focused on this single news story. The *Daily Mail* also published a sixteen page supplement devoted to the Bulger case. As one journalist observed in interview, 'It's impossible to go over the top on a story like Bulger. Everyone on the paper is given their head; especially the subs' (i.e., the sub-editors who devise captions and layout and choose pictures to accompany the journalist's story). Overall, twelve of the *Daily Mail's* nineteen editorial pages (when advertising and television programmes, etc., are discounted) were allocated to the coverage of James Bulger's death. In the broadsheet newspapers, coverage was also extensive. The *Daily Telegraph* (twenty-three articles and two editorials) and the *Guardian* (twenty-two articles) both offered an extremely high news priority to the story. The *Daily Express* published an eight page special supplement exploring various aspects of the story. The death of James Bulger was the front page headline in every national newspaper.

Two papers proved the exception to this general rule. On the day after the verdict was announced, the *Morning Star* published a single brief but factual story on its back page entitled 'Children Guilty of Bulger Murder' (*Morning Star*, 25 November 1993). But by the next day the story had moved up the newspaper's news agenda warranting an editorial which perhaps reflected the high news priority allocated to the story by the other national papers. The

Financial Times seemed largely indifferent to the events which enjoyed such prominence in other newspapers. The paper printed a brief story (9 square inches) in a left-hand column devoted to reviewing the day's news; it also printed a picture of James Bulger. The paper's preferred lead story focused on the changes to the rules of ownership for Channel 3 franchises; 'Battle Begins for ITV' (*Financial Times*, 25 November 1993).

The actual lifespan of the story, however, proved to be remarkably short. Many newspapers offered considerably truncated coverage on the two days following 25 November 1993. Reports in the *Daily Express* for example were reduced from 1,980 square inches on 25 November to a mere 3 square inches two days later. Even the *Daily Mail* which allocated 2,595 square inches of editorial space to the Bulger story on the day after the trial verdict (25 November), believed the story justified no more than 45 square inches by the 27 November. Editors seem to believe that even major stories like the Bulger case have a very short shelf-life; a media obsession and frenzy to report a particular topic can fizzle out into indifference across two news days. The imperatives of modern journalism require stories to be reported in a sensational fashion which will attract the fleeting attentions of readers, momentarily satisfying their insatiable appetites for shocking and tragic news before moving swiftly on to coverage of the next 'human interest' extravaganza. In this constantly moving journalistic roadshow, there is little time for sustained reflection on the significant issues which a particular story might prompt. It's all just news; the profound must be reported with the same glib slickness as the profane.

Second, although the news agenda may have shifted promptly, it retained a clear connection with the Bulger story. On 25 November, newspapers had been concerned to convey details of the Bulger case, the verdict and other details of the trial, as well as to identify and offer some background information about Thompson and Venables. By the next day the agenda had moved on to explore related themes, but these were also reported in similarly sensational fashion. Every single newspaper focused in detail on the alleged (although utterly unsubstantiated) influence of 'video nasties' such as *Child's Play 3* on Thompson and Venables and attempted to draw attention to alleged similarities between this particular video's narrative and details of the Bulger murder. Justice Morland's speculative and contradictory remark, offered during his summation, that 'It is not for me to pass judgment on their upbringing but I suspect that exposure to violent video films may be an explanation,' certainly triggered the kind of imitative behaviour among journalists which is reputed by them to be a consequence of sustained viewing of videos; press speculation and judgment about the issue was rampant. *Today*, on 25 November, reminded its readers that, 'inadequate parents use videos as baby sitters,' and that, 'images of violence are beamed at innocent young minds'. Print journalists, of course, relish the opportunity to attack their rivals in broadcasting, but there is a second irony here. Rupert Murdoch seems to have been persuaded by his journalists' argument in *Today* and in his other papers as he removed *Child's Play 3* from the schedules of his Sky television channel for later that evening; a fact seized upon with some glee by journalists on rival papers (Petley, 1995, pp. 52–8).

Another item reflecting the shifting news agenda was triggered by Minister David Maclean who accused the church of being 'strangely silent' over the need to teach children the difference between right and wrong; politicians and journalists, he argued, had been obliged to assume the church's responsibility in this matter. The Church of England responded angrily describing the Minister's comments as 'bizarre and ill informed' (*Daily Telegraph*, 26 November 1993). The story was explicitly linked to the Bulger case and was clearly part of the press' concern to allocate blame for the child's tragic death; despite all the press venom and abuse heaped upon them, Venables and Thompson on their own were inadequate and insufficient scapegoats. The prominence of the story in news agendas on day two of coverage of the Bulger case is reflected in the front page leading headlines of all the quality and many of the tabloid newspapers: 'Silence of the Pulpits; Storm in the wake of Bulger case' (*Daily Mail*); 'Bulger Case Sparks Row Over Morals; Minister attacks church failure' (*The Times*); Church Fails to Give Lead on Morality' (*Daily Telegraph*); 'Bulger Taunt Angers Church' (*Guardian*) 'Government and Church Clash Over the Teaching of Right and Wrong' (*Daily Express*). It seems remarkable that the death of this very young, small boy should trigger such an acrimonious dispute between those twin moral pillars of society; Church and State. James Bulger's death seemed to symbolize nothing less than the uncertainties, insecurities and moral unease which characterized the central moral infrastructure of society (Hay, 1995).

Third, the brutal and hysterical press vilification of Venables and Thompson spilled over into more generalized assertions about childhood. The essentially 'evil' character of these two boys was projected by press reports onto children in general and the whole notion of childhood, thus metamorphosing the traditional social construct of childhood 'innocence' into its opposite. The notion of children as inherently evil is, of course, not new but enjoys an ancestry which can be traced back to the bible. More recently, pessimistic social philosophers like Freud have offered a vision of human beings as fatally flawed and motivated by the irrational and essentially sensual and uncontrollable appetites of the id. Fortunately, since the seventeenth century more measured counsels have largely prevailed and western societies have constructed childhood differently. A succession of historians have illustrated how the contemporary account of childhood which dates from that time stresses the innocence and weakness of children and bestows on adults 'the duty . . . to safeguard the former and strengthen the latter' (Aries, 1962, p. 329; see also Franklin, 1995, pp. 7–8; Kitzinger, 1988, pp. 77–88; and, James and Jenks, 1994, pp. 4–7).

But many journalists steadfastly refuse to offer any credence to theoretical analysis; articulating populist 'common sense' is the vital tool of their trade (Soothill and Walby, 1991). Consequently, newspaper reports were unrelenting in their denunciation of Thompson and Venables as inherently evil, prompted no doubt by Justice Morland's description of the murder as, 'an act of unparalleled evil and barbarity'. Thus *Today*, 25 November, referred to the friendship between the two boys as 'the chemistry of evil — a lethal cocktail'. It also reported a police officer's recollection that as Thompson and Venables left the court, 'there was eye contact between the two boys. Thompson looked at Venables and smiled . . . It was a cold smile, an evil smile'. Elsewhere in the same paper, Bob Graham sums them up as 'an evil team. Venables with an uncontrollable temper that had made him the demon of one primary school. And Thompson, devious son of a hard drinking mother . . . he was plain wicked.' In yet another article a neighbour of Thompson's states that, 'there was an element of evil in him', while another says, 'I remember thinking there was evil in his heart.' The police officer's remarks were quoted in detail by every other paper. One of the headlines in the *Mail* of November 25th's '16-page Special on the crime that shocked the world,' which boasted of no less than four exclusives, referred to them as the 'boy brutes'. The entire special was headed 'The Evil and The Innocent'. Many newspapers detailed Thompson's alleged cruelty to animals and some even suggested a demonic explanation of his character. Thus the *Mirror* (25 November 1993) reported that 'Amityville', a reference to three horror films of that name, was scrawled on Thompson's boarded up house, while the *Telegraph* (25 November 1993) stated that Thompson's nickname was Damien (a reference to the *Omen* films) and recalled that Venables was born on Friday the 13th.

Newspapers' hatred for the two boys was promptly generalized to embrace all children. The *Mail*, 25 November, dismissed, 'the sentimental view that children are born innocent' as 'relatively modern'. Its editorial cites with approval the view of William Golding expressed in his novel *Lord of the Flies*, that 'any ordinary group of children . . . can turn into pre-pubescent savages capable of killing one of their number'. Those seeking more measured assessments found little comfort in *The Times'* editorial on the same day.

> Popular reaction to the behaviour of James' youthful killers has been conditioned by the belief, prevalent since the Victorian era, that childhood is a time of innocence . . . But childhood has a darker side which past societies perhaps understood better than our own . . . children should not be presumed to be innately good. In the lexicon of crime there is metaphysical evil, the imperfection of all mankind; there is physical evil, the suffering that humans cause each other; and there is moral evil, the choice of vice over virtue. Children are separated by necessity of age from none of these.

Journalists and editors were simply unable to reconcile the view of childhood 'innocence' with the facts revealed in court about the brutal murder of James Bulger. As James and Jenks (1994) argue, 'the imagery of childhood and that of violent criminality are iconographically irreconcilable. It is still difficult to regard the video film of Jamie Bulger's abduction from the shopping mall as anything other than pictures of children holding hands' (p. 4). Police officers found it no easier. Gitta Sereny cites Superintendent Albert Kirby's difficulty in accepting two young boys as the perpetrators of the violent killing of Bulger. 'I just don't think any of us will get over it,' he claimed, 'the violence done to the baby . . . and . . . well . . . the confrontations with the two boys. They were so . . . [he still sounded surprised] . . . so small; they had these nice young, young voices. When I looked at them for the first time, I just thought it's impossible. And in spite of the video we kept thinking, yes, perhaps hoping, that others . . . adults, had been involved' (Sereny, 1994b). The *Sunday Times* addressed the issue directly. If childhood, 'is supposed to be the age of innocence . . . how could these 10 year olds turn into killers' (28 November 1993).

Journalists squared the circle and resolved the evident mismatch between ideal and reality in one of two ways. The first possibility involved what James and Jenks describe as 'conceptual eviction'; some journalists thus defined Venables and Thompson as anomalous exceptions to childhood, leaving the category of childhood as an age of innocence intact. This strategy was adopted by journalists at the *Daily Mirror*, 25 November, and articulated in the headline which branded Venables and Thompson as 'Freaks of Nature'. Lord Denning was a predictable advocate of this view declaring 'such terrible wickedness in two young lads' to be 'a freak incident' (*Sun*, 25 November 1993). *Today* also presented the two convicted boys as exceptions: 'I believe human nature spurts out freaks' claimed a police officer. 'These two were freaks who just found each other. You should not compare these two boys with other boys — they were evil' (*Today*, 25 November 1993). But the great majority of newspapers, like the *Times* and the *Daily Mail* cited above, redefined children as a threat and childhood as containing innate evil.

The fourth characteristic of press reporting of the Bulger case was its unrelentingly retributivist and punitive character. There was a perverse logic informing such sentiments for, if children are as inherently evil as many papers claimed, then containment of evil is society's only appropriate response. Again Justice Morland set the tone by noting that Thompson and Venables should be 'locked away for very, very, many years' (*Daily Mail*, 25 November 1993). Subsequently, Thompson and Venables have been obliged to assume false names to protect them from assaults by other boys in custody; their families have been re-housed and adopted pseudonyms to protect them from possible public hostilities.

For some newspapers, however, the sentence was insufficiently harsh; the 'cold blooded murderers' were getting off lightly. The *Daily Mail*, 25 November, published a story headlined '£2,000 A Week: The Boys' Life on Remand' which explained that 'Thompson is being held in a unit where 7 youngsters are looked after by 25 staff at a cost of £2,000 a week each. He has a small room to himself — locked at night — containing a bed, desk and chair, radio cassette player and a computer his mother brought him from home.' In the same day's *Telegraph* it was reported that since their arrest Thompson and Venables had been, 'held in conditions of comparative comfort. They had continued to receive education, with access to recreational facilities. With regular

meals, each has put on several pounds.' Venables' room is described as resem-
bling 'a student pad'. In an article entitled '£2,000 A Week To Lock Them Up',
the *Express* complained that they, 'Will be locked up in a life of comparative
luxury at state expense. They will be guaranteed three square meals a day, a
warm bed and almost constant attention from adults' (*Express*, 25 November
1993). Similarly, the next day's *Daily Express* resented that the boys would be
'living in comfort'. Bob Graham, writing in *Today*, complained that, 'the places
where they are going are not so much prisons as holiday camps with activities
ranging from soccer, roller skating and pool to fell-walking trips. At the home
where . . . Bobby Thompson will be kept there is even a "holiday brochure"
handbook welcoming new inmates' (25 November 1993). With evident disap-
proval, Graham quotes from the handbook to the effect that 'at weekends you
can have a lie in but people are usually up by 11 am for brunch', as well as
the fact that the boys are referred to as 'guests'. The concluding quote from the
offending book is: 'Most of all try to enjoy your stay at . . . and if you need to
know anything else ask your social worker to ask any member of staff who
will be only too pleased to help.' This unsubtle use of irony, in tandem with
an evident contempt for young people, feeds readers' beliefs that the criminal justice system is too soft on offenders; especially young offenders: press
indignation over 'soft' sentences for young people is commonplace. Journalists
fuelled by such punitive attitudes towards young people still hark back to the
failed policy of offering offenders a 'short, sharp, shock'; they look forward
with restless anticipation to the more rigorous regime promised by the 'boot
camps'.

The most sustained and discursive example of the retributive theme was
published in *The Times*, 26 November, in an article entitled 'Show Me Where
It Hurts' by the BBC's urban affairs correspondent David Walker. He begins
by complaining that these 'boys have become objects of solicitude — a social
worker's shoulder, a council official's hankie. Now for an indefinite period,
they will live in units where their emotional development — autonomy and
self-esteem are preferred words — will be tenderly fostered at an annual cost
of at least £90,000 each.' He then addresses the more general issue of punishment. According to Walker: 'public policy is squeamish. The penal system
demands utter respect for the rights, the human rights of the criminal . . . new
prisons are made more comfortable than a student hall of residence and, for
the young, penal regime is a misnomer.' He continues by attacking the Children Act which, he argues has specific obligations to the autonomy of children
and 'autonomous children cannot, by definition, be chastised. That Act was the
product of a conspiracy; not a ramp of social workers alone but of progressive judges and the Law Commission.' To those who argue that retributive punishment does not work, if measured in terms of recidivism rates for example,
Walker simply responds that, 'punishment exists to satisfy society's sense of just
deserts. This is a nerve ending which material civilisation has not yet anaes-
thetised. To pooh-pooh that yearning to see perpetrators of crime, young no
less than older, are punished is to put social cohesion at risk.' That just such

an argument could be used to justify bringing back the stocks and public executions is a point that Walker seems to prefer not to explore.

Finally, in many of the press reports of the Bulger case, Venables and Thompson were judged to be entirely morally culpable for their actions; there was little, if any, allowance for any extenuating social circumstance. The time was, of course, more than usually propitious for such unforgiving sentiments, following John Major's much reported injunction to 'condemn a little more and understand a little less'. It's extremely significant in the present context that Major's remark was made as a contribution to the national debate about crime which was sparked off by the murder of James Bulger. Equally germane, but rather less well known, is the statement by the then Home Secretary Kenneth Clarke on BBC Radio 4 on the same day (February 21 1993) that 'it is no good [social workers] mouthing political rhetoric about why children in their care are so delinquent. John Major and I believe it is no good that some sections of society are permanently finding excuses for the behaviour of the section of the population who are essentially nasty pieces of work.' But Jon Venables had been referred to a psychiatrist by a primary teacher because he repeatedly banged his head against a wall to attract attention, threw things at other children, cut himself deliberately with scissors, stuck paper over his face, hung himself upside down on the coat pegs at school and, on one occasion, nearly choked another child with a ruler. He was bullied at school for being behind with his lessons. Robert Thompson's family lived in poverty; he was the fifth of seven children. Relations between his parents were bitter after they separated and his mother began to drink heavily. The catalogue of familial unhappiness includes the family home being destroyed by fire and Robert's brother Ian being taken into care after another brother threatened him with a knife; home life was so awful that when he returned, Ian took an overdose of paracetamol in order to pressure social services into taking him back into care. Robert's performance at school was poor; he could barely read and began to truant. After the murder he was diagnosed as suffering from post traumatic shock: hardly the reaction which might be anticipated from someone routinely described by the press as a 'cold blooded murderer'.

The press, however, were not, on the whole, interested in any complicating social mitigation which, as far as they were concerned, served only to blur the clear lines of moral responsibility. An editorial in the *Daily Telegraph* was noticeable for its hostility to what it described as a 'deterministic theory of human behaviour' which should never, 'be allowed to eliminate the need for personal responsibility'.

> The evidence presented has deflected attention from the arguments that the deprived conditions of working class Liverpool housing estates, the frequency of family breakdown and single motherhood, or a neglect in the name of progressive education to teach children the difference between right and wrong, can be held responsible for this awful crime . . . A criminal trial, a formal procedure for holding people

to account for their wrongful actions, refutes the pernicious nonsense of our times that a personal sense of guilt or shame is no more than a curable neurosis. Perhaps for the first time in their lives, these two boys have been held personally responsible for their actions. (25 November)

With a regrettable sociological naivety, but enviable moral certainty, the British press passed sentence on Jon Venables and Bobby Thompson. A similar point was made by Janet Daley in the *Times* (25 November 1993). Dismissing as 'offensive nonsense' the 'social science platitudes of the age' she argued that 'to blame the murder of James Bulger on a litany of social disadvantages is to demean it, to reduce it fatuously to a simple chain, with unemployment at one end and bestiality at the other. What an insulting picture this is, anyway of the poor and disadvantaged: as if they were robbed of any degree of free will by their misfortunes. If they behave badly, at least permit them some pride in their own freedom of action, rather than depicting them as pitiable victims blown hither and thither by blind social forces.' Not, of course, that right-wing newspapers are averse to 'social' explanations but only those which they ignorantly caricature as 'social science' ones. Thus, for example, Daley herself goes on (without a hint of a sense of inconsistency and self-contradiction) to 'explain' the murder of James Bulger as the result of a 'subtle abdication of responsibility: a wilful dismantling of any absolute sense of right and wrong.' The British press offered many other explanations for the death of James Bulger; some of these are considered below.

How Could It Happen? The British Press 'Explains'

The headline in the *Daily Express* on 26 November asked 'How Could It Happen?' The British press offered a number of causal accounts. In the *Telegraph* (26 November) the familiar right-wing bogeyman of 'Sixties permissiveness' is adduced as an 'explanatory' social factor by Anthony Daniels in an article headed 'What's wrong with society is far too many rights.' In that dreadful era, 'one's only duty was to enjoy oneself, and no frustration was to be tolerated.' Consequently many people now live in a state of 'moral solipsism' where 'no-one has a duty except to himself. Everyone has rights, but not a duty to respect the rights of others. This is because to respect the rights of others might curtail one's ability to enjoy oneself, which is one's only true responsibility.' This is a world 'in which moral commitment is rare and unknown. It is a world of the eternal present, where no impediment to the desire of the moment is supportable.' And the conduit through which these alleged ideas have passed into the wider society? Step forward our old friend the '*trahison de clercs*', here in the guise of 'opinion formers' who have 'for a long time now attacked and undermined the idea that people bear the responsibility for their own actions. They have emphasized the social causes of behaviour, and persuaded people that they are the victims of injustice . . . People need to be persuaded there is no escaping moral responsibility, in the same way they were persuaded there is no accepting it.'

One of the main casualties of 'Sixties values', so it is argued, has been the nuclear family. (A Conservative press is hardly likely to look at the adverse effects of Conservative economic policies on family life.) Inevitably it was the *Mail* (25 November) which had to drag this particular ideological favourite into the debate. It comes as the conclusion to a two page article by the Roman Catholic novelist, Piers Paul Read, who states that

> the question posed by the murder of James is not: 'Why did it happen?' but: 'Why does it not happen more?'. The answer, I fear, is that almost certainly it will. The reason has been much in the news: the disintegration of the nuclear family, in particular the absence of fathers for their sons.' His comments are echoed by an editorial in the same day's paper which argues that 'children need love and discipline within a stable family. They have to be watched, trained and corrected . . . if need be, chastised . . . That is harder when their homes are broken and their families fractured.

It's extremely difficult to read much of the press reporting of and comment on the Bulger case without being aware of a strong sense of class dislike. Much of the time it remains implicit and sub-textual (and it's certainly there in many of the pieces quoted in this chapter), but occasionally it rises to the surface quite blatantly. One of the most striking examples is provided by what purports to be a news report, by Wendy Holden and Nigel Bunyan, on the front page of the *Telegraph* (25 November). It's headed 'Yeah, my son's a robber but he's not a murderer,' and this is how it begins: 'The mother of Robert Thompson drew hard on a hand-rolled cigarette, blew smoke above her head and said: "Yeah, my son is a robber. Yeah, my son did play truant. Yeah, he always went to the Strand because he could pinch. My children are all scallies, little scallies, but they are not murderers." Overweight, with red streaks in her shoulder-length hair, Ann-Marie Thompson, 41, a single mother of seven, spoke of the difficulties of keeping her "cheeky and mischievous" son under control. If only the police, his head-mistress and the local authorities had done more to discipline him, she said.' There are actually quite significant differences in the way in which different papers represented Mrs Thompson, some actually giving her a fair amount of uncontested space in which she could speak for herself. The bulk of the coverage could not exactly be described as sympathetic, but the *Telegraph* piece is in a class by itself and deserves to become a textbook example for discursive analysis.

A similar but rather less distaste-filled picture of Ann-Marie Thompson emerges from the *Sun*, in its sixteen pages of coverage on 25 November. Its portrait is headed 'Monster's Mum: I'm not to blame', and begins: 'Thompson's mother has blamed everyone but herself for her son becoming a killer . . .

"They always blame the parents" she moaned. But it is down to bad communication all round.' However, curiously (and in our opinion, quite correctly) it is the *Sun's* own editorial, headed 'The horror we can't ignore,' which suggests that not all of the blame can be heaped onto Thompson's and Venables' parents. Noting that the boys 'cannot just be dismissed as monsters who do not have to be understood' the editorial concludes that 'it should have been clear that something was catastrophically wrong in the lives of both Thompson and Venables. The responsibility lies with their parents, their teachers, social workers, the police and anyone else who had contact with these two misfits . . . The signs were obvious, yet still no-one cared enough to try to rescue their young lives from a fast descent into hopelessness.' Equally interesting is the way in which the *Sun* abandons the Richard Littlejohn column which should have appeared that day in favour of no less than seven commentators, including Gary Bushell, Lord Denning, Nick Ross and the ubiquitous Raj Persaud, from whom a genuine diversity of points of view emerges, some of them taking a broad overview of the kind that is all too often dismissed by the *Sun* as 'blaming society'. For example, Bushell argues that in our inner cities 'we are building a jungle on the altar of despair' and complains that 'community values are dying because communities are dying', whilst Nina Myskow holds that 'something very rotten in our society stinks', citing the underfunding of education and the abdication of parental responsibility as two particular problems. Meanwhile the paper's 'agony aunt' Deidre Sanders warns against creating a moral panic about supposedly violent children and points up factors such as the breakdown of the relationship between home and school, and people's unwillingness to 'get involved' when they see things going wrong.

These sorts of all-encompassing explanations were favoured by the *Guardian*, *Independent* and *Today* — in its leader column at least. Entitled 'A Crime of Our Times', this blames the influence of media violence, the state of the education system, the growing gap between the 'haves' and 'have-nots', the collapse of the family, the 'culture of greed' and 'a breakdown in the mutual respect human beings should have for one another', concluding that we must 'reflect and wonder where Britain in 1993 has gone wrong'. The *Guardian* was keen not to stoke the flames of a panic about delinquency on the rise ('puzzled child care experts view killing as a one-off', 'we are not on a downward spiral'), and headed its leader 'Lessons of an avoidable tragedy.' Like the *Sun* it stressed that the warning signs should have been heeded and, like Deidre Sanders, asked 'What has happened to the active citizen?', noting that people were fearful of approaching children in trouble both because they feared being labelled child molesters and because of police advice to people not to 'have a go'. It concluded that the 'best memorial to Jamie would be a more serious debate about crime.' Elsewhere the *Guardian* was the only paper to comment on the media circus that attended the trial ('the boys from Walton became part of an international freak show') and to cast doubt on the whole nature of the trial, devoting a critical article to the 'law that treats 10-year-old kids like adults'.

The *Independent's* attitude to Thompson and Venables could be summed up in its 25 November headline 'Young Criminals Are "Sad Rather Than Bad"' over a story which portrayed the killers, too, as victims and consisted of a large number of comments by child experts of one kind or another. The following day, in an article headed 'How little savages learn to be citizens,' Andrew Marr attacked what he called the 'Rousseau heresy', arguing that 'there is a dark side to boyish behaviour that can be ameliorated, turned and finally repressed by adult contact and teaching . . . Some repression is the essence of liberalism since without common rules commonly learnt and insisted on, we slide back into illiberal behaviour, all the way from rudeness to murder.' The next day, 27 November, it devoted its second editorial to the murder. This was entitled 'An indictment of fractured Britain,' and was close in spirit to the *Today* editorial quoted above. Whilst not denying the notion of personal responsibility, nor trying to present environmental factors as excuses or total explanations it argued that 'nobody can read about the dismal, empty, broken lives and atrophied feelings of the two boys without concluding that they were let down by those responsible for their upbringing. They did not receive the love, guidance, discipline and education that they were owed by a civilised society. Their surroundings were shoddy, their role models inadequate. They were exposed to neglect and cruelty . . . Their stories are, therefore, bound to be felt as an indictment of Britain today. While no society can banish all evil or control all deviants, a mature and relatively well-off country such as Britain could do better.'

At the other end of the epistemological spectrum entirely were those papers which concluded that the murder was, quite simply, inexplicable or, as has been noted above, explicable only in terms of the boys as 'evil'. These present particularly clear examples of the way in which the popular press tend to present events as 'randomized', 'strongly governed by luck, fate and chance', and as being caused by 'eternal human drives, such as fear, love, hate, and greed' (Curran, Douglas and Whannel, 1980). The main offenders here were the *Mirror*, the *Express* and the *Star*. The *Mirror* (25 November) headed its eight page supplement 'Beyond Belief', and its editorial 'Evil beyond belief'; this asked 'how can two young children be that evil? This is what defies our understanding' and concluded that 'we must accept that we will never know why these two young boys did what they did.' For the *Star* 'when we look at Robert Thompson and Jon Venables we are staring pure evil in the face. Wickedness has existed since the dawn of man. Do-gooders tell us there is no such thing. They are blind, dangerous fools.' And the *Express* suggests that 'this horrendous crime is another demonstration that within the human heart and soul reside dark forces that can, and do, break out with terrible consequences; in all societies, in all times, in all places.' Their reporter who covered the court case concluded that 'after three weeks of evidence we were no closer to knowing why they killed James — and without that there was nothing to be learned from the case, except never let your child out of sight.'

There was one explanation that was barely hinted at in any of the papers:

that the murder was preceded by a sexual assault that had its origins in the fact that Thompson and/or Venables had themselves been sexually abused, either by an adult or an older boy. The *Telegraph*, 25 November, noted that 'some detail was considered too shocking to be heard in open court' whilst both the *Sun* and the *Star* on the same day speculated (though at no great length) that the murder might have been the result of a 'sex fantasy'. The only journalist to deal with this aspect of the case in any detail was Gitta Sereny — and not until February 1994 — in the course of two remarkable articles in the *Independent on Sunday*, now reprinted as an appendix to the 1995 edition of *The Case of Mary Bell*. Sereny reveals that 'the police believe James's clothes were removed before the killing. They undressed James and they manipulated his penis and foreskin.' This the jury was told, though it did not feature in any of the newspaper reports analysed here. Furthermore, Sereny suggests that the batteries found near James' body, whose role always remained somewhat mysterious in press accounts of the murder, were utilized to sexually abuse James. There is also the suggestion (though it is no more than that) that Thompson himself may have been abused at some point in his earlier life.

The possible sexual dimension is also explored by Mark Thomas (1993, pp. 174–7), the Press Association's Merseyside correspondent. On the basis of substantial interviews with David Glasgow, Professor of Child and Adolescent Psychiatry at Liverpool University, and Ann Burgess, Professor of Psychiatric Mental Health Nursing at the Pennsylvania University, both of whom suspect a sexual motivation in the murder, Thomas concludes that 'the removal of his lower clothing may well point to the secret heart of this crime'.

The point of all this, of course, is to suggest that by ignoring this aspect of the case the press (and the broadcasters too) may have ignored a highly significant explanation for the murder, one which would make recourse to notions such as original sin, evil and the like somewhat redundant and beside the point.

It is important to point out that the vast amount of press coverage of the Bulger case before the trial actually began gave Thompson's QC the opportunity to argue, just before the trial, that the whole process should be abandoned. He held that the saturation coverage had gone far beyond the normal pre-trial reporting of a criminal case, that many articles had used highly emotive language, and that the case had become too much of a public debate for any juror not to be influenced by it. The QC had collected a total of 243 articles which he divided up into four categories of unacceptable publicity: 'first, when an editor expressed an opinion of guilt by headline, comment or innuendo; second, publishing an express view of a politician or church leader that the defendants were guilty, or establishing that as the only inference that could be drawn from the article; third, publishing material that was wrong, misleading or prejudicial; and, fourth, publishing sensational or highly prejudicial material' (Smith, 1994, p. 196). He was supported by Brian Walsh, QC for Venables, who called the coverage 'disgraceful' and 'hysterical' and accused papers of 'poisoning the stream of justice'. The judge agreed that the coverage had reached saturation point, and that the nature of the reporting had gone way beyond the norm — indeed, it had caused him considerable concern. However, 'he had come unhesitatingly to the conclusion that it had not been established that on the balance of probability either of these two defendants would suffer serious prejudice to the extent that no fair trial could be held' (Smith, 1994, p. 198). Significantly, only one newspaper (*Express*, 25 November) stressed this particular aspect of the case. Given the ever greater degree of cut-throat competition amongst newspapers, and the role that crime reporting clearly plays in circulation wars, we would guarantee that this is a matter which will recur with ever greater frequency in the future.

Finally, it's worth noting that we appear to owe to the *Daily Mail* the judge's controversial decision to name Thompson and Venables. The edition of 27 November smugly notes that 'the legal moves to name the killers were set in train by Associated Newspapers, publishers of the *Daily Mail*, who applied to the judge for the boys' anonymity to be dropped on conviction.' According to Smith 'the judge said there was a rule that the interests of the child are paramount' (Smith, 1994, pp. 223–4). The Crown had to bear in mind the child's rehabilitation — a task which would be made more difficult if the boys were named and identified, notoriously, worldwide: 'On the other hand this is not merely a case of ghoulish interest in the macabre. This was a ghastly crime, and unbelievable that it could be perpetrated by one or two ten-year-old boys' (Smith, 1994, pp. 23–4). It could be argued that it was in the public interest that the circumstances, the exposure of children today to films, radio, television and newspapers, video and so on may have played their part. There could be a role for legitimate investigation, which would be of interest to 'serious sections of the public'. This seems an extraordinary judgment, given the nature of the reporting which had so troubled QCs Turner and Walsh even before the trial had begun. Furthermore, remarks about the importance of 'rehabilitation' look simply absurd in the light of the permanent campaign by sections of the press to ensure that Myra Hindley can never be released — a fate which may well await Thompson and Venables. As the judge deliberated on the 'public interest', the publishers of the *Mail* were already preparing to print their sixteen page supplement 'The Evil and the Innocent', with its four 'exclusives'. And so, an extraordinarily upsetting and unpleasant affair — the murder of a child by two other children — was sullied further by the spectacle of the British press at full authoritarian-populist throttle, proving once again, as if proof were needed, that nothing is too awful to serve as grist to their ideological mills. For newspaper coverage of the death of a child, even when other children are complicitous, does not have to be like this.

Holding a Mirror to Society

In October 1994 in Trondheim, Norway, the death of 5-year-old Silje Marie Raedergard prompted comparisons with the death of James Bulger. Differences in the British and Norwegian press coverage of these two similar cases were very striking.[1] Press reporting of the Bulger case was sensational, callous and vindictive in its discussions of Thompson and Venables, pessimistic and conservative in its assessment of the nature of childhood, and punitive in its demands for justice. 'Back to Basics' was the political and ideological reaction to the Bulger case. By contrast, Norwegian press reporting of the Silje Raedergard case expressed compassion for all the children and families concerned, attempted to understand the causes of the tragedy and tried to explore ways to prevent future incidents. There is an old adage that 'we get the press we deserve' which suggests that newspapers reflect, as well as help to shape, the views of their readers; newspapers mirror and articulate society's broader social values. The radically different reporting of these similar cases in British and Norwegian newspapers may well reflect the divergent perceptions of childhood prevalent in the two communities and cultures.

On the afternoon of 15 October 1994 a 5-year-old girl was found lying dead in the snow near her home in Tillerbyen, a suburb of Trondheim. By the morning of 17 October, having asked parents in the local area to discuss the incident with their children, the police had established that the girl had died of hypothermia after being beaten unconscious by three 6-year-old boys. Trondheim police chief Per Marum explained that Silje had been playing with the boys when they began to quarrel; she was pushed to the ground and her jacket was removed. She began to cry and tried to run away, but the boys began to kick and punch her. One of the boys later told the police, 'we beat her until she stopped crying' (*Tonsbergs Blad*, 18 October 1994). Distressed by the events, one of the boys led his mother to where Silje had been lying in the snow for more than an hour; the child was dead.

The boys' age required that further investigation of the case would be conducted by the health and welfare authorities rather than by the police. If the parents consented, each of the boys would have a lawyer appointed and would be questioned about the incident by a judge; a procedure known as Dommeravhor. On 21 October, it was announced that the parents of one of the boys had refused to give their permission for their son to be examined in this way; a week later, NRK news announced that all parents had withdrawn permission. No reason was given or required.

There were, of course, points of overlap in press coverage of the Bulger and Raedergard cases. In both cases coverage was extensive, with comment and analysis examining the details of the particular cases, and also exploring broader concerns about society's attitude towards violence and the alleged impact of television and video presentations of violence on children's behaviour.

But press coverage of the two cases differed markedly in at least four respects. First, press reporting of the Bulger case was highly sensational. Photographs of the two boys featured prominently on the front pages of newspapers with captions such as 'Born to Murder' (*Today*, 25 November). By contrast, in the Raedergard case there was little sensationalism in newspaper reports. A sense of collective tragedy was the prominent mood which characterized coverage. On the day after Silje's body was discovered, Norwegian newspapers chose not to publish pictures or descriptions of the dead girl, or even her name. The editorial in *Dagbladet* announced, with a proper regard for legal concerns, 'we do not wish potential witnesses to be influenced by such information circulating in the media.'

Second, while the tenor of much of the coverage of the Bulger trial was adversarial and retributivist, reports of the Norwegian case were considerably more dispassionate, the attitudes of the parents and the community more conciliatory. In Britain the press articulated the view that it was necessary to ensure, 'society is protected from evil individuals of whatever age. If criminals act against society then they must be removed from society' (*Guardian*, 27 November). While Thompson and Venables have had their sentences increased by the Home Secretary to a minimum of fifteen years (an act declared beyond his powers in a decision of 2 May 1996), following the substantial public support for a petition organized by the Bulger family, Norwegian newspapers have reported an extraordinary discourse of conciliation and understanding between the parents involved in the Raedergard case.

On 18 October 1994, the front page headline of *Dagbladet* announced, 'Silje's Mother Says: I FORGIVE THEM. Families seek comfort from each other.' In the text below, Silje's mother explained, 'I forgive those who killed my daughter. It is not possible to hate small children. They do not understand the consequences of what they have done . . . I can sympathise with the boys' parents. They must be going through a lot now. I do not know all of them yet, but they are welcome to contact me if they so wish' (18 October). The mother of one of the boys claimed, 'my son does not understand what he has done. Several times he has said that he did not kill Silje.' The boy's mother asked the local community not to isolate her family. 'Please remember that we are dealing with small children here,' she said, 'I cannot continue living here if my son is to be called a killer for the rest of his life' (*Dagbladet*, 18 October).

Third, British newspapers presented James Bulger's death as a motiveless act, explicable only in terms of an inherent evil within these children who were 'born to murder'. This 'new' (but, in truth, ancient) image of children and childhood stood in stark contrast to traditional constructions of childhood as a period of innocence. The crime was judged to be greater, and the need for punishment likewise, for having been committed by 'innocent' children; or rather children who should be innocent. As Marina Warner has claimed, 'their trial revealed a brutal absence of pity for them as children. It was conducted as if they were adults not because they behaved with adult consciousness, but because they betrayed an abstract myth about children's proper childlikeness' (Warner, 1994, p. 35).

In Norway there was a more concerted attempt to explore the complexities of the event rather than a mere evoking of notions of innate evil. The death of a young child prompted a considerable societal questioning and introspection. The local school convened meetings of psychologists, police officers, teachers, clergy, parents and children from the local community to provide a forum in which local people could obtain information and support. Psychiatrist Michael

Setsaas claimed, 'We have been able to mobilise a vast network of experts . . . to try to answer the question "How on earth could something as awful as this happen?" We do not know the answer. A lot of information will have to be collected in order to solve the mystery of how children can inflict such suffering on each other' (*Dagbladet*, 17 October 1994).

This leads to a fourth but related difference in press reporting. In the Bulger case the two boys were held to be entirely responsible for their actions; there was only occasional discussion of any mitigating circumstances. However, since the British press largely endorses Mrs Thatcher's view that 'there is no such thing as society, only individuals and their families', it is perhaps unsurprising that newspapers consider individuals as, in all circumstances and without exception, wholly and solely responsible for their own actions. Accordingly, the boys were labelled 'bastards', 'evil' and 'killers', and that was more or less that. In Norway more sober judgments tried to eschew the need for blame and individual culpability, preferring instead to investigate the broader social roots of the incident. Trond Viggo Torgerson, the Norwegian Ombudsworker with children argued, 'We must all ask ourselves some pertinent questions in order to prevent similar cases. How should we teach ourselves and our children to distinguish between playing games and committing abuse? How can we make our children want to copy our good habits, our good intentions without also copying our conflicts and inadequacies? This is what the Trondheim **accident** is all about. It does not serve any purpose to blame those who were involved in the accident itself. They are already unhappy' (*Dagbladet*, 22 October 1994).

Press coverage of the Bulger and Raedergard cases by British and Norwegian newspapers reveals the different attitudes of two communities and two cultures towards children, the nature of childhood and the role of punishment in a criminal justice system. In Norway the Trondheim tragedy was compared with the Bulger case. *Dagbladet* commented that 'Government policy concerning young offenders in Britain has become more strict. The British seek to solve their problems by introducing more punishment. They have not tried to prevent tragedies by developing more youth clubs or helping teenagers to find work . . . The two boys who killed James Bulger were both growing up in a depressed area with few possibilities for work or leisure activities' (17 October 1993). It can make uncomfortable reading to discover how others see us; and judge us!

The comparison of the Bulger case with newspaper reporting of another incidence of child murder, again in Britain but this time in 1861, also suggests that responses by both the community and the press to such events are not fixed or immutable and can be sensitive, compassionate and understanding.

On 11 April 1861, two 8-year-old boys, Peter Barratt and James Bradley, abducted 2-year-old George Burgess, removed his clothes, beat him brutally with sticks and eventually drowned him in a brook. The contemporary records offer Police Inspector William Walker's recollections of finding the body:

> The face rested on a large stone in the brook and when I raised the body, the nose appeared as if it had been pressed against the stone.

The body was quite naked with the exception of the clogs. The child's back had dark stripes upon it as if it had been lashed. (quoted in Sereny, 1995a, p. 10)

An inquest was held on Saturday 13 April in the White House Tavern; George Burgess's funeral was three days later. Following police enquiries, Barratt and Bradley were charged with murder and tried at the Chester Summer Assizes on 3 August 1861.

There were a number of points of comparison between the Bulger and Burgess cases beyond the similar ages of the victims and the perpetrators. Neither Bulger nor Burgess were known previously to their assailants and, in both cases, a number of witnesses testified to seeing the young boy being mistreated by the older children but failed to intervene. But it is the differences between the two cases which are more instructive here.

First, the sentencing of Barratt and Bradley was more compassionate. The boys were judged not to have understood what they had done and were accordingly found guilty of manslaughter rather than murder. On 8 August 1861, the jury required only fifteen minutes to return its verdict. The judge, addressing the defendants, stated that, 'I believe that in time, when you come to understand the nature of the crime you have committed, you will repent what you have done. The sentence is that each of you be imprisoned and kept in gaol for one month and at the expiration of that period you be sent to a reformatory for five years' (Sereny, 1995a, p. 12). The members of the public attending the court murmured their approval of the sentence; ultimately both boys were released six months early.

This 'lighter' sentence reflected a second but significant difference. In 1861, the children concerned were not judged to be inherently evil but to have been (temporarily) led astray by the devil. The blame and responsibility for events was judged to rest with an external agent (the devil) and consequently the possibility existed for moral improvement. Work and moral rectitude were the appropriate response to 'invasion by the devil'. The reformatory regime was consciously designed to remove the 'evil' influence and reinstate the offender as a 'normal' child. Judge Crompton struck an optimistic note, 'You have been very wicked and naughty boys,' he claimed, '. . . I am going to send you to a place where you will have the opportunity of becoming good boys' (Sereny, 1995a, p. 11).

Third, despite the murder it was possible for the parents of Barratt and Bradley, unlike the parents of Venables and Thompson, to remain in the community and enjoy its support. Sereny believes this underlines the 'moral stability of society then' (Sereny, 1995a, p. 12). However, such tolerance and support should not be misinterpreted as expressing the community's indifference to the murder of Burgess; the community was shocked and contemporary records illustrate that more than 1,000 local mourners lined the twenty minute route to the cemetery at Burgess's funeral.

Undoubtedly the most striking difference between the Burgess and Bulger cases was the divergent press responses to these very similar events. Sereny describes the editorials in the *Chester Standard* and the *Times* in the week following the Chester Assizes as 'cogent and enlightened' (Sereny, 1995a, p. 12). The *Times* editorial in 1861 certainly displayed greater measure and compassion than the paper's editorial on 25 November 1993 which denounced the evil nature of Venables and Thompson. In 1861, the newspaper did not believe such young people could be held criminally responsible:

> What is the reason then why it should have been absurd and monstrous that these two children [Barratt and Bradley] should have been treated as murderers? . . . As far as it went their conscience was as sound and a genuine a conscience as that of a grown man: it told them that what they were doing was wrong . . . But conscience like other natural faculties admits of degrees: it is weak and has not arrived at its proper growth in children, though it has a real existence and a voice within them, it does not speak with that force and seriousness which justifies us in treating the child as a legally responsible being. (Sereny, 1995a, p. 12)

This brief comparison of newspaper reporting of the Bulger case with similar incidents separated by time (Burgess) or space (Raedergard) reveals a great deal about both the British press and the highly distinctive character of contemporary British attitudes towards children and childhood criminality. Broadly speaking that attitude is relentlessly punitive, harsh and unforgiving. It is also an attitude which seeks to insist — quite contrary to most comparable countries — that, in the domain of criminal justice, children should be treated as adults and be similarly legally responsible for their actions. The press not only loudly articulates such views but bawls its endorsement of them. If we truly get the press we deserve, there is much about which to be properly ashamed in its coverage of the James Bulger case.

Note

1 Norwegian press reports are from *Dagbladet* (a left-of-centre national daily tabloid similar to the *Guardian* in its style of comment and analysis — circulation is approximately 250,000) and *Tonsbergs Blad* (a daily regional paper which circulates approximately 30,000 copies in the county of Vestfold). *Tonsbergs Blad* quoted a good deal of material from Trondheim's local paper *Adresseavisen*.

References

Aries, P. (1962) *Centuries of Childhood*, Jonathan Cape, London.
Curran, J., Douglas, A. and Whannel, G. (1980) 'The political economy of the human

interest story', in SMITH, A. (ed.) *Newspapers and Democracy: International Essays on a Changing Medium*, MIT Press, pp. 288–347.

FRANKLIN, B. (ed.) (1995) *The Handbook of Children's Rights: Comparative Policy and Practice*, London, Routledge.

FRANKLIN, B. and PARTON, N. (1991) *Social Work, the Media And Public Relations*, London, Routledge.

GRANT, L. (1995) 'Beyond Evil', *Guardian*, 8 February, pp. 12–13.

HAY, C. (1995) 'Mobilization through interpellation: James Bulger, juvenile crime and the construction of a moral panic', *Social and Legal Studies*, **4**, pp. 197–223.

HILLS, A. (1980) 'How the press sees you', *Social Work Today*, **11**, 36, 20 May, pp. 11–12.

JACKSON, D. (1994) *Killing the Child in Themselves: Why Did Two Boys Murder James Bulger?* Nottingham, Mushroom Books.

JAMES, A. and JENKS, C. (1994) 'Public perceptions of childhood criminality.' Unpublished paper presented to the ESRC seminar Childhood and Criminality, Keele University, 15 April.

KING, M. (1995) 'The James Bulger murder trial: Moral dilemmas and social solutions.' *The International Journal of Children's Rights*, **3**, pp. 1–21.

KITZINGER, J. (1988) 'Defending innocence: Ideologies of childhood', *Feminist Review*, **28**, pp. 77–88.

PETLEY, J. (1995) 'In defence of "video nasties"', *British Journalism Review*, **5**, 3, pp. 52–8.

SERENY, G. (1994a) 'Re-examining the truth, Part 1', *Independent on Sunday*, 6 February, pp. 4–10.

SERENY, G. (1994b) 'Re-examining the truth, Part 2', *Independent on Sunday*, 13 February, pp. 5–11.

SERENY, G. (1995a) 'A child murdered by children', *Independent on Sunday*, 23 April, pp. 8–12.

SERENY, G. (1995b) *The Case of Mary Bell*, London, Pimlico.

SMITH, D. (1994) *The Sleep of Reason: The James Bulger Case*, London, Century Books.

SOOTHILL, K. and WALBY, S. (1991) *Sex Crime in the News*, London, Routledge.

SPARKS, C. (1993) 'Goodbye Hildy Johnson: The vanishing "serious" press', in SPARKS, C. and DAHLGREN, P. (eds) *Communication and Citizenship: Journalism and the Public Sphere*, London, Routledge, pp. 58–75.

WARNER, M. (1989) *Into the Dangerous World*, London, Chatto and Windus.

WARNER, M. (1994) 'Little angels, little devils: Keeping childhood innocent', in *Managing Monsters*, The Reith Lectures, London, Vintage, pp. 33–48.

YOUNG, A. (1996) *Imagining Crime: Textual Outlaws and Criminal Conversations*, London, Sage.

10 'I've Just Seen a Hole in the Reality Barrier!': Children, Childishness and the Media in the Ruins of the Twentieth Century

Patricia Holland

Invited to put his own question to Bandai executives, six year old Alex astonished Mark Tsuji and Michael Loveland with playground rumours of new toys only just released in the US market and not due here until Christmas 1995. (*Sunday Telegraph Review*, 27 November 1994)

Schools seek to ban 'pro-drug' clothing. These include 'Mr Spliffy' range of jeans, jackets and T shirts, clothing advertising 'Big C', magic mushrooms, Big H and 'Snowman'. Most colleagues don't actually know what these substances are, but the kids know exactly what they are. (*Independent*, 2 June 95)

I've just seen a hole in the reality barrier! (VR Troopers, *GMTV*, 4 August 1995)

Back to the Future

When the kids know more about 'Mr Spliffy' and 'Big H' than their teachers and 6-year-old Alex can challenge the executives more effectively than his journalist parent, many adults feel there is indeed a hole in the reality barrier. Changes in the ways in which children are addressed, by television, new media and even, it seems, clothing, date back at least to the mid-1950s, but have speeded up to such an extent during the 1990s that the phenomenon of contemporary childhood can appear completely new. As more satellite channels come on stream and electronic and digitially-based forms of entertainment are launched — interactive forms that are often mysterious to adults but eminently marketable to kids — the popular discourse claims that it is children who are skilled in the technologies of the future. 'I'm the first cow on the inter-net,' moos Morag, a shaggy Highland longhorn, as she gives out her personal e-mail number on BBC Saturday morning television. She straddles the cosy children's world of puppets and friendly animals and a much more threatening landscape of a technologized future.

The newer media, including deregulated television, virtual reality and computer games, have become the most important sites where the shifting relationships between adults and children are negotiated. The developments are often contradictory, with debates around childhood conducted sometimes at a hysterical pitch in the popular press, often seeming to bear little relation to the changing situation of children themselves.

I will try to unpick some of the tensions which emerge from the public discourse *about* children and the public address *to* them. Anxieties concern children's *knowledge*, which can appear to exclude adults in its orientation to the future, and children's *pleasure*, which, within an increasingly commercialized environment, seems dangerous and euphoric, challenging and destabilizing to adulthood itself.

In the ruins of the twentieth century childhood has become latched onto the future in a significantly new way. For the post-war welfare state, childhood, and therefore actual children, carried the hopes for a new Britain united around an improved education system, universal health care and security benefits. For the progressive movements of the 1970s, childhood, and therefore actual children, bore the vision of a child-centred, spontaneous renewal of society. The children of the 1990s also represent the future, but the optimism of those earlier periods has been lost. In debates that have centred on the power of the media to influence and corrupt, children have become the focus of moral panics which suggest a future that seems bleak and unknowable. Hope for a better world now seems unrealistically utopian and a childish search for the sensation of the minute is placed above future plans. Paradoxically we no longer look forward to a maturing world but to a world of recurring childishness.

Recent developments in children's media have been accompanied by a high level of public anxiety. Over the 1980s, as the government and the national mood balanced free market libertarianism with an increasing demand for a 'return' to a family-based morality, campaigners like Mary Whitehouse gained renewed public attention by putting the protection of childish innocence at the centre of their efforts to 'Clean Up Television'. Subsequent debates led to the Video Recordings Act of 1985, which restricted the distribution of so-called 'video nasties', and to the Broadcasting Act of 1990, which gave a 'lighter touch' to the regulatory structure of British television, both centred on the vulnerability of children (see Tracey and Morrison, 1979; Barker, 1984).

By the mid-1990s, newspapers had become filled with fears of a young people's culture made up of mind bending and destructive drugs, mesmeric computers and corrupting television. Reports in the tabloid press — on the addictive qualities of computer games, on the tendency of children to imitate violent videos, and so on — have been couched in terms of pure hysteria, while those in the responsible press often reflect a mixture of panic, ignorance and denial. We can detect an undertow of concern that the roles of child and adult are being reversed, as worries are expressed over advertising and television programmes that by-pass adults and appeal directly to kids. As the teacher quoted at the head of this article told the *Independent* newspaper, most colleagues don't actually know — and clearly would prefer not to know — things their students take for granted (Messenger Davies, 1989, p. 67). The new knowledges in which children are skilled are sometimes clearly unaccept-able, particularly when they concern 'magic mushrooms' and 'Big H', but more often they are on the borders of legitimacy, difficult for parents and teachers to evaluate. 'Computer games can be as addictive a hard drugs for the most besotted children', reported the *Guardian* under the headline 'Hard drug fear for computer children'. But the sentence folds back on itself, concluding 'how-ever, they can have a therapeutic effect on others' (Boseley, 1995).

When children's knowledge outstrips that of adults, it's hardly surprising that adults become uneasy. Children's television programmes used to reflect the need to learn. They moved at a gentler pace than the rest of the output and were carefully led by responsible adults (Wagg, 1992). Now, GMTV invites its young audience to 'Wake up to the Wuzzles: a psychedelic noise creating extravaganza!' (GMTV trailer, August 1995). Programmes roar along at a hectic speed. Endlessly mobile cameras chase to keep up with fast talking, youthful presenters. Children in the public eye have lost their respectful tone.

Concern about *what* kids know is equalled by concern about *how* they get to know it. Neil Postman described television as a '"total disclosure medium" which effectively undermines adults' control over the knowledge and experiences that are available to children' (Postman, 1983, quoted in Bazalgette and Buckingham, 1995). Many share his fear that knowledge is no longer in the hands of adults who pass it on to children, drip by drip, monitoring its use. Now it is grabbed by them, wholesale and without understanding. They by-pass parents and teachers in the name, not of a children's culture, but of a futurist cyber-culture where the contact is with less responsible adults. News-papers frighten parents with stories of playground crime-rings who down-load porn out of cyberspace. 'An intelligent, determined and computer literate child with a credit card and a flexible phone bill could . . . amass a huge collection of startlingly disgusting and realistic pornography' (Brown, 1994).

Unlike traditional school knowledge, these new knowledges are not put to the service of work and self-improvement, but to that of *pleasure*, and in particular pleasure based on consumerism and home entertainment. The two generational family home, important for the booming post-war consumer-based economy, was secured by the image of the ever-happy child. But that ima-gined child of the 1950s was safely contained within the family group. Accept-able children's pleasures — snap, crackle and pop at breakfast time and the new educational toy — reinforced family cohesion. The electronic pleasures that children of the 1990s desire are outside parental control. Whereas the first television set drew families together in the living room, computer games, vid-eos and the multi-set home are driving them apart. 'Parents who allow their children a TV set in their rooms must be prepared for the fact that children will watch whatever they want,' concluded a market research report ('Class of 94'

SMRC Childwise market research agency quoted in the *Independent*, 6 June 1995). Jiggling their computer games and surfing the internet — where they can down-load drug recipes and cyberporn — these are the incomprehensible children of the new century.

For the Conservative government of the mid-1990s, committed to a cohesive nuclear family, television is a weapon in the generation war and parents are on their own. 'Parents — both parents — have a clear duty to look after the children they bring into this world. They must face up to their responsibilities, not shuffle them off on to the state,' declared Michael Howard, Home Secretary, in what the *Guardian* described as an attempt to 'shore up the Conservative Party as the voice of the family and community by demanding greater respect and discipline in the home.' If television was showing programmes that were a bad influence on their children, parents 'have a fearsome weapon in their hands, guaranteed to strike terror into the heart of every child. It's 100 per cent effective. There's no known defence against it. It's called the off switch' ('Howard calls for more discipline in the family', *Guardian*, 1 April 1995).

For those of a more liberal disposition, including many who study television, the family remains of central importance. Now the punitive use of the off switch is replaced by the presence of a warm, supportive family group, as in Maire Messenger Davies's description of how her own family dealt with her youngest daughter's reaction to the death of Damon Grant in the Liverpool soap opera, *Brookside* (1989, pp. 92–4). When children's activities resist control by family and school, and are supported in that resistance by unregulated media, both moral Conservatives and child-centred liberals feel threatened.

The fear is repeatedly expressed that children no longer represent *childhood*. However, in a paradoxical way, these changes have their own attraction. If adults can *share* childish indulgencies instead of censoring and limiting them, that would extend adults' nostalgic pleasure. The re-assertion of values of play — advocated in a different context by writings from the 1960s, such as Richard Neville's *Playpower* — would provide a pleasurable abdication of responsibility, a relish of childish illusions of omnipotence. Perhaps this is one reason why the values of childish*ness* have made a surprising incursion into the media as a whole (Neville, 1971).

Quality and the Market

I shall be arguing that 'childish*ness*' is an appropriate mode for the supermarket generation of the late twentieth century and that this shift in sensibility is visible in contemporary media both for children and adults. Childishness includes the capacity to seek personal gratification without inhibition or a sense of guilt and does not necessarily imply a greater understanding of actual children. Indeed, the valuing of adult impulsiveness and irresponsibility suggests that children's needs are more likely to be overlooked. At the same time there are new ways in which children have been invited to take part in the adult world.

During the second half of the nineteenth century, children in Britain were progressively excluded from involvement in the economic sphere as producers (see Walvin, 1982). At the end of the twentieth they have been progressively *included* as consumers. Contemporary children's knowledge includes experience in choosing between a wide variety of consumer goods temptingly displayed in High Street and shopping mall. To keep up with their peers, children must recognize branded trainers, the most up-to-date T-shirts and baseball caps, innovations in fabrics and developments in design. They must be able to select amongst flavours, sizes and type of packet, to distinguish between Shreddies and Frosted Shreddies and appreciate the difference between new long Wotsits and the old ones. They must make distinctions which depend on preference and taste with reference to the minutiae of bodily pleasures, sense experiences and a studied self-image.

'Children are very discerning consumers,' said a spokesman for Waddington Games, 'They won't accept inferior substitutes for Pog' (Roffey, 1995). Advertisements which interleave the children's programmes for summer holiday mornings on ITV and Channel Four, sometimes as many as ten on the trot, encourage the purchase of a wide range of items. Few are cheap enough to be within pocket money range, but this is where the fantastic and the disgusting come into their own, from Pogs (coloured cardboard discs that can be collected and swapped) to Super Sour Nerds, described as 'too much for your tongue to take'. Most desirable goods are costly and mean that kids must put pressure on their parents for access to the latest craze. In the run up to Christmas 1994, such was the desperate demand for Power Rangers dolls that there were all-night queues outside Toys R Us. Hamley's rationed their sales to one per customer, and fathers came to blows as supplies ran out. As more satellite and cable television channels become available, more are likely to be aimed specifically at children. 'Kids are . . . marvellous manipulators of parental pockets — a fact that is becoming increasingly clear to the TV industry,' wrote a reporter for the trade magazine, *Broadcast*, on the launch of American owned satellite channels Nickelodeon and The Cartoon Network, both launched in Britain in Autumn 1993 (Fry, 1994).

As childhood was established as a protected category during the nineteenth century, children came to be seen as encapsulating precious and unworldly qualities which may be corrupted by commerce. In the twentieth-century discourse of television regulation, an opposition was established between the self-sufficient values of childhood and those of a market in which all values are subordinated to profit. Not only were susceptible children to be protected from commercial exploitation, but it was made clear that, in a public service regime, there are areas into which commerce may not intrude.

Since the *Radio Times's* editor resolved in 1937 'that everything broadcast shall be fit to appeal to the keen, fresh, unspoiled mind of the child' (Wagg, 1992, p. 154), children have remained a point of appeal in debates around 'quality' in broadcasting, as icons for non-commercial values. In the mid-1950s when the possibility of a television channel financed by advertising became a reality, the Archbishop of Canterbury argued against it 'for the sake of the children' (Wagg, 1992, p. 154). As it happened, the new commerical channels were introduced within a framework of regulation amongst whose basic principles was the need to ensure that children were provided for, and the need to bear in mind the welfare of those children who will be watching adult programmes. At the BBC, Edward Barnes, Head of Children's Television during the 1970s and early 1980s, wrote that the role of children's programmes is to lead children on to 'quality' adult programmes, 'before they are conditioned to believe that they are *Crossroads* fodder' (Bazalgette and Buckingham, 1995, p. 49).

However, the paternalism and comforting tones of those early programmes seemed out of date as long as they eschewed the burgeoning commercial culture that was reaching down the age range. Consumer culture was attractive precisely because it could by-pass the moralizing of teachers and parents. Wagg argues that the shift from the teacherly approach of BBC's *Blue Peter*, launched October 1958, to the Saturday morning mayhem of the *Multi-Coloured Swap Shop* and *Motormouth* of the 1980s, came about by way of the overt sexualization of pop music, together with an increasing commercialization of children's culture itself (Wagg, 1992, p. 165).

At the end of the 1980s, debates centred on the upcoming Broadcasting Act designed to pitch British television into the free market by auctioning off the new franchises to the highest bidder. Children's television itself appeared under threat. Maire Messenger Davies describes 1988 as a low point. Regular young children's programmes were removed from Channel Four by the incoming Chief Executive, Michael Grade. The BBC's much loved *Playschool* ended its twenty-five year run, and was replaced by *Playdays*, produced by an independent company on a short contract, a move that was characteristic of the BBC's introduction of commercial values within its own non-commercial organization. (Dropping the reference 'school' and its educational implications was also a significant change.) Independent television was to be more audience driven and the whole principle of regulation came under attack.

Resistance to the devolution of all broadcasting to commerce once more centred on issues of 'quality', with children as an important point of appeal. In the event, the campaign to introduce 'quality' clauses into licence applications was successful. Children's programmes were part of the package, and the new regulatory body took their duties as seriously as the old. In 1993 ITV was criticized by this new body, the Independent Television Commission, for the 'creeping erosion' of children's television. But things were already changing. Both the ITV companies and Channel Four were greatly expanding their provision for children, and by 1994 three whole satellite channels were dedicated to children; The Children's Channel, Nickelodeon and Cartoon Network. In the view of John Dugdale of the *Guardian*, 'fears that children's TV would be a casualty of the battle for audiences . . . have been replaced by a virtual take over [of the television output] by children's TV.' He included television which is watched by children even when not designed specifically for them: 'Since

Neighbours and *The Big Breakfast* TV bosses know that kids shows can boost and/or define a whole channel' (Dugdale, 1994, pp. 14–15).

So what does this change imply? An important point is that much ideological work had gone into the reconciliation of the concepts of 'quality' and the 'market' so that they no longer stand in opposition to each other. Greg Dyke, at that time Chief Executive of LWT and the man who rescued TV-AM by introducing the thoroughly childish Roland Rat, was one of the most vocal in arguing that 'quality' programmes can still be popular, indeed, that 'quality' should *mean* popular. If childhood is to remain a marker of quality, such shifts in meaning are significant. They have made possible a softening of the boundary between commercial and non-commercial television.

By the mid-1990s children's morning programmes, on BBC as well as ITV, neatly balanced the aspiration for non-commercial 'quality' and the marketing imperative. Magazine programmes are built around pop music and celebrity interviews in which the guests both entertain and promote their tours, tapes, CDs and merchandising. In an August 1995 issue of the BBC's *Over the Wall*, Declan the young designer is busy squirting silver paint over a baseball cap. Silver is definitely in and 'caps will be good for merchandising'. 'It looks like something from a high street shop at a fraction of the price'. Children's programmes have traditionally encouraged activities, showing their young audience how to make things themselves in the 'here's one I made earlier' syndrome, noted by Stephen Wagg. But silvered baseball caps are more than home-based handicrafts. This is definitely 'merchandising' that is being made, and it is placed next to the abundant promotional merchandising that accompanies every new film and pop group and is regularly displayed in the *Children's BBC* studio. In his scarcely ironic comment, eye-on-the-main-chance Decco, the joker in the programme, is more interested in selling than in wearing the new trendy gear. As boundaries become confused and commerical culture becomes part of a direct address to children, the concern to protect children from commercial exploitation is seen as outdated and increasingly irrelevant.

In one of the many paradoxes which characterize the relationship between adulthood and childhood, market values have themselves come together with childish values. The marketing of goods, particularly toys and other goods which are purely for fun and make no pretence at usefulness, depends on the creation and potential gratification of desires. The belief that libidinous pleasure is indeed possible and the ability to throw off constraints in the interests of pure enjoyment are seen as characteristics of childish spontaneity. Thus the assertion that children must be protected from rapacious market forces smooths over a contradiction in contemporary definitions of childhood. On the one hand there is the need emphasized by Neil Postman (1983) that children should be kept in ignorance of corruptions of the world, and on the other there is an adult envy of children's impulsive egoism and their ability to indulge without guilt in pure, selfish pleasure. The moral and the pleasurably amoral aspects of childhood are being fought out in terms of market forces and the commercialization of British television.

Friends and Enemies: Morphs and Mutants

Friends

Paralleling the tension between 'quality' and the market is the tension between an acceptable face of childhood — active, happy and protected — and a darker, wilder side, with its own long, disreputable history in children's media. 'The market' has no qualms about going straight for the id. However, children's television on the British terrestrial channels covers the whole range of programming, from soap operas and drama to news and sport. This varied output is often presented within a quasi-magazine format that encourages the audience to see children's television in its entirety, rather than as a collection of isolated programmes. A structure of friendship and community with the audience is set up, so that the type of material that is criticized as being corrupting and dangerous — those terrifying narratives of fantasy and violent conflict — are contained by linking sequences which bring the audience back to familiar settings, presented by well-known figures who are both informal and reassuring.

Children's programming has long sought to involve its audience in a special sort of relationship with those on the screen. The first children's presenters were caring adults, the uncles and aunties familiar from BBC Radio *Children's Hour* providing the 'surrogate family' of the early 1970s (Noble, 1975). More recently, presenters have been replaced by either the 'trendy older brother and sister or the adult as clown' (Bazalgette and Buckingham, 1995, p. 48). They may be adults disavowing their adulthood, like the zany Timmy Mallett of TV-AM's *Wacaday*, or young people hardly out of childhood themselves, playing up their youthful characteristics. *Why Don't You?* goes the whole hog and uses child presenters. The impression of an extended family has been replaced by an impression of a community of the young-at-heart of all ages, sometimes specifically in opposition to the hierarchical structures of family life. The attitude spills over into the dramas. The teachers in the comedy serial *Mud*, about a school adventure holiday, are companions as much as stern authority figures.

The chief job of the presenter of a children's magazine programme is to *involve* the audience, rather than merely informing or entertaining them. Stephen Wagg (1992) has described how 'participation' became the defining quality of children's television. From the early days 'activities' were encouraged over mere passive viewing. This has implied a certain schizophrenia on the part of the programme makers, for they have tended to have at least some sympathy with the view that their medium is bad for kids. Monica Sims, Head of Children's Programmes at the BBC, voiced the paradox, 'What would make me happiest', she said, 'would be if they went away' (Messenger Davies, 1989, p. 65). Of course, she meant that she hoped her programmes would 'stimulate [children] enough to go away and do something creative themselves.' This is the only programming that has encouraged its audience to turn from the screen, denying its own validity. Indeed, the how-to-do-it programme *Why Don't You?* began life as *Why Don't You (switch off your TV set and do something less boring instead)?* (Bazalgette and Buckingham, 1995, p. 52).

The sense that the programmes must constantly reach out to their audience and remind them that this is only television and no substitute for real life, has led to some interesting developments in the relationship with a very specific audience. It has meant an informal address, directly to those who are watching, and it has meant letting children in on television secrets. Rather than stimulating them to turn away, programmes now draw more of their audience in to the friendly space created on the screen. Making programmes *for* children has come to imply making programmes *with* children. In this way the structure of friendship has pioneered two qualities now eagerly taken over by the mainstream — access and reflexivity.

The magazine format assumes that the audience and those on the screen share a contemporaneous time into which the narrative items are fed. The linking sequences in *Children's BBC* or in ITV's *Scratchy and Co*, provide a setting within which cartoons, serials or mini-dramas can be set, sometimes in their entirety, sometimes broken up by advertisements or interventions from the studio. Familiar friends, multi-cultural and multi-regional, provide a national structure which can contain programmes bought in from America and elsewhere, offering a sense of security, familiarity and anchorage.

The studio sets tend to represent flexible, explorable spaces — a holiday island, a cheerful, disorderly warehouse full of junk and unexpected corners, a mock hotel with a variety of different 'rooms' where unexpected things can happen. There's an assumption of continuity in the audience from one day to the next, as themes develop, earlier high points are remembered and clips re-run (Messenger Davis, 1989). The studio is often filled with young people, mingling actors with 'ordinary kids' brought in for the occasion, to take part in competitions, receive prizes, or meet their favourite celebrity. The children watching the show are invited to repond by letter, telephone or e-mail with requests, jokes, personal messages, competition answers and birthday greetings. As a viewer there's a good chance you will see your picture or hear your voice on screen. Informality of relations with the audience is reflected in the informality of the style, the impression of improvisation and spontaneity, of the sense that the show is unprepared and happening *on the trot*.

Programmes play on children's knowledge of the medium and their assumed refusal to be complicit in the illusion which until recently sustained all television. So if the edges of the set appear and the cameras are shown, that's all part of the style. Boundaries between the 'reality' of the studio, and the reality of performance are not respected. The inclusive style means that the audience are treated as if they were part of the event. Presenters speak sometimes to the camera, sometimes to the camera operator, sometimes to others in the studio, sliding easily in and out of performance and casual chat. Richard of *Reactive* is a prime exponent of the medium. He plays games with the *idea* of television and with the framework of understanding which allows viewers to move in and out of the televisual illusion. 'I'll take something from your room,' he says to the camera, or is it to the watching child? He stretches his hand beyond the edge of the frame. 'Oh! A biscuit. I don't fancy that!' And he tosses it back. Or, 'Come closer.' He beckons to the camera until his looming head bumps an invisible screen. 'Not that close!' In TV-AM's *Wacaday*, Shaky, the cameraman, was a regular, if disembodied, member of the cast. A tele-sophisticated audience is expected to be able to interpret movements of the frame as movements of the camera and hence of the cameraman. Up and down is a nod, side to side is a shaking head. When things get really bumpy it becomes obvious that the camera operator is running to keep up.

Television for children has been a pioneer of such subversive devices. By taking on childish values of informality, impulsiveness and lack of deference to authority it has become a deconstructive delight to postmodernists who discover it for the first time (Davis, 1994). Itself influenced by the hectic reflexivity developed in youth television first by Channel Four's *Network 7* and then the BBC's *Def 2*, the style has been widely taken up across the television output in programmes from *Noel's House Party* to *The Word* which indulge a form of childishness for the 1990s. The question then must be whether a specific address to children is being lost, and if it is, what are the implications of that loss.

Enemies

Tucked within this structure of friendship, jokeyness and complicity, are narratives in which enmities are of supreme importance. The cheery spaces in which children's television is enacted enclose apocalyptic visions of a post-nuclear holocaust future dominated by power hungry forces dedicated to evil and aiming to control the universe. In these more desperate worlds, all creatures and objects are unfamiliar and potentially dangerous. War is a brilliant firework display, nothing is stable and friends are represented by quasi-militaristic bands: The Power Rangers, The VR Troopers, The Exo Squad.

These more frightening fantasies have been the source of recent moral panics, with the *Mighty Morphin' Power Rangers* seen as a watershed. Launched in April 1994, the series, which combined American action with Japanese animation, went straight to number one in the viewing figures and pushed up GMTV's flagging ratings. The Power Rangers are healthy all American multi-ethnic teenagers who spend their time supervising children's parties and taking part in High School jamborees. They are also superb gymnasts and kung fu fighters who happen to have the ability to metamorphose first into face-less and genderless body suits, then into mythical fighting beasts in order to save the world from 'evil beyond all imagination' variously represented by Rita Repulsa, Ivan Ooze or Lord Z. The very popularity of the programme increased its notoriety, coming as it did at a time of moral panics around the corrupting effect of violent programming (see Franklin and Petley in this volume). It was temporarily withdrawn in Canada and in Norway, where the press blamed its influence for the death of a 5-year-old, bullied by her play-mates (Karacs, 1994, p. 21).

However, despite the furore, Power Rangers are far from unique, and certainly not new. They take part in just one of the narratives of a threatened future which have become a regular part of a contemporary media, not just children's television. The simple narrative structures are familiar from the long tradition of action movies, from James Bond to the Terminator films, in which (mostly) male heroes push their humanity beyond its limits with the aid of special powers (Tasker, 1993). Visual styles derive from the superheroes of Marvel, DC and their Japanese equivalents, where streamlined fetishistic bodies gain supernatural strength to overcome the forces of evil. Many long-established superheroes are amongst the stars of early morning cartoon narrat-ives — Batman, Conan, the X-Men, and He-man who 'was summoned to the future by the last of mankind to help them in their hour of need'. The paranoid world view reflected in such films and cartoons, and more recently, computer games, has made familiar an iconography of dungeons and prisons, castles and deserted landscapes where a dystopic future merges with a mythic past. Magic and the uncanny are juxtaposed with lasers and space technology in a fantasy landscape where it is possible to 'disavow the painful consequences of viol-ence' (Kinder, 1995, p. 80).

Narratives in this genre divide friends very strictly from enemies. But the small-scale enemies who are met with on the way should not be confused with the one, major enemy who is so inexpressibly evil that no sympathy or understanding is possible. Only children or adults' residual childishness can conceive of such an enemy. These are enemies that can get inside your mind. They can blast you with electricity, transform you into a different shape, hurl thunderbolts at you. And yet, they are surprisingly often surrounded by bum-bling incompetents and they are susceptible to short-term defeat so that they are ready to attack once more in the following episode. Disturbingly, the major enemy gives rise to many robotic enemies, creatures of his imagination or his magic powers. Thus, when heroes like the Power Rangers face the innumer-able evil mutants spawned by the likes of Ivan Ooze, they may kill, splat or annihilate them with impunity. This type of enemy is out to deceive, and inno-cence is the most deceptive of appearances. The attack may come from where you least expect it and the most dreadful violence may underlie the gentlest of exteriors.

Our screens are teeming with creatures whose morphing ability reflects a childish instability of shape and form. Morphological beings created by the enemy are clearly not human and may melt or explode when attacked. Mean-while the superheroes and the Power Rangers themselves express an infant-ile misrecognition of invincible strength and power. Their capacity to change their form and obliterate their own human characteristics offers a fantasy of disguise so that these imagined powers can be protected, kept secret from adults and parents. As the computer magazine pointed out when advising its readers to avoid the 'gore mode' in *Mortal Kombat 2*, 'You don't want your parents seeing all those gory fatalities' (*Games World* magazine quoted in Berens, 1995).

If a world filled with X-men, Power Rangers and uncontrollable toys signifies the dystopic future today's children will inherit, it also reflects the turbulent and destructive world of infantile fantasy, akin to the paranoid states and illusions of omnipotence of early infancy described by Melanie Klein (Klein, 1946/1986). The assertion that violent narratives will corrupt young minds may well reflect a fear of that fantasy as it persists into adulthood. The popular press rages against narratives that will release children's potential for destruction. *Power Rangers*, it is said, shows violent behaviour that is easy to copy in the playground, and the video, *Childs' Play 3*, was accused of causing two young boys to imitate the deadly attacks made by Chucky, the demonized doll (Chucky's much more frequent effect of frightening children — evidenced by interviews with children in the BBC 2 programme *Children of the Video*, 29 May 1995 — has surprisingly caused much less outrage. (Buckingham, 1996)). Yet such fears reach back beyond the playground and may well stand for the unarticulated chaos of infantile paranoia. The fears are mixed with pleasurable fascination. Gillian Skirrow's analysis of video games and Cathy Urwin's reflections on the Ninja Turtles have demonstrated how children's violent narratives may deal with infantile experience (Skirrow, 1986 and Urwin, 1995). Insofar as similar narratives speak to adults, in such films as the Terminator, Die Hard and the Schwarzenegger series, adult cinema, too, has become infantilized.

Cross-over Media

My argument has been that we are seing a realignment in the relations between adult*hood* and child*hood*, in a way that is rendering even more problematic the relations between actual adults and actual children. Adult media in the 1990s are celebrating childish values in a quite different way from the child-centred utopians of the 1970s. That image of the directness and freshness of childhood is now turned on its head by a postmodern childishness in which the mood is for momentary pleasures and impatient demands. Following the factors I have already discussed — the popularity of narratives of fantastic power, the innovative reflexivity of children's programmes and an appeal to childish impulsiveness in the libidinization of the consumer world — child*ren's* media are now being joined by child*ish* media and the principle of addressing television programmes exclusively to children is changing.

Writing of American television, John Hartley (1987) has argued 'Broadcasters paedocratise audiences in the name of pleasure. They appeal to the playful, imaginative, fantasy, irresponsible aspects of adult behaviour'. In his view, such an approach not only maximizes a programme's appeal, but serves to avoid adult conflicts and adult antagonisms. Marsha Kinder has extended his argument, observing a 'transgenerational address', which bypasses troublesome divisions of class, race, gender and ethnicity, a mode in which even Bill

Clinton can present himself as an oversized teenager. The transgenerational address is accompanied by an apparent intensification of a 'generational war' in which, a 'destabilised definition of childhood' underlies a series of narratives which deal with infantilized adults and precocious children, most of them real life events recaptured as media spectacle. Stories include Michael Jackson's alleged abuse of a young boy, the teenage Amy Fisher accused of murdering her lover's wife, childlike Woody Allen's affair with his adopted daughter. Such stories are symptomatic of a situation where 'not only are adult spectators "paedocratised" but young spectators are encouraged to adopt adult tastes, creating subject positions for a dual audience of infantilised adults and precocious children . . . These subject positions seem to provide an illusory sense of empowerment, both for kids who want to accelerate their growth by buying into consumerist culture, and for adults who want to retain their youth by keeping up with pop culture's latest fads' (Kinder, 1995, p. 77).

As Maire Messenger Davies points out, there is very little television produced specifically for children in the US, which makes the state of affairs Marsha Kinder describes all the more potent (Messenger Davies, 1995). In Britain, the move to 'cross-over media' has taken a different form, balanced by the growing assertiveness of children on television, a move to make more space for them on their own terms, and the efforts of regulators and programme makers to maintain the gap between children and adults. The changes are based on the very success of children's television.

In a 1995 *Guardian* article, John Dugdale commented on the phenomenon. 'Discussion of children's television usually glumly centres on how it can be preserved . . . but it has never seemed so vibrant and self confident . . . TV's best kept secret is that don't-you-dare-zap shows like *Live and Kicking* are more lively, adventurous, interactive and full of ideas than most formulaic adult fare.' He went on to note that, 'Whole swathes of the schedule, particularly in entertainment and light features are now dominated by "cross-over TV" — kids shows viewed by adults and vice versa — and programming influenced by kids/youth practices . . . The all-conquering prankster television of Noel Edmonds and Jeremy Beadle turns the nation into a playground, Margi Clark fronts ITV's wholly adult *Good Sex Guide* with the bossy, camped up camera grabbing style of a children's presenter. This process of rejuvenation (infantilization if you prefer) has gone so far that it's worth asking what's left that can genuinely be called "adult". Certainly not games shows, nor comedy — traditionally schoolboyish — nor soaps or popular drama series, increasingly devoted to Neighbours-style lovably childlike adults . . .' He concludes, 'It may be time to start thinking about preserving adult television' (Dugdale, 1994).

The Big Breakfast signalled the change. In September 1992 Channel Four scooped up the early morning audience and pre-empted the launch of GMTV with the zany magazine show made by the independent company Planet 24 ('The average age of those who work for us is 24'). They were prepared to throw away the formality of early morning chat shows and go for the sort of chaos that children's television was already exploring. To the 'children's' style was added the 'saucy' tone of *Viz* comic and the *Carry On* films. *The Big Breakfast* indulges in such things as a 'get your egg over' competition and invites vets to look at animal shit. The sniggers and rudeness of children's comics became imported into quasi-adult television. *The Big Breakfast* combines crude pub humour, the mock cruelty that Stephen Wagg (1992) noted as a feature of children's programmes of the 1980s, with a positive celebration of silliness.

The ways in which childhood has invaded adult media have taken contradictory forms. The 'cross-over' effect is partly the consequence of television's need to maximize its 'family audience' before the nine o'clock watershed allows programmes deemed unsuitable for children to be shown. It is undoubtedly a sign of a change in popular taste, incorporating the irresponsible fun of the Spanish holiday and the Saturday night out, both now broadly spread across the population. But many of the narratives which are programmed *after* the nine o'clock watershed parallel those of children's television shown early in the morning. This is where childhood has invaded adult media as an expression of an overwhelmingly masculine fantasy of power. On the one hand, playfulness is an imperative, while on the other, the terrifying infantile fantasies of the early morning cartoons and dramas for children are symmetrically balanced by late evening fare in which action movies and narratives of combat and confrontation play a central role.

It becomes clear that the reassertion of childish values for the benefit of adults, does not necessarily mean making space for actual children. Indeed an envy of childhood and the expansion of childishness into adult media in the ways I have described, could either lead to the exclusion of children themselves or to the enforced precocity described by Marsha Kinder. Nevertheless, on British television there have been important countervailing tendencies at work, which I shall now go on to discuss.

Children's Participation

In the contradictory way in which these things develop, the increasing role that ordinary children have played in television programmes has been part of a new willingness to take children on their own terms — a tendency which stands in balance with the overheated fantasies of the narratives discussed above. However powerful those narratives have become, there has remained, at least on British television, a very earthy thread of realism. Some long-running programmes have been highly successful in addressing children in a way that takes them seriously without pandering to adult prejudice or adult fantasy. Maire Messenger Davies quotes the schoolgirl who wrote to the *Radio Times* about adults who watch one episode of a challenging series like *Grange Hill* then launch into a damning critique. 'I'm not saying that adults aren't allowed to watch our programmes, but it was written for us, the children at schools like

Grange Hill, who really understand what they're like' (Messenger Davies, 1989, p. 56).

Over the years, the regulated environment of British television has ensured a space for children's voices where they are freed from the responsibility of being childish for the benefit of adults. This is a different kind of 'hole in the reality barrier'. From *Grange Hill* (1978–) to Channel 4's *Look Who's Talking* (1994 — a season of programmes broadcast in adult television hours but from the perspective of children), a remarkably grounded view of childhood has been part of our television fare. These programmes address both adults and children in terms that engage with children's experience of everyday life.

Watching the *Look Who's Talking* season, one becomes aware of the *burden* of childishness, the weight of adult fantasies about childhood as they are born by actual children. In *Child's Eye*, which launched the season, a group of children in their early teens set out to put together a set of proposals from children around the United Kingdom to present to the Prime Minister in Downing Street and to 'enlighten adults on the fact that children do have valid opinions'. Their agenda involved tackling difficult political issues head on. Topics investigated included the sectarian divide in Northern Ireland, homelessness, the core curriculum, racist attacks and the law around divorce. These are all issues which affect children, but from which children's voices are effectively excluded. As the children in the programme interviewed those in positions of power, their most visible problem was their difficulty in being taken seriously. Nevertheless, discussions on such issues as whether to interview the racist British National Party and the implications of broadcasting such an interview, conveyed the dilemmas as cogently as any adult debate. Unlike a 'paedocracy' which draws on adult fantasy of childishness, this direct address by and on behalf of children cuts through adult illusions. Rather than bypassing issues of gender, race and class, as John Hartley claimed the 'paedocratic regime' was designed to do, it faces them head on.

David Buckingham has written on the impossibility of children's programmes, as they must always be made by adults (Bazalgette and Buckingham, 1995). Clearly this is true, but children have shared with other disempowered groups the advantages of cheap new technology which puts film-making in their own hands, even if the final editorial control remains with adult producers and broadcasters. The producers of BBC2's *Children's Video Diaries* admitted their surprise at the power of some of the material produced by their young diarists, the directness of emotion and expression and the unexpectedness of the shift in perspective to a child's point of view ('Watching ourselves: Real people on television.' Conference organized by BFI TV and Projects Unit, 13 May 1994). Diarists have included the girl who used the opportunity of making a television film to telephone her estranged father, repeatedly and vainly asking him to visit, and the boy whose mother was not allowing him to leave the house, keeping him under close supervision following his conviction for stealing. In this short film, he relayed his thoughts, gave his mother the opportunity to speak to the camera, and put viewers in his position as he argued with her and found ways to cope with his situation.

Anna Home, Head of BBC Children's Programmes, who also chairs the European Broadcasting Union's working party for children and young people, warned broadcasters at the 1995 World Summit for Television and Children in Melbourne 'that children's programmes have a precarious position in schedules around the world'. Her proposed charter, intended as minimum guidelines for broadcasters says:

- Children should have programmes of high quality which are made specifically for them, and which do not exploit them. These programmes, in addition to entertaining, should allow children to develop physically, mentally and socially to their fullest potential.
- Children should hear, see and express themselves, their culture, their languages and their life experiences, through television programmes which affirm their sense of self, community and place.
- Children's programmes should promote an awareness and appreciation of other cultures in parallel with the child's own cultural background.
- Children's programmes should be wide ranging in genre and content, but should not include gratuitous scenes of violence and sex.
- Children's programmes should be aired in regular slots at times when children are available to view and/or distributed via other widely accessible media or technologies.
- Sufficient funds must be made available to make these programmes to the highest possible standards.
- Governments, production, distribution and funding organisations should recognise both the importance and vulnerability of indigenous children's television and take steps to support and protect it. (BBC Press Release, 9 June 1995)

Both adults and children need narratives of fantasy, but as I have tried to demonstrate, the biggest threat to children's media has come from adult fantasies of child*hood*. Fears of demonized children latched into an electronic and fiercely consumerist future are matched by the attraction of childish, irresponsible pleasures which fit well with a market oriented environment. My argument is that the trap of recurring childish*ness* is only escaped by attention to actual child*ren*. Despite the pressures following the commercialization of British television, there has remained a significant commitment to take children seriously. The 1990s have seen an unprecedented number of spaces where those who have been children and have, however precariously, achieved adulthood, momentarily stand aside for those who are children and are striving for some form of workable presence in the world in which they find themselves. As Anna Home argues, such spaces are precious and must be protected. *That* sort of hole in the reality barrier might allow for visions of a less paranoid future.

References

BARKER, M. (ed.) (1994) *The Video Nasties*, Pluto.

BAZALGETTE, C. and BUCKINGHAM, D. (eds) (1995) *In Front of the Children: Screen Entertainment and Young Audiences*, London, BFI.

BERENS, J. (1995) 'Forward forward punch kick', *Independent Magazine*, 18 February.

BOSELEY, S. (1995) '"Hard drug" fear for computer children', *Guardian*, 13 March.

BROWN, A. (1994) 'Doomed!' *Independent*, 6 September, p. 23.

BUCKINGHAM, D. (1996) *Moving Images: Understanding Children's Emotional Response to Television*, Manchester, Manchester University Press.

DAVIS, E. (1994) 'Half Japanese: Power Rangers corrupt absolutely!' *The Voice*, 21 June.

DUGDALE, J. (1994) *Media Guardian*, 3 October, pp. 14–15.

FRY, A. (1994) 'Kids R Us', *Broadcast*, 2 December.

HARTLEY, J. (1987) 'Invisible fictions, television audiences, paedocracy, pleasure', *Textual Practice*, **1**, 2.

KARACS, I. (1994) 'Something died with Silje', *Independent*, 21 October, p. 21.

KINDER, M. (1995) 'Home alone in the nineties: Generational war and transgenerational address in American movies, television and presidential politics', in BAZALGETTE, C. and BUCKINGHAM, D. (eds) *In Front of the Children: Screen Entertainment and Young Audiences*, London, BFI, p. 80.

KLEIN, M. (1946/1986) 'Notes on some schizoid mechanisms', in MITCHELL, J. (ed.) *The Selected Melanie Klein*, Harmondsworth Peregrine.

MESSENGER DAVIES, M. (1989) *Television is Good for your Kids*, London, Hilary Shipman.

MESSENGER DAVIES (1995) 'Babes "n" the hood: Pre-school television and its audiences in the United States and Britain', in BAZALGETTE, C. and BUCKINGHAM, D. (eds) *In Front of the Children: Screen Entertainment and Young Audiences*, London, BFI.

MITCHELL, J. (ed.) (1986) *The Selected Melanie Klein*, Peregrine.

NEVILLE, R. (1971) *Playpower*, London, Paladin.

NOBLE, G. (1975) *Children in Front of the Small Screen*, London, Constable.

POSTMAN, N. (1983) *The Disappearance of Childhood*, London, W.H. Allen.

ROFFEY, M. (1995) 'Wanted: A superhero in a store near you', *Independent*, 15 July.

SKIRROW, G. (1986) 'Hellivision: An analysis of video games', in MACCABE, C. (ed.) *High Theory/Low Culture: Analysis of Popular Television and Film*, Manchester, Manchester University Press.

STRINATI, D. and WAGG, S. (eds) (1992) *Come On Down? Popular Media Culture in Post-war Britain*, London, Routledge.

TASKER, Y. (1993) *Spectacular Bodies: Gender, Genre and the Action Cinema*, London, Routledge.

THOMAS, M. (1993) *Every Mother's Nightmare: The Killing of James Bulger*, London, Pan Books.

TRACEY, M. and MORRISON, D. (1979) *Whitehouse*, Basingstoke, Macmillan.

URWIN, C. (1995) 'Turtle Power: Illusion and imagination in children's play', in BAZALGETTE, C. and BUCKINGHAM, D. (eds) *In Front of the Children: Screen Entertainment and Young Audiences*, London, Hilary Shipman.

WAGG, S. (1992) 'One I made earlier: Media, popular culture and the politics of childhood', in STRINATI, D. and WAGG, S. (eds) *Come On Down?: Popular Media Culture in Post-war Britain*, London, Routledge.

WALVIN, J. (1982) *A Child's World: A Social History of English Childhood 1800–1914*, London, Pelican.

11   Thatcher's Working Children: Contemporary Issues of Child Labour

Michael Lavalette

Many a 14 year old, set to work as a builder's apprentice, an electrician's mate or a stable hand, will learn more than he could ever at school, while acquiring independence, responsibility and self respect. If the pay were sufficiently low, and children were willing to work for quite paltry sums, there would be no lack of employers ready to offer it. (Professor Roger Scruton, The *Guardian*, 13 February 1990)

You . . . say that children always will work. The answer is yes, if the legislation permits it. You continued by saying it gives them a sense of responsibility. There are many ways of achieving a sense of responsibility — working harder at school, gaining better exam results, learning new sports. You say it gives them an income. The amount they earn is so trivial can you honestly regard that as a right and proper reason for children going out to work? . . . Do you not honestly feel that the mass of the time . . . children spend earning money would not better be spent in school. (Emma Nicholson, at the time Conservative MP, criticizing the Low Pay Unit for supporting some limited forms of child labour; House of Commons Employment Committee, May 1991)

There is nothing wrong with children taking on part time jobs so as to earn some pocket money, providing that it is done legally. (Labour MP Anne Clwyd, 1995, p. 3)

Introduction

As Wagg and Pilcher note in the introduction to this volume, there is a contradiction which runs through Conservatism's attitude towards children between the values of 'social conservatism' and neo-liberalism. This contradiction is especially apparent on the issue of child labour as is revealed in the quotations from Emma Nicholson and Roger Scruton. On the one hand, neo-liberals like Scruton have an overarching commitment to the market and believe

any government interference with market mechanisms can produce disequilib-
rium and inefficiencies. The government, therefore, should not introduce bar-
riers which may prevent employers from utilizing whatever types and forms
of labour they wish to engage. Markets should determine the price of labour
and the conditions of work on offer: providing there are people willing to be
employed in such circumstances then politicians should keep well away. In
this interpretation, children, like other groups of marginal workers, should be
free to enter the labour market and undertake whatever types of work they
find available to them. As Scruton acknowledges, the jobs may be unskilled
and poorly paid, but they would, in his view, nevertheless bring moral responsibility and independence.

On the other hand, there is the 'child protectionist' argument of Emma
Nicholson and other One Nation Tories. Here, children are portrayed as vulnerable creatures who must be protected from the adult world and all that is
associated with it. To produce a socially, politically and economically mature
nation it is important that certain welfare needs are met and, in particular,
future generations of citizens are suitably nurtured. Thus children should pursue specifically children's activities such as schooling and appropriate leisure
and recreational activities, their best interests should be guarded by trained
professionals, like teachers and child-care workers, and they should gradually
be introduced and helped into the adult world during an appropriate period of
'transition'. For One Nation Tories like Nicholson (notwithstanding her recent
defection to the Liberal Democrats), work and labour are activities that are performed by adults and definitely not children.

Neither of these positions is new. Historically, the debate over the
regulation of child labour has been dominated by proponents of both views:
laissez-faire capitalists, defending the morally invigorating experience of work,
argued against factory legislation or attempts to control the activities of chim-
ney sweepers; in contrast, philanthropists like Lord Shaftesbury, Richard Oastler
and Edith Hogg were in favour of restricting children's work activities and following strategies which instead emphasized 'family values', education and
adequate skill training for youth (Lavalette, 1994). In essence, the question of
child labour creates a conflict between two pillars of bourgeois society: the
(economic) importance of work and labour; and the (ideological) centrality of
family values, within which the concept of childhood remains crucial.

The tension between these competing perspectives has been reflected in
the policy debate over the last few years. In the face of increasing evidence
that child labour is a significant social problem in modern Britain (Pond and
Searle, 1991; Lavalette, McKechnie and Hobbs, 1991; Lavalette, Hobbs, Lindsay
and McKechnie, 1995) and a developing European legislative programme to
restrict the type of work and associated employment conditions open to children, government ministers have attempted to play down the issue suggesting that the work undertaken by children is 'light', harmless and performed
merely to obtain a little extra pocket money. Further, they suggest the legislative framework in Britain provides an adequate regulatory mechanism to ensure

children are protected from any exploitative labour (cf. European Standing Committee B, 1993; Department of Employment, 1992).

The government case, therefore, is that children in Britain may 'work' but they do so at appropriate tasks, in regulated conditions and for suitable wage rates. These are appropriate children's activities and are qualitatively different from forms of 'child labour' which may occur in the Newly Industrializing Countries (NICs) and Underdeveloped Countries (UDCs), over which we have little control.

The Labour Party (Clwyd, 1994, 1995) and the campaigning pressure group the Low Pay Network (Pond and Searle, 1991) reject this complacency. They argue that while there are unscrupulous employers exploiting children at work, the major problem is that the legislative framework in Britain is badly outdated and has led to confusion on the part of employers, parents and children over what work children should perform. But, for these groups, the problem can easily be solved by updating the legislative programme in line with European regulations. This achieved, it will be possible to focus on the real problem of child labour, that which takes place in the NICs and is apparently growing as a result of global economic pressures. Thus the quotation from Clwyd at the start of the chapter would seem to represent a halfway house between the two extremes of 'always' and 'never'. Yet the consequence of this approach is that the debate becomes narrowly confined to a 'descriptive numbers game'. The assumption is that we can distinguish 'good' jobs from 'bad' jobs, 'work' from 'labour' and the debate is restricted to allocating the 'acceptable/unacceptable' label to differing tasks. Yet apart from our *common-sense* interpretations of what tasks are suitable 'children's jobs', how do we *know* what is good and what is not?

It will be argued in this chapter that each of these premises is mistaken. In the first section, it will be suggested that the policy-driven distinction between 'child work' and 'child labour' cannot be sustained in practice. When children sell their labour as a commodity, they are exploited. However, any such recognition has wider implications than the employment of children: it questions the entire wage labour/capital relationship. It is this feature that makes child employment such a 'political' issue, distinct from other child welfare projects (like child immunization, for example, which has much wider political support), and causes particular problems for the 'reforming' project of Clwyd, the Low Pay Network or, internationally, the International Labour Office or Anti-Slavery International. The second section will offer an explanation of the causes of child labour, rejecting monocausal perspectives which identify poverty and economic underdevelopment as the sole cause of child labour and instead suggesting that what is important is the interaction of economic phenomena with socio-political and ideological factors which historically shape the types of jobs children do. Section three looks at globalization and reviews the types of jobs children do throughout the world. Section four offers a more specific case study of child labour in Britain. Finally, section five looks at the various campaigns against child labour and assesses their likely success.

What is Child Labour?

'Child labour' is a particularly emotive term. In Britain, it conjures up images of the worst excesses of the Industrial Revolution, events which led E.P. Thompson (1968) to write that: 'the exploitation of little children . . . was one of the most shameful events in our history' (p. 384). For whig historians, or those portrayed as 'optimists' regarding the outcome of social processes instigated by the Industrial Revolution, the plight of such child workers produced a progressive legislative programme, instigated by the British political establishment which recognized that child labour was immoral and grossly exploitative (Pinchbeck, 1969; Pinchbeck and Hewitt, 1969, 1973; Fraser, 1984). For these writers, child employment was a feature of pre-capitalist, or certainly pre-industrial, society which continued during the early days of the Industrial Revolution. For Pinchbeck (1969), however, the visibility of child labour in this period provoked government action. Gradually, children were prohibited from climbing chimneys, going down mine shafts and working in factories and, with the development of the education system, children increasingly spent most of their days within a 'healthy learning environment', away from the evils of exploitative labouring activities. Hence, they were prohibited from performing work tasks which were regarded as harmful and were expected to attend school and expend their energies on gaining an education. Child labour, therefore, was no longer viewed as a social problem (Lavalette, 1994). Of course, children continued to undertake work tasks but from the turn of the twentieth century they have been identified with a particular type of employment, part-time 'out of school' work, performed before or after school, at weekends or during school holidays. These jobs are not normally identified as exploitative child labour but as 'light work tasks', particularly suitable for children. Thus they are more commonly perceived to be invigorating and healthy pastimes which children carry out for a little extra pocket money. Performing these jobs, it is thought, shows ingenuity on the child's part and allows them some first-hand experience of the world of work. As Michael Forsyth (1989) said (while he was UK Employment Minister):

> . . . our traditions . . . [are that] children must attend school until they reach the minimum school leaving age. They cannot take on permanent full time jobs before then . . . But school years should help young people prepare for working life . . . That is why, in this country, most older children take part in limited employment outside school hours. (*The Glasgow Herald*, 3 November 1989)

Alternatively, 'child labour' may be used to refer to a set of practices which today occur in the Newly Industrializing Countries (NICs) or Underdeveloped Countries (UDCs). Thus Mendelievich (1979) claims: 'We may say that child labour persists in inverse relation to the degree of economic advancement of a society, country or region' (p. 4). For developmentalist writers, the only hope given to children in these countries is to wait for the inevitable economic and social advance that will free them from their burden.

Yet the transposition of child labour to the past or to distant shores is problematic for a number of reasons. First, within the advanced capitalist societies, it reifies the types of jobs performed by children, treating them as idyllic and harmless *work activities*: not '*labour*'. Secondly, and as a result, it ignores the *effects* that this work may have on children, their education and those around them (Lavalette, *et al.*, 1991). Thirdly, it treats 'child labour' as an aberration from the norm, that is, not as part of a 'normal childhood' but as an activity performed by a minority of children. Hence it is viewed as a peculiarity which has little to do with the economic, social and political structures and forces of advanced capitalist societies: it is not a consequence of the development of capitalist social relations but of the reverse, their underdevelopment. Fourthly, within the NICs and UDCs, child labour is treated as an outcome of local cultural traditions or specific national problems which can then be abstracted from global socio-economic processes. As a consequence it can be identified as 'a problem not of our making'. Finally, the imagery of child labour in the NICs and UDCs is used to undermine debate over child labour in Britain. In tones that mirror much of the poverty debate (Novak, 1995), real (or absolute) child labour is assumed to occur in the cities and towns of the Asian sub-continent, in Latin America or in Africa. In this perception, the jobs performed by children in Britain are not part of the same problem: there is no such thing as relatively exploited child labour. While we may expect government ministers to espouse this position it has also coloured the argument of the critics of child employment practices. For example Fyfe (1985, 1989) has tried to draw a distinction between 'obvious' labouring tasks which children in Britain still, on occasions, perform, like working in a factory, which he terms 'child labour' and part-time out of school jobs, like milk and newspaper delivery, which he refers to as 'child work'. A similar approach is adopted by Anti-Slavery International who try to identify three categories: child slavery, child labour and child work, the distinction based on how severe we think the exploitation of the child is (Anti-Slavery International, 1995). Meanwhile, Grootaert and Kanbur (1995) argue that the key determinant of identifying something as child labour is:

> whether the arrangement is 'exploitative'. In the extreme, it can take the form of bonded labour, quasi-slavery, or a feudal relationship . . . It can also be considered exploitative when a child starts full-time work at too early an age, or works too many hours, or when the work imposes excessive physical, social and/or psychological strains. (p. 188)

But here the debate merely moves to one where the focus becomes based around a notion of 'relative exploitation', defined not in terms of the extraction of surplus labour (Wright, 1979) but according to how bad we think the work may be on psycho-social development. Further, this approach conflates activities and social experiences which are clearly different (for example, wage labour and slavery) while assuming differences exist in similar wage-labouring activities because they occur in different global locations. To emphasize the point, it is perhaps worth asking if commentators, academics and politicians would make such claims if the workers were women or migrants and not children?

In the existing literature, the major concern has been to establish a policy-directed operational definition of child work to the neglect of an analytical definition of what child labour is and where it fits within capitalist social relations. Further, the work/labour distinction is based on little research material, but reflects political value judgments about how we treat our children and where the real problem of child labour lies. In Britain, the consequence has been to play the game on the government's terrain: the argument becomes a narrow one of identifying and debating which jobs are 'good' (whatever that means) and which jobs are not. Now, clearly some jobs and some conditions of employment are better than others. This is true whether we are discussing child workers, women workers or male workers and, further, it is important that state policy remains in place and is strengthened to protect the employment and working conditions of all employees. But the focus on listing 'good' jobs or 'appropriate hours' tends to mean that the exploitative nature of all wage labour is lost. The point, therefore, is that child workers sell their labour power to the advantage of their employer, they do not own or control the production process within which they work and they are involved, either directly or indirectly, in the general process of surplus value extraction, as it is shaped by the modern, complex division of labour.

This conclusion can be applied to child workers in the carpet industry in Morocco (Anti-Slavery Society, 1978) or India (Guirajani, 1994), brick workers in Colombia (Salazar, 1988), construction workers in Nigeria (Ukpabi, 1979), service sector workers in Indonesia (Socrato, 1979), children working in the tourism and travel industries (Black, 1995), telesale operators in Manchester (Edwards, 1995) and child factory workers in present day Thailand (Prachankhadee, Nelayothin, Intrasukporn and Montawan, 1979) or Preston (*Lancashire Evening Post*, 1994). But it should also apply to child workers in the service sector of the advanced economies delivering newspapers and milk. To separate these last two tasks as different in kind would be to idealize both the work and the employers' motivations, assuming, ultimately, that the employers are doing it for the good health, well-being and general development of the children and not for their own economic needs or requirements. Any distinction between 'work' and 'labour' is unsustainable (Lavalette, 1994). Our starting point should be that child labour is a particular form of marginal 'poor work' (Brown and Scase, 1991) within capitalist society.

What Causes Child Labour?

The second issue to address is: What causes child labour? Most interpretations of child labour in Britain draw heavily on the substantial literature which focuses on the NICs and UDCs. Writings on these regions are substantial and often at an advanced theoretical level (Rodgers and Standing, 1981; Bequele and Boyden, 1988a). In this literature, local political, cultural, ideological and social aspects are often stressed to account for the *particularity* of child labour in various societies. However, for the majority of writers the core factor is an economic one: the restrictions and poverty which families find themselves facing, force them to utilize all their various sources of labour power, including their children. This is occasionally combined with a perspective which suggests that local employers themselves are constrained by the circumstances in which they operate: their subordinate position, with regard to multinational capital, forces small local employers to employ children if they are to compete with more efficient units of capital (Mehata, Prabhu and Mistry, 1985).

These assumptions have informed many of the recent writings on child labour in Europe (MacLennan *et al.*, 1985; Fyfe 1989; Valcarenghi, 1981). However, when applied to the 'advanced' economies, much of the emphasis on social, cultural and ideological factors is lifted. Instead, child labour is reduced to a purely economic category and can be assessed by adopting a simplistic economic axis. High unemployment and low wages, it is suggested, force families to utilize the labour of their children to supplement the family income. Fyfe (1989), for example, suggests that, 'where parents are unemployed or on low incomes there may be added incentive for their children to work' (pp. 42–3) and Forrester (1979), writing about Birmingham, has claimed that 'economic decline in the Midlands has led to a massive increase in child employment . . . The pressure on living standards and unemployment in the home has forced large numbers of children to take part-time jobs' (p. 259). The essential cause of child labour, therefore, is poverty.

Alternatively, some writers have utilized the economic axis to suggest that, in 'advanced' economies, children will exist as an example of a 'reserve army of labour'. Children, it is suggested, have been marginalized in the production process and will only be drawn into employment when there is an excessive demand for labour. Equally, they will be among the first to be expelled when the market becomes overstocked. Moorehead (1987) suggests that this is the case. She has claimed that, in Glasgow, 'high local unemployment, the fact that small businesses are trying to cut costs and do without part time help and the introduction of . . . Government . . . Training Schemes have driven most young people out of work' (1987, p. 47). Here the essential cause of child labour is not poverty but rapid economic expansion.

Elsewhere I have argued that the existing evidence supports neither of these monocausal explanations for the continuing existence of child labour and that they must be rejected (Lavalette, 1994). Rather, to comprehend fully the present form of child labour in different societies it is necessary to look at the historical interaction of economic factors with an array of political, ideological, cultural and social features. Thus, in trying to understand and determine the social position of the child labourer, we must recognize that the child enters the labour market from a disadvantaged position within the 'age hierarchy', a socially constructed phenomenon: 'a system of seniority in which those in junior positions are unable to achieve full social status in their own right' (Elson, 1982, p. 491). The ideological construction of childhood and the age hierarchy is based on a number of assumptions. Among the most important are that children are:

1 Incapable of supporting themselves and must be protected by individuals further advanced in the age hierarchy.
2 Members of a family unit one of whose members will be earning a 'family wage' capable of supporting the entire family.
3 Primarily involved in social activities deemed suitable for children, such as gaining an education.
4 Protected by state legislation and government agencies from abuse, oppression and exploitation, including protection from harmful labour activities.

It is worth emphasizing that these are ideological assumptions and do not necessarily match the reality of children's lives.

Within Britain, the age hierarchy became more fully embedded in capitalist social relations towards the end of the nineteenth century with the growth of the 'interventionist state' (Hall, 1984), the removal of children from the world of adult work (Cunningham, 1990) and the growth of the education system (Simon, 1960). The result, as we noted, was not to stop children working but to restructure their labour market activities in the sphere of 'out of school' work. The consequence is that, today, the majority of children work at jobs which are commonly viewed as 'children's'. They are jobs which require little training and hence are assumed to be particularly suitable activities for them to perform. Further, because they are assumed to be dependent on adults, their jobs tend to be poorly paid with their wages often characterized as a form of 'pocket money'. These features are mutually reinforcing with the result that even when children are employed in other sectors of the economy — performing illegitimate 'adult' jobs — their inferior position within the age hierarchy will affect their pay and conditions of employment. Thus, the labour activities of children are devalued and cheapened. This has little to do with the actual economic activities performed by children, but instead reflects social phenomena and assumptions.

Thus when looking at the issue of child labour it is crucial to focus on the interaction of economic features with the full array of ideological, cultural and socio-political factors in society and the contradictions created by such interaction. In particular, such complexities produce differing interpretations of both what the 'problem' is and how it should be 'solved'. With regard to child labour, for example, this means that the conflicting perspectives of Nicholson, Clwyd and Scruton are not peculiar to Britain, but shape the dominant thinking of politicians and state officials in most nation states.

Globalization and Child Labour

Social theory and the social sciences have, over the last decade, increasingly focused on changes to the international capitalist economy and its consequences for both national state structures, institutions and individuals in different countries (see, for example, United Nations Research Institute for Social Development (UNRISD), 1995). Understanding these complex processes requires recognition of 'structural' changes and their interaction with political ideals and actions which attempt to 'control' or coordinate these changes. This means we must be aware of two competing, and, at times, apparently contradictory, structural pressures. First, pressures brought by the operation of the international capitalist economic system — the increasing integration of which has brought huge pressures on national economies to 'compete' and encourage large units of capital to locate within their borders. Secondly, however, despite the economic pressures associated with globalization, the nation state remains crucially important within the capitalist system (Harman, 1991, 1993): the structural requirements of the global age clearly do not simply dictate the forms and practices of local governments and states. There is, therefore, room for 'local' solutions (national and sub-national) to the problems of the modern age: local populations, governments and organizations are more than mere pawns of international capital. Thus, what is important is the outcome of the interaction of both the 'global' and the 'local' (Giddens, 1991).

As well as these structural changes, we need to acknowledge the role of individual and collective 'agency' in shaping responses to these changes (Callinicos, 1987b). Such responses can come from a range of institutions and/or social forces. Thus it may be national or international agencies keen to ensure that the consequences of the socio-economic structural changes do not threaten the process of surplus value extraction, or it may be a response from sections of society keen to resist the changes and their social consequences (the French 'winter of discontent', 1995–96 could be one such example). The question we must address, however, is how has the interaction of 'structure' and 'agency' affected child workers in differing global locations? We will start to address this issue by reviewing the evidence of the extent and form of child labour in the NICs before looking at Europe and North America.

The Case of the NICs

The process of capitalist development in the NICs over the last forty years has not prevented very high levels of unemployment and under-employment. This was because within the various NICs, industrialization failed to involve the entire (potential) labour force. Instead, industrialization tended to remain limited to various 'enclaves'. These societies became marked, therefore, by the process of uneven and combined development, containing both 'advanced' and 'backward' features. But as Callinicos (1987a) has noted:

The failure of industrialisation to involve the entire workforce in wage labour has its most important effects on the urban areas, with the creation of vast pools of 'marginals', unemployed or under-employed, scraping an existence thanks to the handouts from wage earning relatives, forms of petty capitalism and crime. (p. 108)

To this list can be added irregular or marginal employment or employment in small unregulated workplaces, where there is little concern for such legal niceties as employment regulations. Child labour fits into this picture as one form of marginal activity performed to meet, or partially to meet, the material needs of the child or his/her family.

The global economic crises of the last twenty years has brought increasing social problems to working-class families throughout the globe, and working children in particular (UNRISD, 1995). These problems have been exacerbated by the dominance of the neo-liberal economic paradigm within the international finance institutions (IFIs), the World Bank and International Monetary Fund (IMF). From the early 1980s 'stabilization and structural adjustment programmes' (SSAPs) have become preconditions for any help given to individual states with balance of payment or debt problems. The consequences, as the UNRISD (1995) report 'State of Disarray' notes, have been that:

In almost all cases, adjustment required deflationary policies and cutbacks in welfare services, which resulted in hardship for the poor . . . [as a consequence] . . . the societies of the third world have . . . become more highly polarised: a few people have been able to take advantage of the new market opportunities, but the mass of the poor are worse off. (pp. 10–11)

In these circumstances, Boyd (1994) has argued:

Child labour is not just limited to the poor countries of the world, it is rather a part of the life of poor sectors in all societies . . . And, it is my view, that the global economic context for this phenomenon, [with child workers] as a highly vulnerable, marginalised sector of the labouring poor . . . will be exacerbated in the coming years. (p. 154)

The last two decades have witnessed a growth in child labour research, reflecting concern that it is an escalating problem (Mendelievich, 1979; Challis and Elliman, 1979; Rodgers and Standing, 1981; Bequele and Boyden, 1988a). Boyd (1994) quotes international labour office figures which estimate that at least one in four children between the ages of 10 and 14 works in the Third World. As she notes:

Children constitute about 18 per cent of Brazil's workforce. An estimated 12 million children work in Nigeria. But the highest number of child workers is to be found in the countries of Asia. India has an estimated 44 million working children; Pakistan's estimates range from 7.5 million to 10 million child labourers. In Indonesia, conservative estimates claim that almost 3 million children work between the ages of 10 and 14 years. (1994, p. 155)

These figures emphasize the scale of the problem of child labour internationally, but we should be aware of two things. First, these figures are only the tip of the iceberg, since they represent the 'official' figures given to the ILO by national governments. If illegal and unreported instances of child labour were added the figures would increase substantially. Second, the figures do not reveal the full plight of child workers who are very often employed in harsh and hazardous employment (Bequele and Myers, 1995) in the most appalling conditions (Bequele and Boyden, 1988a), for little financial return (Challis and Elliman, 1979).

Child labourers can be found in all societies performing a wide range of tasks. Prachankhadee *et al.* (1979) described the plight of child factory workers in Thailand (an economic 'success' story of the 1980s and 1990s). The children are employed in the glass, cold storage and canned food industries. Here, the conditions of employment are unregulated and very poor; tasks are repetitive, hours long and, in a throw back to the 'prentice houses common in Britain during the early Industrial Revolution, many of the children live at the factory where they work. As is the norm, as far as child employment is concerned, the children's pay is poor, even in relative terms. In India, Nangia (1986) found children working in agriculture, the service sector and in manufacturing and processing. They were employed as furniture makers, book binders, motor mechanics, tyre inflators, construction labourers, brick kiln workers, stone breakers, shoe blacks, vendors, newspaper hawkers and rag pickers. Similar findings are available in the work of Sengupta (1975) and Mehta *et al.* (1985). Burra (1987), in a more focused study, looks at child workers in India's lock industry, where he estimates that children represent between 7,000 and 10,000 employees out of a total workforce of approximately 80,000. Children are employed throughout the production process on hand presses, undertaking electrical plating and performing the various finishing trades such as polishing, spray painting and packaging. The hours are long, the work is dangerous, and it remains very badly paid.

Guirajani (1994) focuses on what she considers to be the biggest employer of children in the manufacturing sector in India: the carpet industry. This is an industry which produces almost exclusively for the export market and is firmly tied to global capitalism. In 1991, India faced severe debt and inflationary problems as the world crisis took hold. The result was a programme of 'stabilization and structural adjustment' whose consequences were: compression of government industrial spending programmes, which increased unemployment; and cuts in government welfare and anti-poverty measures. These measures, says Guirajani (1994), exacerbated the poverty situation faced by many families which encouraged:

Children to drop out of school and enter the labour market, depressing the wage rates and reducing the supply price of child labour . . . [The conclusion is that] child labour is no relic from the pre-capitalist days, and may in fact grow, as the link of the poor economies with the world capitalist system grows. (pp. 195–6)

A similar pattern exists in Africa and Latin America. Abdalla (1988) undertook a survey of training workshops in Egypt's leather industry and found only one workshop where children were not being employed. The children were generally employed in monotonous tasks in the leather preparation side; tasks, however, which were 'essential to the production process' (Abdalla, 1988, p. 33). Ukpabi (1979) notes the role of children in Nigeria's construction industry, while Verlet (1994) and Ravololononga and Schlemmer (1994) note the effects of both globalization and adjustment programmes on, respectively, Ghana and Madagascar. For Verlet (1994), a decade of structural adjustment programmes has had clear and negative effects on the urban working class: higher levels of unemployment, poverty and deregulation of the labour market. As a consequence of all these changes there has been an increase in child labour.

A number of studies have looked at Latin America. Bensusan (1979), in a study of child workers in Mexico, noted that most children were likely to be employed by smaller businesses. He notes that: 'The conditions of extreme poverty in which many children live make it necessary for them to carry out various kinds of jobs from about the age of 5 or 6' (1979, p. 104). Guillen-Marroquin (1988) undertook a study of children employed in the gold extraction industry in Peru, where the seasonal nature of the job was thought particularly suitable to children who could combine it with some form of schooling. Salazar (1988) looked at the extent of child labour in Colombia. Child labour (for children under 14) was made illegal there in 1982, but nevertheless 'child labour is common . . . mainly because of widespread poverty' (Salazar, 1988, p. 54). All that has happened, he suggests, is that it has been forced underground: 'even though child labour is widespread . . . there is a general tendency to conceal it since . . . [it] was prohibited by law' (Salazar, 1988, p. 49). Colombia is also the focus for Sastre and Zarama (1994) who look at child miners in the charcoal industry. They, too, note that the problem of child labour appears to be increasing throughout Latin America despite legislation aimed at curtailing the practice.

Global economic pressures, SSAPs and economic crises have clearly had an impact on working-class families throughout the NICs, with child workers bearing some of the consequences. The result is often to instigate a 'cycle of poverty', with poor working-class families forced to send their children out to work instead of attending school. As a result, the children from these families obtain an inadequate education and training and so become permanently located in the poorly paid, unskilled and less secure sectors of the economy, where, as they get older, their poverty and insecurity will force them to send their children out to work (Mendelievich, 1979). As a consequence, there is some evidence of a growing divide between the IMF and World Bank over the social consequences of SSAPs. According to Deacon (1995), the IMF remain firmly wedded to the neo-liberal position but the World Bank may be moving towards a position which supports minimal welfare provision (including some restrictions on child labour) and a focus on education and training as the way for NICs to promote and sustain long-term growth. Aspects of the Nicholson/ Scruton dichotomy, therefore, seem to be replicated within the IFIs.

The plight of child workers throughout the NICs is stark. This is often portrayed as a consequence of their cultural and political backwardness (Mendelievich, 1979), but that is too simplistic. Local capital and states are often prepared to follow the most vicious social and public policies to exploit, intimidate and control their populations. Such policies meet their own immediate short-term interests, but they also, directly or indirectly, match the interests of multinational capital. In the area of child labour, the influence of the IFIs and globalizing economic pressures have exacerbated the position of child workers. In this sense, the problem of child labour in the NICs is clearly shaped by the operations of multinational capital and should not be portrayed as a manifestation of Third World 'peculiarism': in a very real sense it is a problem of 'our' (that is, British, American, European, etc., capital's) making.

There is also increasing evidence that some multinationals are benefiting from the exploitation of child labour in the NICs in a more direct sense. The Granada television programme *World in Action* (8 January 1996) revealed the case of the Siccome factory in Morocco. Here, they claimed girls as young as 10 worked up to 55 hours a week for as little as 20 pence an hour. They worked in a textile factory performing tasks which had been subcontracted from the Northern Irish company Desmond's, who in turn were supplying the goods to Marks and Spencer. Similarly, the extensive use of child labour in the Indian and Pakistani carpet industry produces goods which are sold extensively throughout Britain and Europe (*New Internationalist*, 1995, p. 19). In China, there is extensive use of young workers in the toy production industry where goods are made for, among others, Fisher-Price and Chicco (ETUYM, 1994). Similarly, the tea and coffee picking industry is renowned for poor pay and working conditions and the extensive use of child labour (ETUYM, 1994). The employment of children in the NICs, therefore, is a central problem within modern, international capitalism of which we are all a part.

Europe and North America

In general terms, recent studies of child labour in Europe and North America seem to report the growth of child labour exploitation. However, it is not clear whether this growth is real and that child employment is spreading, or whether children have worked in large numbers throughout the history of capitalism and, therefore, what we are witnessing is simply renewed interest in the issues surrounding children and work. In Europe, much of the focus on child employment has been on the 'peripheral' regions like Greece (Papaflessa, 1979), Spain (Searight, 1980) and southern Italy (Valcarenghi, 1981). Searight (1980) notes the range of work activities performed by children throughout Spain. She claims, children still work in the metal industry, in textiles and in the shoe industry. Extensive subcontracting means that children are employed by 'small groups outside the factory . . . the factory owner simply pays for work produced; he has no responsibility for social security, health and safety precautions, hours of work or wages' (Searight, 1980, p. 19). Children were also identified as working in a range of service jobs: in hotels, bars, cafes and small shops.

Mendelievich (1979), Valcarenghi (1981) and Goddard (1995) have all looked at the position of child workers in Italy. Mendelievich (1979) found children working in agriculture, small industry and, more generally, throughout the service sector. Valcarenghi (1981) suggests that children's labour is extensively used throughout Italy, not just in the poor south, and that the 'problem is becoming more serious' (p. 10). She lists children as working in the glass grinding industry, in the manufacture of television components, in button and lace factories, and throughout the selling and service sector. She notes that:

> Children . . . are hardly ever employed in large modern industries. The complicated technological machinery and trade union presence in such enterprises act as deterrent to employers. However . . . through the process of decentralising production . . . children are 'slotted' into the production cycle of large firms. (Valcarenghi, 1981, p. 11)

The effects of subcontracting is the focus of Goddard's (1995) work. In particular, she notes the spread of outwork in Naples and the hard work, for little financial return, provided by workers in backstreet factories, shops and homes.

There is also increasing evidence that child labour is a problem in the 'heart' of the system in west-central Europe and the USA. Light, Hertsgaard and Martin (1985), Greenberger and Steinberg (1986) and Taylor (1973), for example, note the extent of child labour in the USA and the range of tasks performed by children there. They can be found in the service sector working at fast food outlets, cafes and retail stores, in manufacturing performing manual labour, in clerical work and child-care tasks. Steinberg, Greenberger, Vaux and Ruggerio (1981) found children working up to 24 hours a week on top of schooling. In Europe, Hansen (1992), looking at Denmark, Hertmeijer (1992), focusing on the Netherlands, and Weinold's (1992) work on Germany all note the large numbers of children working in continental Europe in a range of service, manufacturing and specifically 'children's' jobs. The evidence, therefore, would seem to emphasize that child labour is not a peculiarity of the NICs development but a common and constant feature of modern global capitalism.

Thus, the conclusion of this review would appear to be that child labour is increasing throughout the world. The development and expansion of capitalism has brought severe problems for the urban working class in the NICs and UDCs. Severe poverty and the imposition of the cash nexus onto all aspects of their lives has increasingly forced them to utilize all the labour resources available to them, including that of their children. World recession, globalization and various SSAPs have made the situation worse. The market system, a system based on commodity production for profit and including the commodification of labour, will not solve the problems of the poor, or of child workers, throughout the globe; rather than a solution to this form of labour exploitation, it is its base cause.

In Europe and North America, poverty and globalizing pressures have made the plight of some child workers worse. But poverty cannot be identified as the sole cause of child labour. In Germany, America, Denmark and, as we shall see, Britain, large numbers of children work, but not all of them come from the poorest sections of the community. Rather, historical development has restructured the child labour market with certain jobs being located within a particular niche: they are identified as children's jobs. Nevertheless, the children's labour is exploited, their remuneration and conditions of work are poor and the jobs reflect wider structural inequalities within these societies.

Thus, although changing economic structural factors have had an international impact on child workers, they have not produced uniform results. The way in which these pressures have been played out within particular nation states reflects their interaction with local cultural, political, social and ideological 'commitments'. For example, the working patterns of boys and girls are often different (Aghajanian, 1979; Levy, 1985) and the types of jobs and general employment conditions may reflect the impact of local settlements between employers and unions (Callinicos, 1987a). The point of interest, therefore, is the extent to which international, structural *tendencies* are off-set or reshaped within local contexts. As a result, it is important to look at the general pressures and trends within the area of child labour, together with specific nation state studies of how this is worked out in practice.

We will now move on to look at one specific nation-based study, child labour in Britain, where, it will be suggested, the interaction of economic structural pressures has historically been shaped by the 'local' response to produce the present form of child labour.

The Global/Local Dichotomy: A Case Study of Child Labour in Britain

In this section we will look at a specific example of the global/local interaction by addressing the child labour question in modern Britain. We start by looking at whether there is a child labour problem in Britain: to reiterate what was noted earlier, many academics and government ministers assert that there is not.

In recent years there has been a steady increase in the number of press reports which have revealed examples of children working in factories, warehouses and offices in Britain. In 1995, the *Manchester Evening News* discovered large numbers of young workers employed as tele-sales operators, working long hours for little money (Edwards, 1995). In 1994, the *Lancashire Evening Post* (unnamed article) was able to report that children as young as 12 and 13 were working in a textile factory in Preston, while Channel 4's 'Look Who's Talking' found children working in a box factory on machines that had been adapted and had their safety shields removed allowing young hands to get closer to the guillotines. In 1991, the Newcastle based *Sunday Sun*, found 10-year-old boys starting work at 3 am delivering milk (Oxley, 1991). While in Glasgow in 1990 the *Evening Times* discovered a pie factory where children were working up to 40 hours a week, for £1 an hour (Hildrey and McLaws, 1990).

These are just a few examples of media revelations about child labour in Britain. It would seem that the government's complacency is misplaced. But, of course, it could be argued that these examples are so shocking and receive press coverage because they are atypical. This would undoubtedly be the government's position but research produced by a number of groups over the last ten years has emphasized that the exploitation of children at work is unfortunately alive and well in the British labour market and 'part-time out of school work' remains a significant feature of children's lives (Lavalette, 1994; McKechnie, Lindsay and Hobbs, 1994; McKechnie, Lindsay and Hobbs, 1993; Balding, 1991; Pond and Searle, 1991; Lavalette, McKechnie and Hobbs, 1991; Finn, 1987; Moorehead, 1987; MacLennan *et al.*, 1985).

In a series of surveys of working children from 1987 onwards, the universities of Paisley and Liverpool have been able to plot the extent of child labour in a number of different regions of Britain. Using the same questionnaire in each region, the surveys have asked school students about jobs they may have at the time of the survey, previous paid work experiences, conditions of employment and pay rates. The data obtained will be presented in the following pages to assess the government's claims that working is a minority activity, carried out in well regulated circumstances and undertaken for a little extra pocket money. We start by looking at the extent of child labour in Britain. Table 11.1 gives a breakdown of the number of school students reporting work as either a 'present' or 'former' activity. The research suggests that at any given time, somewhere between a third and a half of school students in their last two years of compulsory schooling will be working and, among the same cohort, approximately two thirds will either be working or will have worked in the recent past (cf. Lavalette, 1994; McKechnie *et al.*, 1994, McKechnie *et al.*, 1993, see also Balding, 1991). The first thing to note, therefore, is that child labour is not a minority experience but rather an activity that the majority of children will experience by the time they leave school.

Table 11.1: Work status of children in Britain (%)

| Region | Source | Work status | | | N* |
		Currently working	Formerly working	Never worked	
Stratchclyde 11 schools	Lavalette (1994a)	36	26	38	567
Urban Scottish 2 schools	Hobbs *et al.* (1993a)	35	29	36	347
Cumbria 4 schools	·McKechnie *et al.* (1993)	50	22	27	490
North Tyneside 2 schools	Hobbs *et al.* (1993b)	46	33	21	281
Dumf. & Galloway 3 schools	McKechnie *et al.* 1994	35	35	30	259
Greater Manchester 4 schools	Lavalette (1994b)	48	27	25	697
Lancs. (urban) 1 school (year 11)	Lavalette *et al.* (1995)	47	21	32	161

* N = Total number

Clwyd (1994, 1995) argues that the major problem associated with child labour in Britain is that the majority of it is illegal, on one count or another, and, therefore, represents a threat, to some degree, to the child's well-being. To assess this claim, we will need to outline the existing legal position of child workers in Britain — not a simple task. The regulation of child employment is through a mixture of national statute and local authority bye-law. The Employment of Children and Young Persons Act (1933), and its equivalent Scottish Act of 1937, are the major pieces of law in this area.

Although dated, the laws provide a framework for the regulation of child labour. With a few exceptions, children are not allowed to work prior to the age of 13. The Acts prohibit a range of tasks, including working in factories, warehouses and garages, working from moving vehicles and generally performing tasks which are deemed to hinder the child's educational and social development. Strangely, it also prohibits specific jobs such as ice-cream making, which reveals how dated the legislation has become and may also reflect an anti-Italian bias within the 1930s legislation. More generally, children are prohibited from working before 7 am or after 7 pm. On school days and Sundays, children can work for no more than two hours, but on Saturdays and school holidays this is increased to 5 hours (for 13- and 14-year-olds) and 8 hours (for 15-year-olds), up to a weekly maximum of either 25 or 35 hours. Finally, all children who work must first obtain a work permit, signed by the educational authorities and a medical officer, which should ensure that the job the child wishes to do will not have a detrimental effect on the child's development. Beyond this, Councils are free to tighten the legislation in any way they see fit and to produce bye-laws which reflect local employment traditions. However, rather than rationally tightening and updating the law to meet changing circumstances, bye-laws have been used very unevenly; resulting in

Table 11.2: Types of jobs performed by children in the UK (%)

	Del	Shp	Bab	Wai	Frm	Cat	Other
				Types of Jobs (%)			
Urban Lancs							
Year 7	80	3	3	—	—	—	13
Year 8	67	13	8	2	6	2	2
Year 9	60	4	15	4	—	—	17
Year 10	40	22	14	17	2	1	4
Year 11	16	27	16	20	—	5	16
Total	47	16	12	11	2	2	10
Rural Lancs							
Year 7	63	6	12	—	—	—	19
Year 8	62	7	10	3	7	—	10
Year 9	31	3	19	13	16	3	15
Year 10	28	23	5	23	8	5	8
Year 11	9	15	9	32	6	28	—
Total	32	12	11	18	8	11	9

Del = delivery; Shp = shopwork; Bab = babysitting; Wai = waiting on; Frm = farmwork;
Cat = hotel and catering

a system marked by dramatic geographical variation and widespread confusion. This is a situation which is made worse by the fact that 'policing' of the legislation is covered by three agencies: the police, the factory inspectorate and the educational welfare service (MacLennan *et al.*, 1985; Lavalette *et al.*, 1991; Pond and Searle, 1991).

To assess the adequacy of existing law we will focus on results from the latest survey of child workers in two schools in Lancashire, comparing where appropriate with previous research material. First we will look at the types of jobs performed by children. This is given in Table 11.2, broken down by school and year of student. The common-sense picture in Britain is that children perform a limited range of light tasks. Yet Table 11.2, in common with most studies undertaken, points to the fact that while the *main* sectors employing children coincide with those normally viewed as 'children's jobs' (e.g., delivery work), children can be found working in a wide range of activities and often compete with adult workers for jobs (e.g., in shop work and in restaurants). Further, although small in number, the survey found children working in areas not normally regarded as appropriate for children: factories; building sites and warehouses (listed under the 'other' category in Table 11.2). Again, this is replicated in other studies which consistently show a small number of children working at these types of tasks (Lavalette, 1994; McKechnie *et al.*, 1994; Balding, 1991; Lavalette *et al.*, 1991; Pond and Searle, 1991; MacLennan *et al.*, 1985).

Of the tasks listed in Table 11.2, babysitting, hotel and catering and all the 'other' tasks are illegal. However, the figures do not reveal the whole picture. Delivery work is consistently the most popular job that children (especially younger boys) perform. These are the ideal type of 'children's job'; from Michael Forsyth's perspective the typical 'light, harmless work' performed for extra pocket money. However, further investigation questions this idealistic conception of children's delivery work. Children performing these tasks include those delivering milk door to door, but development in sub-contracting of milk rounds to drivers have increased the pressure associated with such work. It starts very early in the morning (often at 3 or 4 am) and is often performed 'at running pace'. Further, the need for drivers to submit low bids for potential rounds means they utilize the cheapest labour they can find and, if they can, 'understaff' their rounds. The children, therefore, work hard, in poor conditions, at illegal times and are employed, consciously, as a cheap labour source.

Paper rounds are another typical children's job. Yet again, idealistic notions about what this involves must be questioned. Early morning paper rounds almost always start before 7 am and are, therefore, illegal. But more than this, paper rounds quite often place extensive physical demands on children. A report in the *Observer* newspaper entitled 'Paper Weight Lifters' claimed some newspaper bags carried by the delivery workers 'weigh . . . from 21.5lbs to 68.5lbs — nearly five stones' (Cooper, 1988). By comparison, an agreement between the Post Office and the Union of Communication Workers prohibits postal cadets (16- to 18-year-olds) from carrying more than 20lbs on foot or 26lbs on a suitably adapted bike. Newspaper deliverers, therefore, are expected to carry heavier weights than older postal cadets and it is questionable how many do so on suitably designed bikes. To emphasize the danger such weights can bring, the *Glasgow Herald* reported in 1990 that a boy was undergoing serious back surgery, the result, his doctor claimed, of regularly delivering newspapers on a Sunday round (MacDiarmid, 1990). Finally, of course, newspapers, like milk, must be delivered in all weather conditions, but again, unlike postal workers or many other delivery and outdoor workers, children rarely obtain appropriate waterproof clothing.

The evidence shows that, in the range of tasks performed by children, the conditions of work are very often poor. In catering, children can be involved in unpleasant tasks like washing dishes all day, or preparing food around busy and dangerous kitchens. 'Waiting on', often involves very late finishing times or split shifts. Shop work, for children under 16, is rarely in large chain supermarkets where conditions can be better, but in small retail outlets where breaks are irregular and facilities poor. Further, children are often employed in direct competition with other groups of discriminated workers like, for example, women, but children have the 'advantage' of being cheaper.

With regard to the age of child workers and their hours of employment, research reveals a fairly consistent picture. Many children work prior to the age of 13, many as young as 10 or 11 (McKechnie *et al.*, 1994; Balding, 1991; Pond and Searle, 1991; MacLennan *et al.*, 1985). With regard to hours, while relatively few children work more than the weekly maxima (25 or 35 hours depending on age), significant numbers start their jobs earlier in the morning and finish later in the evening than they are legally allowed to (some, as we noted, starting work as early as 3 or 4 am, while others can finish at 11 pm or

12 midnight) (Lavalette, 1994; McKechnie *et al.*, 1994; McKechnie *et al.*, 1993; Hobbs *et al.*, 1992; Pond and Searle, 1991; Lavalette, 1991).

Finally, the key regulatory mechanism to assess the extent of child labour, the types of jobs they perform and ensure the jobs keep within the law and do not detrimentally affect the child's well-being, is the local authority work permit. However, evidence has shown repeatedly that the permit is completely inadequate for the task. In most studies, approximately 90 per cent of the working children did not have, or had not heard of, this permit (Lavalette, 1994).

The final issue to consider is the question of children's wages. Government sources, and even Labour MPs like Ann Clwyd, often portray these as a form of 'pocket money', reflecting the assumption that the tasks are not really work. It should be clear by now that this perspective does not stand up to much scrutiny and that children are expected to work hard, in a range of tasks and in poor conditions. In return for this hard labour, most children earn very poor rates of pay. In most studies, something under £2 per hour is the norm (Lavalette, 1994; Lavalette *et al.*, 1991; Pond and Searle, 1991; MacLennan *et al.*, 1985). How does this compare with other workers? This, of course, is not an easy question to answer. The abolition of Wages Councils and the government's refusal to consider any form of minimum wage means that there are many adults working for similar sums, but surely this in itself does not justify the apparent poor levels of children's wages? For guidance, we could perhaps look at the proposals being discussed by the Labour Party for a minimum wage, should they win power at the next election. Although the Labour Party have refused to state what the minimum wage should be, the consensus seems to be that it should be no less than £4 per hour. However inadequate this may be, if we take this figure then it would apply to those over 18, with 17-year-olds getting 90 per cent of it and 16 year olds getting 80 per cent (i.e., £3.60 and £3.20). If we follow this process logically we should expect a minimum wage for children to be 70 per cent of the adult rate (i.e., £2.80). Whether this is likely or not, it does emphasize that most child workers receive less than any (conservatively set) 'minimum wage' level and further confirms that the tasks they undertake are a particular form of what Brown and Scase (1991) call 'poor work'.

The types of jobs performed by children, their condition of work, their wage rates and the fact that, on one count or another, the majority of children work illegally, has led to a growing campaign to force the government to introduce new legislation. The Low Pay Network have adopted a twofold strategy. First, they have argued that a piece of legislation which has been passed by parliament, but never implemented, The Employment of Children Act (1973), should be immediately enforced. While this legislation is itself now rather dated, it would have the benefit of introducing uniform national laws and encourage the government to take the issue seriously. The chances of this occurring, however, remain slim. Secondly, they argue for Britain to ratify immediately the European directive on the protection of young people at work, from which the government managed to obtain a six year opt-out (DoE, 1993). The government's position remains that the directive is an unacceptable inter- ference by Europe in British law-making and that this is an area where the principle of subsidiarity should take precedence. Nevertheless, by the end of 1995, the Department of Health had published a consultation document on child employment. Clearly with an eye on Europe, the document proposed that, for 13- and 14-year-olds, there should be a list of jobs children were per- mitted to do (reversing previous practice of a list of proscribed tasks), that employers would be responsible for obtaining the necessary permits and that children should be allowed to work longer on Sundays (which cynics might suggest has more to do with Sunday Trading than any concerns for the child). How the consultation proceeds from here is unclear, but it will not stop chil- dren from being exploited at work or performing jobs in questionable circum- stances (many of the tasks, we noted, children already perform are on the 'acceptable' list, although not, interestingly, milk rounds). Finally, the fact that the vast majority of children work illegally means that simply passing laws is unlikely to solve the problem.

As we have noted, child labour is a feature of capitalism. Children are exploited, as a cheap source of labour, in a range of activities, many of them illegal. Further, the development of capitalism in Britain has created a niche within the labour market which is identified as the preserve of specifically children's jobs. Tightening the law may make it easier to regulate some types of jobs children perform, it may make it clearer to children what their rights at work are, but under present circumstances it will not stop children being exploited at work.

The campaigns against the exploitation of children at work in Britain are mirrored by similar ones in other countries (Vuzina and Schaffer, 1992). But child labour is also the focus of a number of cross-national campaigns, it is to these that we now turn.

Campaigning Against Child Labour

The inequities that child labour exploitation brings has led to a number of campaigns by various supra-national bodies, NGOs and pressure groups to restrict child employment and to promote a 'childhood' free from oppression and exploitation. However, many of the campaigns bring with them a num- ber of contradictions and, so, need to be viewed with a more critical gaze. In this section we briefly review some of these campaigns, and note their suc- cesses and the possible conflicts they promote. These campaigns operate at different levels and have different goals, we can identify three broad types: (i) campaigns 'from above', organized by quasi-governmental bodies and various NGOs which aim to tighten state laws or promote child social welfare and education within particular nation states; (ii) campaigns 'on behalf of children', which may be based outside of the country of focus and promote consumer boycotts and moral purchasing strategies; (iv) and, finally, the far less common or 'obvious' campaigns 'from below' which focus on the children and their social experiences and are often led by children themselves. We will look at each in turn.

The agency with the longest history of child labour research and standard setting is the International Labour Office (ILO). Founded in 1919, the ILO has consistently attempted to regulate the work children do throughout the world. It does this by framing policy conventions and recommendations which member states *can* sign if they wish. Once ratified, they become binding on signatory states who are then expected to provide annual reports on their compliance.

The first convention on child labour was passed in 1919 and prohibited children under the age of 14 from doing regular industrial work. Other conventions followed, gradually introducing age restrictions for seafarers, in agriculture and mining and in non-industrial sectors. However, in 1973 the ILO replaced these existing conventions with a more embracing and inclusive policy framework: Convention 138 and Recommendation 146. According to Fyfe (1989) these are: 'the most comprehensive international instrument[s] and statement[s] on child labour' (p. 132).

The proclaimed aim of Convention 138 and Recommendation 146 is to abolish child labour, although this is not quite true as 'light' work is allowed. The Convention and Recommendation prohibit children under 15 from working (in 'non light' work); they prohibit under-18-year-olds from taking part in work that may detrimentally affect their health, safety or morals; and they prioritize children's health and welfare within national policy developments. Articles 28 to 35 of the UN's Convention of the Rights of the Child follow similar themes; and again the exclusion of 'light work' has allowed the UK government to sign the UN Convention and take no action over child labour. Despite the evidence, the UK government claims the existing framework is adequate and the country meets the work requirement.

The ILO Convention and Recommendation set a high standard which clearly the ILO want governments to follow by becoming signatories. The ILO campaigned extensively for ratification, especially in the run up to the International Year of the Child (1979). Research projects and publications which focused on the problems faced by child workers and the need for ratification were undertaken (Mendelievich, 1979; Rodgers and Standing, 1981). But the campaign, apart from raising awareness in some circles, was not a great success: by 1979 only thirteen countries were signatories and by 1988 it was still only thirty-six (Fyfe, 1989). Furthermore, many of those countries which did sign were unable to fulfil, or even monitor, the conditions set within the Convention (Fyfe, 1989). Initially ratification came close to being seen as an end in itself, with sections of the ILO's own research establishment warning against policy prescriptions and blueprints being put in place within nation states and little attention given to implementation on the ground (Standing, 1982) — clearly an important warning regarding the abstract use of both ILO and UN Conventions.

In the face of these concerns the ILO altered direction slightly, adopting a multi-level approach which directs demands at governments while also attempting to educate children, their families and communities about the possible dangers of child labour (Myers, 1991). More recently still, the campaign has narrowed to deal with those jobs which are commonly seen as exploitative. The First Things First campaign is aimed at stopping work that is 'detrimental' to children's physical, social and educational development (Bequele and Myers, 1995). The aim is to involve children, child welfare workers, state officials and employers in an awareness campaign about the harm labour can cause and hence attempt to restrict the worst practices. The campaign has moved, therefore, to accept less universalistic goals and to adopt a gradualist perspective of slow reform on the issue.

Problematically, the recent campaign seems to accept that we all know, and can agree, what types of jobs are detrimental and exploitative and which are less so. This perspective is not helped by the continuing use of the work/labour distinction within the ILO. The various NGOs, such as the Anti-Slavery International, Defence of Children International and the International Working Group on Child Labour again replicate this problem, often denying that there is an issue because we all *know* work and labour are different (IWGCL, forthcoming). As was argued at the beginning, the work/labour distinction is not helpful and the evidence from the British case study shows that apparently harmless and light tasks can be exploitative and threaten children's health, welfare and educational development. Clarity of definition will be necessary to focus research and practice on the various types and forms of employment performed by children in various regional settings.

A second approach to the problem of child labour is those campaigns 'on behalf of' children which promote consumer boycotts of goods produced by children. The two most significant cases of note are the attempts by US Senator Harkin to promote legislation that will prohibit the sale of goods within the United States made by children (Donovan, 1995) and the 'Rugmark' campaign which aims to promote a cross-national voluntary consumer boycott (ETUYM, 1994; ASI, 1995).

The aim of both campaigns would seem to be to force 'unscrupulous employers' to stop employing children. But certainly in the case of Senator Harkin, the motives are perhaps less philanthropic than they may at first seem, part of his reasoning being that American workers were losing jobs because of the cheap labour (including child labour) embodied in foreign goods (Donovan, 1995). Certainly, Harkin's moves have been interpreted as motivated by protectionism by many writers in the NICs (Guirajani, 1994). Further, the boycotts may be a questionable strategy. If poverty is a central cause of child labour in the NICs, then of course it means that poor, working-class families rely on the wages of their children for their families survival and, in the dire circumstances in which families find themselves, what is the alternative? Boycotts will only affect the export sector within national economies and therefore will not stop child employment and may make the situation worse by increasing competition between children for jobs. The solution is not to be found in strategies which increase poverty and hardship but instead must be based on structural transformations which redistribute income, wealth and provide adequate welfare. Such strategies of course, cannot be built on SSAPs and the neo-liberal economic paradigm aimed at increasing poverty and inequality. They require a transformative political agenda, not just in terms of North/South relations, but in terms of 'internal' class relations.

Finally, within this transformative project we should note that children themselves are important actors (Schibotto and Cussianovich, 1994). Children can, and do, withdraw their labour (Hoyles, 1979), shape their work environment (Van Hear, 1982) and join with other (adult) workers to resist wage cuts or government policy (*Socialist Review*, 1996). Over recent years there have been examples of children acting together to shape and improve their work environment, their rights at work and emphasize that children can be active social agents in socio-political processes (Otiv, 1994). The potential power that child workers have was perhaps emphasized by the murder of Iqbal Masih, a young carpet worker from Pakistan, who was killed after leading a campaign against conditions in the Pakistani carpet industry (*New Internationalist*, 1995).

The fact that child labour is a phenomenon of capitalist development and intimately bound to capitalist social relations means that reform strategies are difficult to achieve but, nevertheless, the plight of child workers throughout the globe emphasizes the importance of the struggle to both obtain recognition of the problem and take steps to solve it.

Conclusion: Child Labour in the Capitalist Labour Market

In this chapter it has been argued that child employment is a particular form of labour exploitation under capitalism and that as capitalism has spread throughout the globe so has the problem of child labour. In the NICs and UDCs, child labour is associated primarily with poverty in urban working-class communities. Families, desperate to meet their material living requirements, are forced to utilize the labour power of all their members, including their children. Children work wherever and whenever the opportunities arise to do so. In the manufacturing sectors they tend to be employed in small under-capitalized sectors (Bequele and Boyden, 1988a), but extensive use of sub-contracting means that their employment is often part of the general cycle of production which leads up to many large 'western' multinational corporations and retailers. In these sectors, the employment of children takes no account of their special needs or requirements, they are employed as individual proletarians, but paid according to their status as children. Where the employing unit of capital is small, the number of employees small and unorganized, and the employer pushed by the competition of larger and more efficient units of capital, one way the employer has to make profits is to exploit cheap, sweated labour. This might mean paying low wages to migrants, to married women or to children. In other words, the employer will exploit whatever source is available, all that is required is people desperate enough to work for the money on offer. The combined effects of economic crises, globalization and the various SSAPs instigated by the major International Financial Institutions has been to make the plight of the poor worse and lead to an increase in the extent of child labour.

In the 'advanced' economies (like Britain) children still occasionally work in factories, warehouses, garages and machine shops, but more common are a number of 'specifically children's jobs' performed alongside schooling. These jobs are overwhelmingly in the service sector but are, nevertheless, exploitative, often illegal and harmful to the children involved. In these societies, the types of jobs children perform have been shaped, historically, by the interaction of social, political and ideological factors with changing economic criteria: these jobs have been structured and restructured by the development of capitalism.

Hence, it is clear that working-class children's situation is not exactly the same across the world, that the actual experiences of children will differ in particular 'local' settings and thus that the particularity of the local/global interaction is important in shaping the specific form of childhood and child labour in different societies. Nevertheless, it is the case that child workers across the globe are all victims of exploitative capitalist labour relations and that child labour should be seen as a structural phenomenon within capitalist societies. It also means that child labour is a particularly difficult political problem for governments to address. In essence, it combines two concepts which apparently should not go together: 'childhood' and wage labour. For the New Right, both nationally and internationally, the problem is seemingly intractable. On the one hand, their commitment to family ideology means that children are portrayed as a group to be nurtured and protected within the home, while their obvious commitment to wage labour and relatively 'free' labour markets (that is, free from state interference or trade union influence) means that they are often against regulation of children at work. Their solution is to deny that the jobs children do are a form of labour but instead portray it as a light and harmlessly socializing experience. The evidence clearly undermines such an idealistic conception and leaves the New Right exposed on the issue of the rights of children at work.

References

ABDALLA, A. (1988) 'Child labour in Egypt: Leather tanning in Cairo', in BEQUELE, A. and BOYDEN, J. (eds) *Combating Child Labour,* ILO, Geneva.

AGHAJANIAN, A. (1979) 'Family economy and economic contribution on children in Iran: An overview', *Journal of South Asian and Middle Eastern Studies,* **3**.

ANTI-SLAVERY INTERNATIONAL (1995) 'World trade and working children', ASI Briefing notes, London.

ANTI-SLAVERY SOCIETY (1978) *Child Labour in Morocco's Carpet Industry*, Anti-Slavery Society, London.

BALDING, J. (1991) 'A study of working children in 1990', *Education and Health*, **9**, 1.

BENSUSAN, G. (1979) 'Children at work: Mexico', in MENDELIEVICH, E. (ed.) *Children at Work*, ILO, Geneva.

BEQUELE, A. and BOYDEN, J. (eds) (1988a) *Combating Child Labour*, ILO, Geneva.

BEQUELE, A. and BOYDEN, J. (1988b) 'Working children: Current trends and policy responses', *International Labour Review*, **127**.

BEQUELE, A. and MYERS, E. (1995) *First Things First in Child Labour*, ILO, Geneva.

BLACK, M. (1995) *In the Twilight Zone: Child Workers in the Hotel, Tourism and Catering Industry*, ILO, Geneva.

BOYD, R. (1994) 'Child labour within the globalizing economy', *Labour Capital and Society*, **27**, 2.

BROWN, P. and SCASE, R. (1991) *Poor Work: Disadvantage and the Division of Labour*, Open University Press, Milton Keynes.

BURRA, N. (1987) 'Exploitation of child workers in the lock industry of Aligarh', *Economic and Political Weekly*, 11 July.

CALLINICOS, A. (1987a) 'Imperialism, capitalism and the state today', *International Socialism*, **2**, 35.

CALLINICOS, A. (1987b) *Making History*, Polity Press, Cambridge.

CHALLIS, J. and ELLIMAN, D. (1979) *Child Workers Today*, Quartermaine House, Sunbury.

CLYWD, A. (1994) *Children at Risk: An Analysis of Illegal Employment of Children in Great Britain*, The Labour Party, London.

CLYWD, A. (1995) *Illegal Employment of Children*, The Labour Party, London.

COOPER, E. (1988) 'Paper weight lifters', *Observer*, 18 December.

CUNNINGHAM, H. (1990) 'The employment and unemployment of children in England c.1680–1851', *Past and Present*, **126**.

DAVIN, A. (1982) 'Child labour, the working class family and domestic ideology in nineteenth century Britain', *Development and Change*, **13**.

DEACON, B. (1995) 'The globalisation of social policy and the socialisation of global politics', in BALDOCK, J. and MAY, M. (eds) *Social Policy Review*, **7**, SPA, London.

DEPARTMENT OF EMPLOYMENT (1992) *European Commission Proposal For a Council Directive on the Protection of Young People at Work: A Consultation Document*, DoE, London.

DEPARTMENT OF EMPLOYMENT (1993) *The United Kingdom in Europe: People, Jobs and Progress*, DoE, London.

DONOVAN, P. (1995) 'All work and no play', *Guardian*, 7 February.

EDWARDS, A. (1995) 'Slave work for girls, 13', *Manchester Evening News*, 13 November.

ELSON, D. (1982) 'The differentiation of children's labour in the capitalist labour market', *Development and Change*, **13**.

EUROPEAN STANDING COMMITTEE B (1993) *Protection of Young People at Work*, Parliamentary Debates, Wednesday 19 May, HMSO, London.

EUROPEAN TRADE UNION YOUTH MAGAZINE (1994) 'Child Labour in Europe', Onion No. 1 10/11/12.

FINN, D. (1987) *Training Without Jobs: New Deals and Broken Promises*, Macmillan, Basingstoke.

FORRESTER, T. (1979) 'Children at work', *New Society*, 1 November.

FRASER, D. (1984) *The Evolution of the British Welfare State* (Second Edn) Macmillan, London.

FYFE, A. (1985) *All Work and No Play: Child Labour Today*, TUC, London.

FYFE, A. (1989) *Child Labour*, Polity Press, Cambridge.

GIDDENS, A. (1991) *Modernity and Self-Identity*, Polity Press, Cambridge.

GODDARD, V. (1995) 'Child labour in Naples: The case of outwork', *Anthropology Today*, **6**.

GREENBERGER, E. and STEINBERG, L.D. (1986) *When Teenagers Work: The Psychological and Social Costs of Adolescent Employment*, Basic Books, New York.

GROOTAERT, C. and KANBUR, R. (1995) 'Child labour: An economic perspective', *International Labour Review*, **134**, 2.

GUILLEN-MARROQUIN, J. (1988) 'Child labour in Peru: Gold panning in Madre de Dois', in BEQUELE, A. and BOYDEN, J. (eds) Combating Child Labour, ILO, Geneva.

GUIRAJANI, M. (1994) 'Child labour in the Indian carpet industry', *Labour, Capital and Society*, **27**, 2.

HALL, S. (1984) 'The rise of the representative/interventionist state', in McLENNAN, G., HELD, D. and HALL, S. (eds) *State and Society in Contemporary Britain*, Polity Press, Cambridge.

HALL, S. and SCHWARZ, B. (1985) 'State and society, 1830–1930', in LANGAN, M. and SCHWARZ, B. (eds) *Crises in the British State 1880–1930*, London, Polity.

HANSEN, O.N. (1992) 'Children at work: A study of health risks in a Danish school population', in VUZINA, D. and SCHAFFER, H. (eds) Kinderarbeit in Europa Ministerium fur Arbeit, Gesundheit und Sociales des Landes Nordrhein-Westfallen, Dusseldorf.

HARMAN, C. (1991) 'The state and capitalism today', *International Socialism*, **2**, 51.

HARMAN, C. (1993) 'Where is capitalism going: Part 2', *International Socialism*, **2**, 60.

HERTMEIJER, H. (1992) 'Child labour in Netherlands', in VUZINA, D. and SCHAFFER, H. (eds) *Kinderarbeit in Europa Ministerium fur Arbeit*, Gesundheit und Sociales des Landes Nordrhein-Westfallen, Dusseldorf.

HILDREY, M. and McLAWS, A. (1990) 'Scandal of the Posil Pie man', *Evening Times*, 12 February.

HOBBS, S., LAVALETTE, M. and McKECHNIE, J. (1992) 'The emerging problem of child labour', *Critical Social Policy*, **34**.

HOBBS, S., LINDSAY, S. and McKECHNIE, J. (1993) 'Part-time employment and schooling', *Scottish Education Review*, **25**.

HOUSE OF COMMONS EMPLOYMENT COMMITTEE (1991) 'Child labour', Minutes of Evidence, HMSO, London.

HOYLES, M. (ed.) (1979) *Changing Childhoods*, Writers and Readers, London.

IWGCL (forthcoming) *World Report of the International Working Group Child Labour*.

JAMES, A. (1984) 'Children's experience of work', ESRC Newsletter, **51**.

LANCASHIRE EVENING POST (1994) 'Child sweat shop probe', 12 April.

LANDRIGAN, P.J. (1993) 'Child labor: A re-emergent threat', *American Journal of Industrial Medicine*, **24**.

LAVALETTE, M. (1994) *Child Employment in the Capitalist Labour Market*, Avebury, Basingstoke.

LAVALETTE, M., HOBBS, S., LINDSAY, S. and McKECHNIE, J. (1995) 'Child employment in Britain: Policy, myth and reality', *Youth and Policy*, **47**.

LAVALETTE, M., McKECHNIE, J. and HOBBS, S. (eds) (1991) *The Forgotten Workforce: Scottish Children at Work*, SLPU, Glasgow.

LEVY, V. (1985) 'Cropping patter, mechanization, child labour and fertility behavior in a family economy', *Economic Development and Cultural Change*, **33**.

LIGHT, H.K., HERTSGAARD, D. and MARTIN, R.E. (1985) 'Farm children's work in the family', *Adolescence*, **20**.

MACLENNAN, E., FITZ, J. and SULLIVAN, J. (1985) *Working Children Low Pay Unit*, London.

McKECHNIE, J., LINDSAY, S. and HOBBS, S. (1993) *Child Employment in Cumbria: A Report to Cumbria County Council*, University of Paisley, Paisley.

McKECHNIE, J., LINDSAY, S. and HOBBS, S. (1994) *Still Forgotten: Child Employment in Rural Scotland*, SLPU, Glasgow.

McNALLY, D. (1993) *Against the Market: Political Economy, Market Socialism and the Marxist Critique*, Verso, London.

MEHTA, M.N., PRABHU, S.V. and MISTRY, H.N. (1985) 'Child labour in Bombay', *Child Abuse and Neglect*, **9**.

MENDELIEVICH, E. (ed.) (1979) *Children at Work*, ILO, Geneva.

MINISTERIUM FUR ARBEIT, GESUNDHEIT UND SOCIALES DES LANDES NORDRHEIN-WESTFALEN (1992) *Kinderarbeit In Europa*, NRW.

MOOREHEAD, C. (1987) *School Age Workers in Britain Today*, Anti-Slavery Society, London.

MURRAY, J. (1991) 'Working children', in LAVALETTE, M., McKECHNIE, J. and HOBBS, S. (eds) The Forgotten Workforce: Scottish Children at Work, SLPU, Glasgow.

MYERS, W. (ed.) (1991) *Protecting Working Children*, Zed Books, London.

NANGIA, P. (1986) 'Determinants and consequences of child labour: A cyclical relationship', *Philosophy and Social Action*, **12**.

NEW INTERNATIONALIST (1995) 'Carpet mafia: Campaigner killed for speaking out', October.

NICHOLLS, T. (1992) 'Different forms of labour', *Work, Employment and Society*, **6**, 1.

NOVAK, T. (1995) 'Rethinking poverty', *Critical Social Policy*, **44/45**.

OTIV, R. (1994) 'Children demand right to work', *Morning Star*, 14 August.

OXLEY, K. (1991) 'Why I send my boys out to work in the middle of night', *Sunday Sun*, 2 June.

PAPAFLESSA, T. (1979) 'Children at work: Greece', in MENDELIEVICH, E. (ed.) *Children at Work*, ILO, Geneva.

PINCHBECK, I. (1969) *Women Workers and the Industrial Revolution 1750–1850*, Virago, London.

PINCHBECK, I. and HEWITT, M. (1969) *Children in English Society: Volume 1*, Routledge, London.

PINCHBECK, I. and HEWITT, M. (1973) *Children In English Society: Volume 2*, Routledge, London.

POND, C. and SEARLE, A. (1991) *The Hidden Army: Children at Work in the 1990's*, LPU, London.

PRACHANKHADEE, B., NELAYOTHIN, A., INTRASUKPORN, N. and MONTAWAN, V. (1979) 'Children at work: Thailand', in MENDELIEVICH, E. (ed.) *Children at Work*, ILO, Geneva.

RAVOLOLONONGA, B. and SCHLEMMER, B. (1994) 'L'enfant au travail a Madagascar', *Labour Capital and Society*, **27**, 2.

RODGERS, G. and STANDING, G. (eds) (1981) *Child Work, Poverty and Underdevelopment*, ILO, Geneva.

ROSDOLSKY, R. (1977) *The Making of Marx's 'Capital'*, Pluto, London.

SALAZAR, M.C. (1988) 'Child labour in Colombia: Bogota's quarries and brickyards', in BEQUELE, A. and BOYDEN, J. (eds) *Combating Child Labour*, ILO, Geneva.

SASTRE, B.C. and ZARAMA, M.L. (1994) 'Le travail des enfants dans les mines de Colombie', *Labour, Capital and Society*, **27**, 2.

SCHIBOTTO, G. and CUSSIANOVICH, A. (1994) *Working Children: Building an Identity*, Manthoc, Lima, Peru.

SEARIGHT, S. (1980) *Child Labour in Spain*, Anti-Slavery Society, London.

SENGUPTA, P. (1975) 'Children work to live', *Social Welfare*, **22**.

SIMON, B. (1960) *Studies in the History of Education 1780–1870*, Lawrence and Wishart, London.

SINHA, R. (1995) 'Economic reform in developing countries: Some conceptual issues', *World Development*, **23**, 4.

SOCIALIST REVIEW (1996) 'France's Redhot Winter', Special Issue, February.

SOCRATO, F. (1979) 'Children at work: Indonesia', in MENDELIEVICH, E. (ed.) *Children at Work*, ILO, Geneva.

STANDING, G. (1982) 'State policy and child labour: Accumulation versus legitimation', *Development and Change*, **13**.

STEINBERY, L.D., GREENBERGER, E., VAUX, A. and RUGGERIO, M. (1981) 'Early work experience: Effects on adolescent occupational socialization', *Youth and Society*, **12**, 4.

TAYLOR, R.B. (1973) *Sweatshops in the Sun: Child Labour on the Farm*, Beacon Press, Boston.

THOMPSON, E.P. (1968) *The Making of the English Working Class*, Penguin, Harmondsworth.

UKPABI, B.E. (1979) 'Children at work: Nigeria', in VUZINA, D. and SCHAFFER, H. (eds) Kinderarbeit in Europa Ministerium fur Arbeit, Gesundheit und Sociales des Landes Nordrhein-Westfallen, Dusseldorf.

UNRISD (1995) *State of Disarray: The Social Effects of Globalization*, UNRISD, Geneva.

VALCARENGHI, M. (1981) *Child Labour in Italy*, Anti-Slavery Society, London.

VAN HEAR, N. (1982) 'Child labour and the development of capitalist agriculture in China', *Development and Change*, **13**.

VERLET, M. (1994) 'Grandir a Nuna (Ghana)', *Labour Capital and Society*, **27**, 2.

VUZINA, D. and SCHAFFER, H. (1992) Kinderarbeit in Europa, Ministerium fur Arbeit, Gesundheit und Sociales des Landes, Nordrhein-Westfallen, Dusseldorf.

WEINOLD, H. (1992) 'Sociological aspects of child labour in Germany', in MINISTERIUM.

WHITTAKER, A. (1986) 'Child labour and its causes', *Third World Now*, Spring.

WRIGHT, E.O. (1979) *Class, Crisis and the State*, Verso, London.

12 Child Prostitution and Tourism: Beyond the Stereotypes

Julia O'Connell Davidson and Jacqueline Sanchez Taylor

In May of 1995, Christian Aid published a short report on child prostitution in the economically underdeveloped world which suggested that there may be as many as 200,000 child prostitutes in Thailand, over 200,000 in India, 60,000 in the Philippines, 15,000 in Sri Lanka and an unknown further number in other South East Asian countries, Latin America and Africa (Christian Aid, 1995). The report was concerned to highlight links between child prostitution and tourism and to provide support for a Private Members' Bill, tabled by Lord Hylton, which was designed to make it possible for British tourists accused of committing sexual crimes against children whilst abroad to be tried for their offences in British courts. Such legislation had been adopted in a number of other European and Scandinavian countries, as well as in Australia and the United States, following a rash of cases in which their nationals had been charged with sexual offences against children in Thailand, Sri Lanka and the Philippines, but had escaped to the safety of their own country before being brought to justice. Despite the fact that Britons are the second or third largest group of men deported from the Philippines and Sri Lanka for sexual offences against children (Ireland, 1993), and the fact that in June 1995 a Swedish national was successfully tried and convicted in Sweden for child sex offences committed in Thailand, the Major government refused to support Lord Hylton's Bill, arguing, among other things, that it would be technically difficult to secure convictions for extra-territorial crimes.[1] The Christian Aid report, the Bill and the government's response to it generated fairly extensive media coverage of the phenomenon of child sexual exploitation by tourists. A spate of news articles, radio programmes and television documentaries devoted to the topic appeared, many of which implicitly assumed that the problem consisted mainly of 'paedophiles' travelling to poor countries in order to secure safe and easy sexual access to very young children and reinforced a set of stereotypes about child prostitution in the economically underdeveloped world.

Prostitutes do not generally receive a sympathetic press. Because sexual purity is demanded of women, while male sexuality is typically understood as a biologically determined 'drive' or 'appetite', it is prostitute women, and not their clients, who are usually the focus of moral indignation. The client is often presented as an almost pitiful victim of his own biology, while the 'free choice' prostitute is viewed as cynically exploiting his moral and physical weakness for her own economic ends (see McIntosh, 1978). Western discourses around prostitution do allow for the possibility of a 'morally blameless' prostitute, but an essential precondition for this state is that the woman was coerced into prostitution by someone or thing she could not have resisted. It is in the context of such attitudes towards prostitution in general that the stereotypes of child prostitution we are concerned with here need to be understood, for there are two particular stereotypes which enjoy a good deal of popular currency in the West at present.

One involves an image of child prostitutes enslaved in brothels, often having been sold into slavery by their own parents. When this image is presented by reporters, it often carries with it an implication that responsibility for the problem lies in large part with the culture and/or government of the countries that host sex tourists. What kind of culture produces parents who would do such a terrible thing as to sell their own flesh and blood into sexual slavery, journalists implicitly ask, and how can their government allow this vile traffic to continue? The second stereotype involves an assumption that child prostitutes are prepubertal (which removes all ambiguity from their status as children) and that their clients are preferential abusers of prepubertal children. This serves to set child prostitution apart from other forms of prostitution. A child cannot be 'complicit' in her own degradation and dishonour, nor can she consciously exploit the frailty of men, for, according to western ideologies around sexuality and childhood, children are both asexual and innocent (see Ennew, 1986; Kitzinger, 1988). Since a child is held to be an inappropriate object for a normal male's sexual attentions, the clients of child prostitutes can then be assumed to be 'paedophiles', a category which is treated unproblematically and which clearly demarcates these clients both from the respectable 'majority' and from other men who buy sexual services at home and whilst holidaying in economically underdeveloped countries.

Employing these stereotypes enables journalists, politicians and Joe Public to express abhorrence for the men who exploit child prostitutes in economically underdeveloped countries, without having to question or condemn the motives and actions of those who exploit adult prostitutes, either at home or abroad. (It was notable, for example, that the extensive press coverage of the white British actor Hugh Grant's misadventure with an African-American prostitute in the US drew no parallels with the phenomenon of sex tourism that was simultaneously receiving so much attention.) The stereotypes of child prostitution in economically underdeveloped nations are not entirely without basis, but the reality of the phenomenon is far more complex.

This chapter begins from the premise that popular stereotypes about child prostitution effectively serve to detach the phenomenon from its broader social, political and economic context. We will therefore examine these stereotypes against empirical data on child prostitution in two very different settings, Thailand and Cuba,[2] and argue that the sexual exploitation of children in the economically underdeveloped world cannot be meaningfully separated from the sexual exploitation of adults (especially adult women) in these countries. This more general phenomenon of sexual exploitation is not something alien to western culture, nor is it something practised by a small minority of aberrant 'monsters'. Rather, it is an expression of economic, gendered, 'racialized' and aged power relations and ideologies that are widely accepted as 'natural', 'normal' and 'proper' in contemporary capitalist societies.

Varieties of Child Prostitution

It is child prostitution-slavery and the traffic in children that feeds it which, for obvious reasons, tends to command the lion's share of the international community's (as well as the western media's) attention and concern. It is very difficult to obtain reliable data on the average age, or even the age range, of the women and children who are subjected to this existence, and the exact total of the global population of debt-bonded and enslaved prostitutes is unknown. It is widely believed that in Thailand, tens of thousands of Thai and Burmese girls and women (as well as girls from Laos, Cambodia, Vietnam and China) are debt-bonded or otherwise enslaved by brothel owners, and there are also estimated to be over 210,000 enslaved child prostitutes in brothels in India and Sri Lanka, with unknown numbers of children in Brazil, Colombia and other parts of the southern hemisphere who are being prostituted under conditions of virtual slavery (Christian Aid, 1995).

Playing the numbers game is peculiarly repellent in relation to the phenomenon of prostitution-slavery, since, as Ennew (1986) points out, to know that one human being is being kept in such conditions should be enough to prompt concern and action. The knowledge that we live in a world where thousands of women and children are enslaved is surely unbearable, regardless of the age of those individuals. But it is also important to recognize that eradicating systems of debt-bondage and the kidnap, traffic and sale of children would in no sense imply an end to either the phenomenon of child sexual exploitation or that of prostitution-slavery. For in reality, large numbers of enslaved prostitutes are not children, and large numbers of child prostitutes are not enslaved to brothel owners.

Prostitution is not a unitary phenomenon. Its social organization, like that of wage labour, varies enormously. In both economically developed and underdeveloped countries, there are adult prostitutes who work as independent entrepreneurs, as well as those who are involved in a range of, usually indirect, employment relations with third parties (see Delacoste and Alexander, 1988; Phoenix, 1995; O'Connell Davidson, 1995a and 1996a). It is also the case that in both economically developed and underdeveloped countries, there are adult women who are prostituted under conditions of actual or virtual slavery. The same diversity is to be found in the phenomenon of child prostitution. Children may be directly coerced into prostitution by a third party who exercises powers of ownership of them; they may be compelled by economic and/or other circumstances to enter into some kind of employment relation with a third party; they may be prostituted by their own relatives; or they may prostitute themselves independently. A consideration of the organization of child prostitution in two very different settings, Thailand and Cuba, illustrates this diversity clearly.

Though girls can, with their parents consent, marry at the age of 15 in Thailand, unmarried girls remain sexual minors until the age of 18. In Thailand there exists fairly extensive local as well as tourist demand for prostitution, and the organization of child prostitution varies according to which segment of the market the child prostitute is being forced to serve. In the town of Ranong on the Thai-Burmese border, for example, O'Grady (1994) reports that there are brothels which cater to the several thousand illegal Burmese migrant workers who live and work there, and brothel owners make money by minimizing overheads (Ranong brothels are dilapidated buildings surrounded by high walls and defended by armed guards, which consist of as many as '102 small cubicles jammed together with little sanitation, poor lighting and a few broken ceiling fans,' (O'Grady, 1994, p. 19)); by paying no wages to the women and girls they have effectively kidnapped and imprisoned; and by maximizing the through-put of customers.

In the backstreets of towns and cities that attract large numbers of tourists there are also some brothels that are run along these lines. Such establishments cater primarily to local demand but also obtain a certain amount of custom from foreign men who are prepared to stray from the regular tourist haunts. It is also the case that some of the establishments which rely primarily on tourist demand provide men with sexual access to children. However, it would be an exaggeration to claim that sex tourists who stick within tourist areas of Bangkok are immediately faced with ready access to very young children in the Go Go bars, clubs and brothels that cater to them. A sex tourist with a specific and focused interest in prepubertal children will often rely, therefore, on the assistance of yet another person who benefits financially from the child's sexual exploitation. There are taxi drivers, hotel staff, even street touts, who will take the tourist to the brothels in locations well away from tourist centres where younger prostitutes are kept. Such establishments are generally known and protected by corrupt police, and a guidebook written by a sex tourist for sex tourists describes the 'guide's' fourth party involvement in the following way:

> When you get into a cab or Tuk-Tuk and the driver says, 'I have a special girl for you' ... he's trying to entice you to go to a brothel with him. Not only does he make his cab fare, but he gets a kickback from the brothel's owner ... Your driver will be waiting for you to finish, hoping you had a good time so that you'll tip him too. If you can remember the location, which is difficult because these brothels are always in some back alley, you can save 20% on your next trip,

about what the taxi driver gets as his finder fee. (Cassirer, 1992, pp. 180–1)

But brothels are not the only setting in which sex tourists can satisfy a sexual desire for children. They also obtain sexual access to children, especially very young children, through more informal types of prostitution. In Pattaya, for example, there is a strip of beach about a mile and a half long where tourists lounge on deck chairs beneath palm-thatched sun shades, and large numbers of independent, 'freelance' prostitutes of both sexes (many of whom are minors) come here during the day to pick up custom. Without being formally arranged or orchestrated by any owner or manager, this open air 'market' is divided into sections, with male prostitutes congregating along one stretch, female prostitutes grouped together in the next, and there is also a patch of the beach which appears to cater to those who are interested in younger children. Here prepubertal as well as older boys and girls mill around amongst male sex tourists, occasionally returning to the row of Thai adults (male and female) who sit in the shade at the rear of the beach. The sex tourists can be observed approaching children, offering them money to buy soft drinks from the stalls that line the beach, splashing, 'tickling' and fondling them in the sea, sitting next to them on the beach with an arm around their shoulders or caressing their thighs, and so on. Sex tourists can also be observed negotiating with the Thai adults at the back of the beach before leading children away in the direction of the hotel complexes behind it.

Western men also secure sexual access to prepubertal children through informal networks that operate in the most desperately poor areas of Bangkok and Pattaya. Montgomery (1994) undertook research in an impoverished slum community on the outskirts of Pattaya, where many households contained within them 'three generations all of whom have worked as prostitutes starting with the grandmother during the Vietnam War'. One of her chief informants was a child who had been introduced to commercial sex at the age of three by an 8-year-old child who was regularly having sex with a foreign businessman in the city. There are also stories of western men, living in Bangkok, who 'adopt' street children in order to obtain unlimited and continuous sexual access to them. The real point is that child prostitution in Thailand does not take a unitary form, but is arranged in a number of different ways.

In Cuba (where the age of sexual consent is 16), third party organization of any form of prostitution, including child prostitution, is rare (see O'Connell Davidson, 1996b). There are no brothels and no indirect employment of either adult or child prostitutes. However, a combination of severe economic problems and rapid tourist development means that large numbers of women and teenagers are currently prostituting themselves in order to subsist. In the absence of formal, organized prostitution serving the interests of an established market, tourists obtain sexual access to girls in their early teens in one of two ways. First, there are girls of 13, 14 and 15 who prostitute themselves independently, approaching tourists in bars and on beaches in the hope of earning dollars, or receiving gifts. Second, there are intermediaries who offer to arrange sexual access to young girls in exchange for a fee. Each of these will be considered in turn.

The experience of independent prostitutes (known as *jiniteras* in Cuba) differs sharply according to whether or not they are legitimate residents of a tourist centre or have migrated to it in search of dollars. Because legitimate residents generally have housing and some form of income (however meagre) other than that from prostitution, they are typically a great deal less vulnerable than migrant prostitutes. The following description of the experience of 'Anna-Bel', a 14-year-old girl, is fairly typical of the stories told by migrant prostitutes. Anna-Bel is the eldest of five children and had been working as a prostitute in Varadero (Cuba's most established tourist resort) for three months when we interviewed her in March 1995. She comes from a village in Ciego de Avila, a poor inland province about 500km away from Varadero, where her father earns, on average, 350 pesos per month. This sum probably guarantees a bare subsistence in the rationed peso economy, but the shortages caused by the US blockade and other economic pressures mean that many staple goods are only available on the 'black' market with dollars. Anna-Bel's father's income translates into around US$100 per month — with this, he must support a family of six. Anna-Bel ran away from home and travelled to Varadero, a tourist centre, in the hope of securing enough hard currency to buy herself a pair of shoes. On arrival, she immediately faced enormous problems. Not only was she effectively homeless and penniless, she was also entirely without experience or knowledge of prostitution. In Cuba, it is this, rather than the existence of formal brothel-based prostitution, which makes young girls vulnerable to forms of hyper-exploitation.

In the first instance, they are open to exploitation by 'black' market rentiers. There is a chronic shortage of housing in Cuba, and only official residents of any given town or city are entitled to accommodation. Though it is possible to own private property, it is illegal to rent it out, so that unless people migrate for official work, there is no legitimate way to obtain housing. Anna-Bel managed to find a room to share in a flat with four other girls in Miramar, a town 2km from Varadero. Each girl paid US$1.50 per night to the landlady who also lived in the flat. Though illegal to rent out space in this way, the incentive to do so is great. By exploiting the situation of young girls and women who had migrated to Varadero in search of dollars, Anna-Bel's landlady was making over US$400 per month, roughly four times the average Cuban wage. A great many Cubans who own or rent property in tourist areas currently sub-let it, to tourists if it is in reasonable condition, to prostitutes and hustlers if it is substandard. So far as the prostitutes are concerned, this effectively locks them into prostitution as a means of survival, for there is no alternative means of securing the dollars necessary to pay for their accommodation.

Young girls who migrate to tourist centres to prostitute themselves are also vulnerable to a form of hyper-exploitation by sex tourists. None of the young girls we interviewed spoke any language other than Spanish, and this, in combination with a lack of experience and the confidence that brings, meant that they found it very difficult to negotiate transactions with tourists. Anna-Bel, for example, never contracted to provide specific sexual services (indeed, even after three months' experience as a sex worker, she remained astonishingly naive about sexual matters and expressed confusion and amazement at the acts that she and her friends were asked to perform), and rarely managed even to negotiate a specific price for her services. Instead, she would accompany tourists back to their hotel rooms, acquiesce to their demands and accept anything that they chose to give her the following morning. In general, they paid her the 'going rate', between $30 and $50 per night, but there had been occasions when tourists had given her nothing at all.

One way in which experienced independent prostitutes the world over defend themselves against the stress and general unpleasantness of their work is to take a professional and businesslike approach to it (see Delacoste and Alexander, 1988; Hoigard and Finstad, 1992; O'Connell Davidson, 1995a). They tend to work regular hours and to find ways of sharply demarcating their work from their private life, for example, thus adding to a sense of control over and distance from the job. None of the young *jiniteras* we observed and interviewed in Varadero did this. Most would spend the entire day, every day of the week, 'hanging out' at the beach or an open bar, and the entire evening, often until 2 or 3am, in tourist bars and discos, waiting to be picked up. In other words, most of these girls are effectively working all of their waking hours. They are never 'off duty', and must constantly be prepared for stressful and intrusive sexual encounters with any man who happens to pick them. Experienced prostitutes also employ a range of techniques which enable them to separate sexual acts with punters from their own, private sexual and emotional life (for example, refusing to kiss, keeping their eyes closed during intercourse, 'switching off' to a point whereby they do not even register what a punter looks like, etc.). Again, the young girls we interviewed in Varadero did not have these skills with which to defend themselves, and children like Anna-Bel gave the impression that each and every encounter with a client was experienced as a fresh, demeaning and horrible violation, rather than an impersonal, if unpleasant, job.

Because many of the younger *jiniteras* are inexperienced and lack confidence they are also often relatively passive in terms of initiating contact with prospective clients. In the bars, these girls tend to spend their time dancing, joking, giggling (sometimes weeping) with each other, trying to catch the attention of male tourists but rarely approaching them directly. This opens the door for yet another variant of third party involvement. Older and more experienced *jiniteras* will assume the role of intermediary, effecting introductions and negotiating on the child's behalf, charging a fee for so doing. Children like Anna-Bel are especially vulnerable to this added layer of exploitation. She is physically very immature, standing about 1.47 metres, with hands and feet the size of a child much younger than her 14 years. She dresses in a childlike fashion which emphasizes her diminutive stature and her mannerisms are those of a little girl rather than a teenager. She is thus ideal fodder for men with specifically paedophile interests, and older *jiniteras* who recognize this type of demand are quick to exploit an acquaintance with girls like this.

Some older prostitutes move from this into more direct forms of procuring. 'Milagros', for example, is in her early 20s and works as a prostitute in Varadero, having been introduced to the work by her aunt, herself a prostitute there. Milagros is experienced and worldly enough to recognize that she can make money not only from prostituting herself, but also from arranging sexual access to others, especially very young girls. She thus acts as a procurer for regular sex tourists to Varadero and has built up a small network of Canadian, German, Argentinian and Italian clients who return to Cuba every two to three months. She recruits these clients by trawling the lobbies and bars of smart hotels (if younger girls went to these places themselves, they would almost certainly be thrown out by the hotel security, whereas because Milagros is relatively well dressed, sophisticated and confident, she can quickly attach herself to a tourist or group of tourists and thereby avoid such unwanted attention). Milagros will approach tourists in the hope firstly of getting their custom for herself. If this fails, she asks them what kind of girl they are interested in, promising to arrange their 'ideal' partner in terms of age, looks and 'racialized' identity in return for a small payment. Though she does not negotiate a price for the girls or take a cut from their earnings, in the high season she claims to earn an average US$100 dollars per week (and has earned US$300 in a single day) through such 'business arrangements' with tourists. Sometimes, the tourists' demands can be met through girls who are already working as prostitutes in Varadero, but Milagros is one of the growing number of procurers who return to their poorer home villages, towns and cities and encourage young girls to travel to tourist centres where, they are promised, they will find that the streets are paved with dollars. The reality is, of course, somewhat different. Competition between *jiniteras* is intense, and what money the girls make is largely swallowed up by the cost of living in a town like Varadero. Many are also robbed by their 'friends', and end up without even the fare home, let alone any dollars to give their family.

Sex tourists to Cuba are not only able to obtain sexual access to girls of 14 and 15 by approaching them directly or through a *jinitera* who acts as intermediary. There are also hustlers, usually men in their 20s who are involved in a range of 'black' market activities, who offer to arrange sexual access. They will approach tourists and offer them cheap cigars and/or drugs, or to change money at an advantageous rate, or to arrange a car and driver, or cheap meals or accommodation in a *casa particular*, or to fix them up with a woman or girl. Unlike pimps and brothel keepers, these men do not usually involve themselves in the details of the transaction between the prostitute and the client, but simply charge a fee for effecting the 'introduction'. If the hustler manages to set up a longer term relationship between a tourist and a prostitute who is a relative or friend of his, he may secure some further, on-going benefits from the relationship in terms of being taken out for drinks and meals with the 'couple', and being in a position to milk the tourist by arranging other 'deals'. This was the case with one young man we interviewed, 'Petter', who proudly told us about his Canadian 'friend', a man of 65 who visits Cuba two or three times a year and stays in accommodation arranged by Petter, with a 16-year-old girl, also procured for him by Petter when she was 14 or 15 years old. Sometimes these young male hustlers financially exploit child prostitutes, generally from within the context of an abusive relationship with them. Anna-Bel had a 'boyfriend', for example, who demanded sex from her, along with half of the money she earned from prostitution, and beat her when she failed to find clients.

As well as these hustlers and *jiniteras*, there are older women, who usually claim to be the child's aunt, who offer tourists sexual access to the bodies of the children in their care. It is difficult to know the precise conditions under which such children are working — whether they are treated as chattels by such women, whether they are bound to them by some sense of family loyalty, or whether they have entered into some kind of 'voluntary' employment relation with them. The only thing that is certain about such arrangements is that the child enjoys virtually no protection, either from the adult's economic exploitation or the tourist's sexual exploitation.

In general, it is assumed that prostitutes who work independently are better off than those who work for third parties. In practice, however, the situation of Cuban girls like Anna-Bel who work independently is little different from that of Thai girls who work for bar owners, in terms of the degree of economic exploitation by third parties and of sexual exploitation by tourists that they are subjected to. (Indeed, the latter are often at least assured a meagre income and/or subsistence from their formal 'employment' in the bar, so that if a client fails to tip them, they are not immediately faced with hunger and homelessness.) Both groups are subject to several layers of financial exploitation in the sense that the money a tourist is willing to part with in order to have sex with them does not all end up in their pocket, instead, the bulk of it goes to the intermediaries who are parasitic on the child's sexual exploitation — brothel keepers, rentiers, taxi drivers, procurers, hotel porters, relatives and 'friends'.

Neither can it be assumed that independent prostitutes exercise greater control over their working life than do brothel-based prostitutes. Take, for example, the issue of whether or not a prostitute is in a position to turn down a particularly repellent or intimidating client. For both Thai bar prostitutes and independent Cuban *jiniteras*, this control rests on economics. A bar prostitute who is reasonably successful and regularly brings her employer a goodly income in the form of bar fines can afford to be selective on occasion. Likewise, an independent prostitute is only ever in a position to turn down a client if she has recently had a good 'run' and has thus been able to pay her rent well in advance and has a little money in her pocket. When times are hard, neither is in a position to refuse.

This section has attempted to make two main points. The first is that child prostitution is organized in a number of different ways. It is true that some child prostitutes are enslaved, having been either kidnapped or debt-bonded, and the life that they endure is unimaginably horrific. However, not all child prostitutes are physically coerced into prostitution. Some are driven by dull economic compulsion alone to enter into employment relations with third parties or to prostitute themselves independently. The second point is that all of the different ways of organizing child prostitution are profoundly exploitative. We do not wish to suggest that the experience of child prostitutes is uniformly as grotesque as that suffered by the women and children in the brothels of Ranong mentioned above, but we do want to argue that there are no forms of child prostitution which can be excluded from concern on the grounds that they are somehow more acceptable, not *really* exploitative, or not *really* prostitution.

The attraction that the stereotype of child prostitutes as necessarily enslaved and/or sold into sexual slavery by their parents has for journalists is, presumably, that it allows them to talk about a form of prostitution that has not been actively chosen, as if people who select prostitution from a bunch of equally horrible alternatives are making a 'free' choice. Children in their early teens, indeed, even younger children, are not without a sense of responsibility for their families, nor are they without personal desire for the dignity that poverty denies human beings. If they are forced to watch their parents and younger siblings suffer endless privations and simultaneously to know that sufficient value is placed on their bodies to put them in a position whereby, potentially, they can alleviate the suffering of their family and/or obtain for themselves the material things that confer worth in any given society, many are capable of making a decision to do just that. But choosing between watching a sibling or parent starve and prostituting yourself, or even between walking barefoot and prostituting yourself, cannot be described as a meaningful *choice*, and it is unhelpful to the task of stemming sexual exploitation to ignore the fact that more than one form of compulsion can operate on children in such a way as to force them to prostitute themselves. Unless we recognize first, the existence of these economic pressures, and second, the fact that children are able to experience them as pressures, we will fall into the trap of imagining that it is possible to put an end to the sexual exploitation of children by eradicating systems of debt-bondage and the traffic and sale of children.

Varieties of Demand for Child Prostitutes

Childhood is, as many authors have pointed out, a socially constructed condition, rather than one which can be clearly defined through reference to biological fact or chronological age. Its perimeters vary cross-culturally and historically, and even within any one nation state, its boundaries are often indistinct. So far as the issue of sexual exploitation by tourists is concerned, defining 'childhood' is made still more difficult by the fact that the age of sexual consent differs both between and among sending and receiving countries. For the international community to concern itself with the condition and experience of children around the globe, however, it must necessarily employ some universal definition of childhood, and the United Nations and many other international bodies define a child as a person under the age of 18. Some are critical of the Eurocentrism which informs this definition (Ennew, 1986), but rather than become bogged down in a discussion of the problems and issues surrounding the definition of childhood, we will simply note here that there are few cultures wherein childhood is constructed in such a way as to include *only* prepubertal persons. It is therefore possible to employ the concept of childhood in relation to postpubertal individuals without automatically providing a narrowly Eurocentric analysis, and we can then make the point that not all child prostitutes are prepubertal. In fact, prepubertal child prostitutes are almost certainly greatly outnumbered by postpubertal child prostitutes, and this has implications for our understanding of who sexually exploits child prostitutes and why.

Used by clinicians, the term 'paedophile' generally refers to an adult who has a specific and focused sexual preference for prepubertal children. Given that not all child prostitutes are prepubertal it follows that, employing this narrow, clinical definition, not all of their clients are paedophiles. The term is also employed by academics, journalists and lay people (as well as by groups of men who seek to defend their own sexual interest in children, such as the North American Man Boy Love Association (NAMBLA) and the Paedophile Information Exchange (PIE)), in such a way as to include adults who are sexually attracted to postpubertal teenagers. There are, in fact, enormous definitional problems surrounding the term, for as Howells (1981) observes:

> Pedophilic acts vary in terms of a multitude of important dimensions, and to such a degree that it is unreasonable to treat them as forming a homogeneous group. In general, for example, little attention is paid to the question of whether pedophiles with female victims differ from those with male victims; whether pedophiles whose deviance is restricted to fantasy differ from those who act out their sexual interest; whether pedophiles whose acts involve an aggressive component differ from those involved in what might be classified as 'sex play'; or whether the age structure of pedophiles . . . requires different theories for different age groups. (pp. 62–3)

Despite definitional problems and debate as to its true nature and aetiology, however, paedophilia is a term which implies that a certain group of people can be bracketed off as sexually, psychologically and/or emotionally distinctive from the rest of the population through reference to their preferred sexual objects. As Plummer (1981) observes, 'Pedophilia is so often hived off from its social context that it becomes the property of people rather than a form of experience. *Activities* become *beings* and the talk is no longer of pedophilia

— but *the* pedophile' (p. 228, original emphasis). For a number of reasons, it seems to us problematic to assume that all those who sexually exploit child prostitutes in economically underdeveloped countries could be meaningfully bracketed off as 'paedophiles', even if this was taken as an umbrella term for a complex variety of sexual practices and interests.

To begin with, it is necessary to bear in mind that we are talking about men who are buying sexual access to prostitutes. Men's motivations for buying commercial sex vary, and there are certainly some who use prostitution as a means of securing sexual access to groups of people who, by virtue of their age, 'racialized' identity, or physical characteristics, they could not hope to obtain non-commercial sexual access to (see O'Connell Davidson, 1996a and 1995b). It is also the case that there are some men for whom the idea of sexual access to a female who is especially vulnerable and powerless (very young, very old, very obviously brutalized, pregnant, or enslaved, for example) carries an intense erotic charge. However, there are also men who use prostitution solely as a means to satisfying what they imagine to be a biological need on their own part (see, for example, White, 1990), or as a means of bonding with other men, as well as men who derive sexual and psychic pleasure from the transgressive nature of any sexual act with any prostitute. For these latter types of client, the physical appearance, age and situation of the prostitute is often entirely irrelevant.

There are places in the world, for example Bombay, Sri Lanka and certain parts of Thailand, where a large proportion of prostitutes in the cheapest brothels are in their early teens and the mass of clients are low paid migrant workers (see O'Grady, 1994; Dunham and Carlson, 1994). It cannot simply be assumed that all these men are motivated to exploit such children *because* they are children. It may be cost considerations and availability as much as any specifically focused sexual preference for children that lead them to these particular brothels (indeed, Montgomery, 1994, suggests that in Thailand, child prostitutes are the 'poor man's' substitute for the older and more expensive females he would prefer, and the authors found the same to be true in Costa Rica[3]). Likewise, it cannot be taken as read that all the foreign sex tourists who visit this type of cheap brothel are doing so because they attach sexual value only to the extreme youth of the inmates. As will be seen, there are other motivations for seeking out brothels which provide sexual access to young girls. In short, it cannot be automatically assumed that men who sexually exploit child prostitutes constitute a homogeneous group classifiable through reference to a specific sexual preference for *children*.

The idea that all the clients of child prostitutes suffer from some kind of clinically recognizable personality disorder is also dubious given the numbers of men involved and their very diverse social, cultural and economic backgrounds. We have no wish to exaggerate the scale of the phenomenon, or even to suggest that it is possible to come up with a meaningful estimate of the numbers of men who have ever paid or who do pay for sexual access to child prostitutes. However, if we accept that globally there are presently some hundreds of thousands of prostitutes under the age of 18, and consider the fact that individual prostitutes typically service several hundred different clients annually, then the number of men who are willing to pay for sex with children must be a significant multiple of that figure. It is also known that these men are not a homogeneous group in terms of their economic, social or cultural background. There is local demand for child prostitutes from wealthy citizens in Thailand and India as well as demand from low paid migrant workers in these countries (see Cox, 1993, cited in Shrage, 1994), and there is demand from tourists from Japan and the Gulf States, as well as those from Australia, North America and Europe. Any explanation of the behaviour of all these men which turns on the idea that they share a common psychological abnormality is less than convincing. Even when considering foreign demand alone, to explain it in terms of individual pathology is to assume that there is some clear and absolute dividing line between the tourists who sexually exploit children, and those who sexually exploit adults while holidaying in economically underdeveloped countries. The remainder of this section provides some empirical data to demonstrate the diversity to be found amongst sex tourists who exploit child prostitutes.

Sex Tourists and Prepubertal Children

It is clearly the case that there are men who conform to the clinical definition of 'paedophilia' who travel to Thailand in order to obtain safe, easy and cheap sexual access to prepubertal girls and boys. It is less certain, however, that such men pursue this access through visiting brothels. Indeed, it seems more likely that men who might be classified as 'paedophile' would prefer to use other routes. If, as a number of authors suggest, many such men are motivated by a form of narcissism, seeing some lost part of themselves in the 'innocent' and 'lovely' child, and veer toward an 'excessively sentimental' regard for children, then they would almost certainly prefer to arrange sexual access in ways that allow them to delude themselves as to the child's interest in and affection for them. The sight of small children playing around on a beach, splashing in the sea, drinking coca colas and so on is easier to reconcile with a sentimentalized vision of childhood as a time of charm and innocence than is the sight of a bruised and half starved child in a small cubicle, or even the sight of a child dancing in a Go Go bar.

There are also some foreign men who have a sexual (and often commercial) interest in subjecting young children to violence, pain and/or humiliation and for whom the child's 'racialized' Otherness is something degrading and dehumanizing, rather than romanticized and idealized. Though their crimes are more extensively documented than those committed by sex tourists whose hostile impulses take more muted forms of expression, these men are without doubt in a minority. Again, in saying this we do not wish to minimize the horror of those crimes or to suggest that finding a way of preventing them is not of the utmost urgency, merely to point out that this type of abuse is only one part of the problem.

Sex Tourists and Postpubertal Teenagers

Although there are, no doubt, men who travel in order to satisfy a narrowly focused sexual interest in children who are at the cusp of physical maturity, we want to argue that the sex tourists who exploit independent postpubertal child prostitutes and those who work in bars and brothels are not, in the main, classifiable as 'paedophiles'. Why then do they fuck children? To understand this it is necessary to recognize that narrowly postpubertal girls often conform to Western ideals of *feminine beauty*, and not western ideals of childish innocence. Sex tourists who select 15-year-olds from the prostitutes on display in bars or brothels, or from the 'freelances' who approach them in other settings, are sometimes satisfying a taste for a particular physical 'type' which is normally, but not invariably, associated with girls in their mid-teens, rather than a specific sexual interest in children. Indeed, one of the generalizations that sex tourists make about Thai women is that 'They' look very youthful. This is partly a self-serving belief. It means that they do not feel a need to enquire too closely into the age of the prostitutes they have selected. (A group of Macho Lads sitting by a swimming pool in Pattaya one day were laughingly accusing one of their members of being a 'child molester' and asking him how old the girl he had fucked the previous evening was. He said she had claimed to be 16, and when his mates laughed, he remarked, 'You can't tell how old they are, they all look really young for their age'.) But it is also the case that many Thai prostitutes, regardless of their age, have physical characteristics that western men associate with youth and feminine beauty, and in this sense, it is a matter of indifference to many sex tourists whether the girl they take back to their room is 14, 15, 16, 17 or even in her early 20s. As one remarked:

> It's hard to tell their age. I took one off the streets, she said she was 18 but I saw her passport and she was 30. But she looked so young, she looked well fit. So you can't tell. They all lie anyway.

Another sex tourist describes a visit to a Thai brothel thus: 'God, what a selection . . . the one thing in common was long jet black hair and perfect complexions. There were no Harley Davidson tattoos to be found, no needle marks, no gum chewers, no inch-thick make up, no old women, and no ugly women.'

The same is true of many sex tourists in Cuba. Though some seek out physically immature girls like Anna-Bel, others are merely interested in slim, firm, 'fit' girls who typify what is considered to be a sexually attractive (usually Black) female. Their chronological age is unimportant. The following extract from an interview with a 37-year-old market trader from Fulham illustrates this well. His Cuban 'girlfriend', who is 17 years his junior, was 15 years old the first time he met her:

> It's funny, but in England the girls I fancy never fancy me, and the ones that do fancy me, I don't fancy. They tend to be sort of fatter and older, you know, 35 but their faces, they look 40. But in Cuba, really beautiful girls fancy me . . . My girlfriend's jet black, she's beautiful. She's a ballerina. She's so fit it puts me to shame really. I don't get much exercise.

If the label 'paedophile' were to be attached to all those who are attracted to narrow-hipped, small firm-breasted, relatively hairless, smooth-skinned girls, then, judging by the models used by the fashion industry and the film and pop stars iconized by the entertainment industry, paedophilia would have to be judged a fairly mainstream condition, rather than an extraordinary 'perversion'. 'Normal' heterosexual men are rarely to be heard expressing an erotic interest in the physical characteristics of mature women, and the idea that a man who is sexually aroused by the sight of a postpubertal 14- or 15-year-old girl is somehow marked off from the mass of 'ordinary blokes' is unsustainable. Moreover, there are elements of 'normal' male heterosexuality which precisely mirror elements of what is considered to be 'paedophilia'. Having reviewed the main studies of paedophilia, Weeks (1985) concludes that the chief distinguishing characteristic of the 'paedophile' is 'an intense, but often highly affectionate and even excessively sentimental, regard for young people' (p. 227). If the words 'young people' were replaced by 'young women', this description would capture well the essence of what is widely considered to be 'normal' male heterosexuality. It sits perfectly happily with one popular image of masculinity, that of the man who both 'protects' and 'worships' a smaller, weaker, younger, beautiful 'girl'.

Sex Tourists and Brothel and Bar Prostitutes

Sex tourists who visit brothels are making a very explicit and conscious choice to buy sexual services from a prostitute, and this is something which can be experienced as pleasurable and affirmative for a number of different reasons. For a certain subgroup of sex tourists (the Macho Men), their annual or biannual trips to Thailand are like passing through the looking glass into a world wherein all their masturbatory fantasies are miraculously embodied and attainable. This is partly because sexual access to prostitutes is extremely cheap in Thailand, partly because the array of different forms of commoditized sex on offer is so extensive that they are in a position to command 'anything and everything'. But it is also important to recognize that they feel able to live out their masturbatory fantasies because they are disinhibited by their sense that, in Thailand, prostitutes are 'commodities' and they themselves are sexual 'consumers'.

On the one hand, their racism makes it easy for them to dehumanize Thai prostitutes. On the other, the organization of brothel and Go Go bar prostitution in Bangkok and Pattaya further objectifies and deindividualizes prostitutes. As Wilson's (1995) interesting and original discussion of commoditization and the nature of demand in the tourist sex trade in Bangkok shows, such places present sex tourists with a sense of prostitutes not only as somehow 'mass produced', but also as highly standardized commodities (for example, large numbers of girls and women of roughly similar physical proportions are displayed in matching costumes, and often have numbers pinned to their clothing). Meanwhile, the live sex shows which Macho Men visit (generally featuring girls and women performing acts which involve expelling air or objects from their vaginas, or pulling long strands of cloth, or strings of bells or razor blades from them) further reinforce the idea of Thai females as nothing more than animated sexual organs.

Not all sex tourists like this kind of very explicit commoditization (again, Wilson's comments on this are useful; see also O'Connell Davidson, 1995b and 1996b on the different 'types' of sex tourist), but there are significant numbers who do. The pleasure they derive from it appears to be linked partly to the hostility they feel toward women in general, partly to their fear of/fascination with the idea of sexual abandon, partly to a form of homoerotic voyeurism. Elsewhere in the world, men drive around red light districts to look at street prostitutes (this 'peeping' can serve either as a prelude to an eventual transaction or as a sexual pleasure in and of itself: see Hoigard and Finstad, 1992), and there are large numbers of men for whom the sight of a real live prostitute, even a mere phone conversation with a prostitute or her receptionist, is hugely sexually stimulating (O'Connell Davidson, 1995a). Through these men's eyes, Thailand is itself nothing more than one vast red light district, and they are aroused both by the sight of large numbers of sexually available persons and by the idea that they are surrounded by all manner of 'perversity' and sexual excess, by other men's 'animalistic' and unbridled sexuality. Though they publicly condemn any form of non-heterosexual or 'deviant' sexual activity, they are clearly fascinated and excited by it. Just as, at home, straight heterosexual men masturbate to magazines and videos which depict the acts they consider to be perverse, so in Thailand these Macho Men want to see the transsexuals, the live lesbian acts, the 'dirty poofters' walking arm in arm with male prostitutes and so on. They are likewise excited by the idea of the objectified brothel 'whore' not just because she is 'degraded' and available to them personally, but also because she is publicly available and has been sexually used by numerous other men. To see women and girls lined up in a brothel, numbered and available to any man who picks them is to see them dominated and humiliated, stripped of their power to 'withhold' the sexual access that Macho Men imagine is so central to their own well-being.

As the following extracts from an interview with one man, 'B', shows, brothel-based prostitution furnishes this type of sex tourist with a sense of power as a consumer, as a sexual being, as a man, and as a white person:

B: There's no pressure on you [in Thailand], you don't have to worry about going out and getting someone, because you know any time, day or night, you can have anyone you want within seconds. You feel so powerful, you feel you're in control of your sex life . . . One night, I went to, like, a brothel . . . They sit you down on these nice couches at the brothel, and then pull the curtains back and there are all the girls sitting there behind this glass screen and they've all got numbers on, round the neck like, and the guy says, 'Which one would you like then?' And you look at the girls and see which one you fancy and you take it from there. You say, 'Oh I like number 7 or 8' and you say 'Is she good girl?' and he says, 'Yes, any problems phone me up and I'll sort it out.'

O'CD: So then he goes and gets number 7 or 8 and brings her round and sends her out with you?

B: Yes. They get a microphone, a walkie talkie out to speak through the screen, sends through for her like, says 'Number 7 go and get dressed', because they're just in bathing suits, and she knows she's been took, and then they go with you. They'll go with anyone, even if you're a big fat Arab . . . You pay the gaffer before you take her. You might give her a tip in the morning, £1 or so, if you're a decent guy or if the girl was good. These girls seem to work for the bar for about a year at a time, and they don't get paid see, until the end of the year. Because through the year, they eat and sleep at the brothel . . . so at the end of the year, when it's time to go home they'll pick up the money. It won't be as much as if they'd gone freelance, but it'll be a fair amount of money to them. It'll be a lump sum.

O'CD: What kind of girls work in those places?

B: Some of them are kidnapped from the north of Thailand and brought down to Pattaya to work . . . I think some of the families sell the kids so as to keep the fathers in heroin, because they are drug addicts, you see. Well, that's the society they live in . . .

O'CD: And what kind of age do you think they are? Do they look younger than freelances?

B: Some do, yes. But its hard to tell their age . . . The difference [between Pattaya and red light districts in Britain] is the scale, its on such a scale, you've got such a choice, thousands and thousands of girls. My thirty-five what I've had is just a drop in the ocean to what is there . . . its just so vast. There's just thousands of bars and thousands of girls, you could never get round all of them.

O'CD: And do you worry about that it isn't right, that some people say it's exploiting the women?

B: No, because with the Thais, they've done this a long time, even before tourism, its just their way of life. A different girl a week, it's their way.

This man believed that some of the girls he had taken from bars and brothels were under the age of 16, but it should be clear from the above that he does not visit such places *only* because he attaches sexual value to the youth of the prostitutes therein. Furthermore, the cheap brothels in backstreets which are more likely to provide sexual access to young girls are seen by some sex tourists as providing just one more sexual experience in the range that is on offer to them as 'consumers'. An anonymous contributor to a 'World Sex Guide' available on the Internet, for example, provides descriptions of six 'adventures' he had in Bangkok, the last of which features a visit to a brothel where 12-year-old girls were on offer. The sexual acts he performed upon a physically small and immature child are recounted as nothing more or less than another new and exciting 'commodity/service' purchased during the course of his trip. There are also sex tourists who find the 'seediness' of backstreet brothels alluring, as well as those who imagine that there is something more 'authentically' Thai about them than there is about the Go Go bars which cater primarily to tourists. Cassirer (1992) describes such establishments in the following way in his sex tourist's guide:

> Basically these brothels are no-frill massage parlours with no massage . . . [The prostitutes] are village girls from Burma or China who are barefoot and who knows how old. They don't speak any English other than Hi and are as foreign to you as you are to them. If the service is good, tip; if extra special, tip more. These girls live here and are *owned* by the hotel. Your tip is their spending money, so let your conscience be your guide. (p. 180, original emphasis)

In their descriptions of such places, then, sex tourists emphasize not just the youth of the prostitutes, but their utter powerlessness — they *have* to go with whoever pays for them, they are *owned* by the hotel. The idea of the girl's powerlessness has erotic value in its own right, but it is also an idea which helps to disinhibit the sex tourist and enable him to justify his own exploitative behaviour. Cassirer (1992) makes this explicit when he says, 'One way to rationalize it [the sexual exploitation of debt-bonded women and children] is to say, if it's not me, then it's the guy behind me, and who's more likely to be the gentler of the two?' (p. 181). But it is also implicit in 'B's' references to the supposed 'Thai way of life' and belief that he is made 'decent' by giving the enslaved child he has fucked a tip of £1. Indeed, many sex tourists view themselves as benefactors of the poverty stricken peoples they sexually exploit, and often, the more vulnerable a prostitute is, the more grateful she will be for the paltry sums of money left by her foreign clients. Any guilt such a sex tourist might feel is, of course, much assuaged by these signs of 'pathetic gratitude'.

The real point is that for many sex tourists, the age of the brothel- and bar-based prostitutes they use is not, on its own, the prime source of sexual excitement, and even though these men do fuck children, it is both misinformed and misleading to describe them as 'paedophiles'. The explanation for their attitudes and behaviour is not to be found in western beliefs about childhood, nor in some pathological quality these individual men possess, rather it lies in widely accepted ideas about gender and sexuality and in the kind of white racism that is routinely propagated in European, Australian and North American society.

The Economics and Ideologies of Sexual Exploitation

All of the countries which currently host large numbers of sex tourists are experiencing some combination of the following: the rapid devastation of traditional or established economies, such that large numbers of people are suddenly severed from the means of subsistence they had previously relied upon; a heavy burden of debt to world financial institutions; a desperate need for foreign exchange revenue. Over the past twenty-five years, governments of economically underdeveloped countries have been encouraged by the World Bank and the International Monetary Fund (IMF) to use tourism as a means of securing the foreign exchange they so urgently need both to service debts to the 'first' world and to finance economic 'development'. Tourism is now *the* major foreign exchange earner in a number of Asian and South East Asian, Caribbean and Latin American countries, and is fast becoming so in others. Many former communist countries, as well as those which are currently struggling to remain so, are now under similar economic pressures to develop tourism.

The economic benefits of mass tourism are not evenly spread, however. For a start, the vast bulk of the profits from it go to the huge, transnationally owned air travel and tourism conglomerates rather than to locally owned companies in the countries which receive tourists. Indeed, as Truong (1990) observes, 'given their weak position, many developing countries have not been able to retain a very large proportion of the foreign exchange earned from tourism' (p. 115). Within these countries that are now so dependent on tourism, what benefit there is from the industry does not and cannot alleviate the problems of poverty they face. Moreover, in many such places, the global institutions that are promoting tourist development are simultaneously 'encouraging' other forms of export-oriented economic 'development', much of which involves the turning over of vast swathes of subsistence land to the production of cash crops (Mitter, 1986). This in turn implies an ongoing dispossession of the rural peasantry, which then supplies labour to the 'prostitution economy' that develops or expands alongside mass tourism, for there is simply not enough waged work in these countries to absorb the 'surplus labouring population' that the annexation of subsistence land creates.

Not every single tourist to economically underdeveloped countries is a sex tourist, but sex tourism does represent a sizeable portion of long-haul tourism. Contrary to popular belief, the men who purchase sex tours run by small firms are not the only people who sexually exploit local women, men and children whilst on holiday. It is large, reputable corporations that transport the majority of sex tourists around the world, for sex tourists are essentially a cross-section of 'ordinary' people, including among their ranks the young and the old, heterosexual and homosexual, package tourists, independent travellers and hippie backpackers, working class and middle class, women as well as men. Because *all* forms of long-haul tourism yield profits for transnational corporations involved in air travel and tourism by exploiting the cheap labour of local people (usually women: see Enloe, 1989), and because all involve not just the provision of hotel and leisure services and guaranteed access to sun, sea and sand, but also the commodification of cultures and people, tourism in general, and sex tourism in particular, can be seen as another feature of the profoundly exploitative relationship between countries at the core and those at the periphery of what Cohen (1987) refers to as 'regional political economies'.

Furthermore, it is impossible to understand sex tourism without reference to the legacy of colonialism and imperialism and to white racisms. US military involvement in South East Asia is directly responsible for the infrastructure of the sex industries in both Thailand and the Philippines, for example, and the US economic blockade of Cuba (imposed on an economy that was still struggling to recover from the deleterious effects of centuries of colonial rule and slavery) makes a substantial contribution to creating the conditions under which women and children are compelled to prostitute themselves. Meanwhile, it is racist myths and stereotypes about the sexuality of 'Others' (see hooks, 1992; Collins, 1991; Shrage, 1994; McClintock, 1995) which fuel a large part of the demand for sex tourism.

Unless western commentators, activists and academics set the phenomenon of child prostitution in this more general context, it will remain a conceptual as well as a moral challenge to them. For prostitution involves the exchange of sexual license for an economic benefit, and since the dominant western ideal of childhood is as a period of the life course in which an individual is neither sexually nor economically active, the term 'child prostitute' embodies very fundamental contradictions. This concept of childhood denies the economic and social reality of many of the world's children (see Ennew, 1986; Kitzinger, 1988), a reality that is also a profoundly 'racialized' one. Though the situation may be changing with the sexual exploitation of people from former communist eastern Europe, it is not, by and large, white women and children who face a 'choice' between sexually servicing tourists or penury.

The stereotypes of child prostitution that are currently popular in the West deflect attention from its economic basis and its relation to sexual ideologies that are 'racialized', gendered and aged. Instead of being faced with uncomfortable questions about why it is that prostitution represents the sole means of subsistence for so many children and adults in so much of the southern hemisphere, and why it is that so many men from economically developed nations are so eager to exploit this fact, these stereotypes turn child prostitution into something that is terrible and tragic but somehow also aberrant, discrete and quite separate from the economic, 'race', age and gender power relations that are viewed as natural or inevitable in capitalist societies.

For reasons of political strategy, it is necessary to make child prostitution and prostitution-slavery the first targets of campaigns against sexual exploitation. Ultimately, however, it is only by acknowledging the fact that child prostitution is indivisible from the broader phenomenon of 'Third World' sexual exploitation and by challenging the power relations that underpin this and other forms of economic exploitation, that we can hope to live in a world wherein no individual, adult or child, is under economic compulsion to become the living embodiment of a richer person's sexist and racist masturbatory fantasies.

Acknowledgments

The support of the Research Committee of the Social Science Faculty of Leicester University, which financed Julia O'Connell Davidson's fieldwork in Thailand and Cuba, is gratefully acknowledged. We would also like to thank The Coalition on Child Prostitution in Tourism, and especially Anne Badger, its Campaign Coordinator, for support and information.

Notes

1 The Home Secretary then proposed legislation that would focus on sex tour operators rather than individual offenders, thereby revealing his own ignorance not only of the extremely limited role in sex tourism played by such companies but also, and rather more surprisingly, of the technical difficulties associated with securing convictions on charges of conspiracy and incitement.

2 The data on Thailand comes from fieldwork undertaken by Julia O'Connell Davidson in 1994, as well as other referenced sources, the data on Cuba comes from fieldwork undertaken by both authors in 1995.

3 Fieldwork investigating child prostitution in Costa Rica was undertaken for ECPAT (End Child Prostitution in Asian Tourism) in August 1995.

References

CASSIRER, B. (1992) *Travel and the Single Male*, Channel Island CA, TSM Publishing.
CHRISTIAN AID (1995) *An Abuse of Innocence: Tourism and Child Prostitution in the Third World*, PO Box 100, London SE1 7RT.
COHEN, R. (1987) *The New Helots*, Aldershot, Gower.

COLLINS, P. HILL (1991) *Black Feminist Thought*, London, Routledge.

COX, T. (1993) *The Badi: Prostitution as a Social Norm Among the Untouchable Caste of West Nepal*, Kathmandu, Asian Ethnographer Society Press.

DELACOSTE, F. and ALEXANDER, P. (eds) (1988) *Sex Work: Writings by Women in the Sex Industry*, London, Virago.

DUNHAM, C. and CARLSON, K. (1994) 'Sex slavery', *Marie Claire*, September.

ENLOE, C. (1989) *Bananas, Beaches and Bases*, London, Pandora.

ENNEW, J. (1986) *The Sexual Exploitation of Children*, Cambridge, Polity Press.

HOIGARD, C. and FINSTAD, L. (1992) *Backstreets: Prostitution, Money and Love*, Cambridge, Polity Press.

hooks, b. (1992) *Black Looks: Race and Representation*, London, Turnaround Press.

HOWELLS, K. (1981) 'Adult sexual interest in children: Considerations relevant to theories of aetiology', in COOK, M. and HOWELLS, K. (eds) *Adult Sexual Interest in Children*, London, Academic Press.

IRELAND, K. (1993) *Wish You Weren't Here*, London, Save the Children.

KITZINGER, J. (1988) 'Defending innocence: Ideologies of childhood', *Feminist Review*, Spring, No. 28.

McCLINTOCK, A. (1995) *Imperial Leather: Race, Gender and Sexuality in the Colonial Contest*, London, Routledge.

McINTOSH, M. (1978) 'Who needs prostitutes?: The ideology of male sexual needs', in SMART, C. and SMART, B. (eds) *Women, Sexuality and Control*, London, Routledge & Kegan Paul.

MITTER, S. (1986) *Common Fate, Common Bond*, London, Pluto.

MONTGOMERY, H. (1994), 'Child prostitution in Thailand.' Paper presented to the Seminar on the Plight of Street Children, The Welsh Centre for International Affairs, Cardiff, 16 November.

O'CONNELL DAVIDSON, J. and LAYDER, D. (1994) *Methods, Sex and Madness*, London, Routledge.

O'CONNELL DAVIDSON, J. (1995a) 'The anatomy of "free choice" prostitution', *Gender Work and Organisation*, **2**, 1, pp. 1–10.

O'CONNELL DAVIDSON, J. (1995b) 'British sex tourists in Thailand', in MAYNARD, M. and PURVIS, J. (eds) *(Hetero)sexual Politics*, London, Taylor & Francis.

O'CONNELL DAVIDSON, J. (1996a) 'Prostitution and the contours of control', in WEEKS, J. and HOLLAND, J. (eds) *Sexual Cultures*, London, Macmillan.

O'CONNELL DAVIDSON, J. (1996b, forthcoming) 'Sex tourism in Cuba', *Race & Class*.

O'GRADY, R. (1994) *The Rape of the Innocent*, New Zealand, Pace.

PHOENIX, J. (1995) 'Prostitution: Problematizing the definition', in MAYNARD, M. and PURVIS, J. (eds) *(Hetero)sexual Politics*, London, Taylor & Francis.

PLUMMER, K. (1981) 'Pedophilia: Constructing a sociological baseline', in COOK, M. and HOWELLS, K. (eds) *Adult Sexual Interest in Children*, London, Academic Press.

SHRAGE, L. (1994) *Moral Dilemmas of Feminism*, London, Routledge.

TRUONG, T. (1990) *Sex, Money and Morality: Prostitution and Tourism in Southeast Asia*, London, Zed Books.

WEEKS, J. (1985) *Sexuality and Its Discontents*, London, Routledge.

WHITE, L. (1990) *The Comforts of Home: Prostitution in Colonial Nairobi*, Chicago, University of Chicago Press.

WILSON, A. (1995) 'Commoditization and the nature of demand in the tourist sex trade in Bangkok', in FINK, C. and FORSHEE, J. (eds) *Travellers and Tourists in Southeast Asia*, Berkeley, Center for Southeast Asia Studies.

Notes on Contributors

Paul Connolly is a lecturer in sociology at the University of Ulster. He is author of two books to be published by the Open University Press: *Growing Up in the Inner City: Racism, Gender Identities and the Primary School* and *Researching 'Race' in Educational Settings: Politics, Theory and Practice* (the latter with Barry Troyna).

Annie Franklin is Director of the Sheffield Children's Information Service. She has co-authored several publications on children and childhood.

Bob Franklin is Reader in Sociology at the University of Sheffield. His books include *The Rights of Children* (1985, Basil Blackwell), and *Packaging Politics* (1994, Edward Arnold). He is the editor of *The Handbook of Children's Rights*, published in 1995 by Routledge.

Patricia Holland is a writer and filmmaker and lectures in communications at Goldsmiths College, London. Her study of the imagery of childhood, *What is a Child?* was published by Virago in 1992.

Michael Lavalette is lecturer in social policy at the University of Liverpool. His book *Child Employment in the Capitalist Labour Market*, was published by Avebury in 1994.

Ruth Lister is Professor of Social Policy at Loughborough University. She is a former Director of the Child Poverty Action Group and sat on the Commission on Social Justice. She has published widely on issues around poverty, income maintenance and citizenship and is currently writing a book on feminist perspectives on citizenship for Macmillan.

Tim Newburn is Head of Crime, Justice and Youth Studies at the Policy Studies Institute. He is the author of numerous books including: *Permission and Regulation: Law and Morals in Postwar Britain* (Routledge, 1991) and *Persistent Young Offenders* (with Ann Hagell, PSI, 1994), *Young Offenders and the Media* (with Ann Hagell, PSI, 1994), *Democracy and Policing* (with Trevor Jones and David Smith, PSI, 1994), *Just Boys Doing Business: Men, Masculinities and Crime*, (edited with Betsy Stanko, Routledge, 1994), and *Crime and Criminal Justice Policy* (Longman, 1995). He is co-editor of the journal, *Policy Studies*, and general editor of a new series of criminology books to be published by Longman.

Julia O'Connell Davidson is lecturer in sociology at the University of Leicester. She is the author of *Methods, Sex and Madness* (with Derek Layder, Routledge, 1994), *Privatization and Employment Relations: The Case of the Water Industry* (Mansell, 1993), and numerous chapters and articles on prostitution and sex tourism.

Carey Oppenheim is a senior lecturer in social policy at South Bank University. She is a former research officer and acting deputy director at the Child Poverty Action Group and author of a wide range of publications about poverty and income maintenance.

Nigel Parton is Professor in Child Care at the University of Huddersfield. A qualified social worker, he has been involved in researching and teaching on child welfare and child protection since the late 1970s. He is the author of numerous publications in this field including *Child Protection: Risk and the Moral Order* (with David Thorpe and Corinne Wattam, 1996, Macmillan). He is also the editor of *Social Theory, Social Change and Social Work* (1996, Routledge) and *Child Protection and Family Support: Tensions, Contradictions and Possibilities* (forthcoming, Routledge).

Julian Petley teaches in the Department of Human Sciences at Brunel University and, with James Curran, is the author of *Loony Tunes: The Media and Local Democracy* (forthcoming, Routledge).

Jane Pilcher is lecturer in sociology at the University of Leicester, where she teaches the sociology of age. Her book *Age and Generation in Modern Britain* was published by Oxford University Press in 1995.

Jacqueline Sanchez Taylor is co-researcher on a series of research projects funded by ECPAT (End Child Prostitution in Asian Tourism) which examine the relationship between tourism and child prostitution in a number of economically underdeveloped countries.

Stephen Wagg is senior lecturer in the Department of Sport Studies at Roehampton Institute, London. He writes regularly on childhood, and on a variety of other topics including sport, the mass media and comedy. His most recent book is *Giving the Game Away: Football, Politics and Culture on Five Continents* (1995, Leicester University Press).

Karen Winter is currently employed by South and East Belfast Health and Social Services Trust as a social worker in a family and child care team. She previously worked in a similar team in Leicester.

Index

Truong, T. 219
TV-AM 161, 162

UK Agenda For Children 23, 95, 104–5
UK First Report to the UN Committee on the Rights of the Child, 103
Ukpabi, B.E. 183
UN Convention on the Rights of the Child (1989) 23, 95, 96, 98–9, 102, 104–7, 111, 129, 193
UN Research Institute for Social Development 180
UNICEF 99
Union of Communication Workers 190
Union of Moslem Organisations 110
Urwin, Cathy 166

Valcarenghi, M. 185
Valles, Jean 96
Vaux, A. 185
Vegetarian Society 94
Venables, Jon 134, 136–43, 145–53
Verlet, M. 183
Video Recordings Act (1985) 156
Viz 168

Wacaday 162, 164
Wages for Housework Campaign 125
Wagg, Stephen 160, 161, 162, 168, 172
Wald, M. 99, 100
Walker, David 141
Walker, William 151
Walkerdine, Valerie 21
Walsh, Brian QC 147–8

Warner, Marina 118, 134, 150
Weeks, J. 215
Weinold, H. 185
welfarism 44–6, 48, 65
White Lion Free School 23
Whitehouse, Mary 156
Whitelaw, William 63
Who Cares? Scotland group 95, 100
Whose Schools? (pamphlet) 17
Why Don't You 162, 163
Williams, Raymond 22
William Tyndale affair 16
Willis, Paul 12
Wilson, A. 216
Windlesham, Lord, 62, 67
Woodcraft Folk 95
World Bank 181, 184
World Summit for Television and Children (1995) 170
Wright, Patrick 19

Young Offender Institutions 67–8
Young Offender Psychology Unit (Home Office) 63, 67
Young Offenders (White Paper, 1980) 63, 65
Youth Council for Northern Ireland 95
Youth Court 68
Youth Custody Order 63
Youth Trade Union Rights Campaign 97
Youth Training Schemes 97
Youthaid 95

Zarama, M.L. 183